THE ASSOCIATIONAL ECONOMY

Firms, Regions, and Innovation

PHILIP COOKE and KEVIN MORGAN

OXFORD
UNIVERSITY PRESS

OXFORD

UNIVERSITY PRESS

Great Clarendon Street, Oxford OX2 6DP

Oxford University Press is a department of the University of Oxford.
It furthers the University's objective of excellence in research, scholarship,
and education by publishing worldwide in

Oxford New York

Athens Auckland Bangkok Bogotá Buenos Aires Calcutta
Cape Town Chennai Dar es Salaam Delhi Florence Hong Kong Istanbul
Karachi Kuala Lumpur Madrid Melbourne Mexico City Mumbai
Nairobi Paris São Paulo Singapore Taipei Tokyo Toronto Warsaw

with associated companies in Berlin Ibadan

Oxford is a registered trade mark of Oxford University Press
in the UK and in certain other countries

Published in the United States
by Oxford University Press Inc., New York

© Philip Cooke and Kevin Morgan 1998

First published 1998
Reprinted new as paperback 2000

British Library Cataloguing in Publication Data

Data available

Library of Congress Cataloging in Publication Data
Cooke, Philip (Philip N.)
The associational economy: firms, regions, and innovation /
Philip Cooke, Kevin Morgan.
p. cm.
Includes bibliographical references and index.
1. Europe—Economic conditions—1945—Regional disparities.
2. Regional planning—Europe. 3. Research, Industrial—Europe.
4. Technological innovations—Economic aspects—Europe.
5. Competition, International. I. Morgan, Kevin. II. Title.
HC240.C6182 1998
330.94—dc21 97–41147
CIP

ISBN 0–19–829018–7 (hbk.)
ISBN 0–19–829659–2 (pbk.)

1 3 5 7 9 10 8 6 4 2

Typeset by Graphicraft Ltd., Hong Kong.
Printed in Great Britain on acid-free paper by
Bookcraft (Bath) Ltd.,
Midsomer Norton, Somerset

ACKNOWLEDGEMENTS

This book could not have been written without the assistance of a variety of colleagues and organizations to whom we would like to declare our heartfelt thanks. First, we express gratitude to all the firms and organizations who gave freely of their time in assisting us in conducting interviews. In particular, we thank specific intermediary figures who often explained roles and functions of target firms or organizations and helped us make important contacts. In Baden-Württemberg we were particularly assisted by Josef Esser, Stefan Kuhlmann, Dieter Klumpp, Joachim Edelman, Heather Malone, Dietrich Munz, Günter Meyerhöfer, and Hans Tümmers; in Emilia-Romagna, Patrizio Bianchi, Annaflavia Bianchi, Paolo Buonaretti, Fabio Sforzi, and Nicola Bellini; in the Basque Country, Goio Etxebarria, Mikel Gomez Uranga, Ricardo Alaes Aller, Arantxa Rodrigues, Jaime del Castello, and Roberto Velasco; and in Wales, David Griffiths, Gerhard Turner, Ian Courtney, and Penny Mitchell.

A second group of colleagues we would particularly like to thank are those who shared advice, information, and, often, unpublished manuscripts which helped us compose the book. Here, we are especially grateful to Charles Edquist, Amy Glasmeier, Gernot Grabher, Martin Heidenreich, Charlie Jeffrey, Bob Jessop, Horst Kern, Gerd Krauss, Bart Nooteboom, Keith Pavitt, Charles Sabel, and Mari Sako.

Thirdly, we sent chapters to colleagues who read them and sent us their comments upon them, for which we are enormously grateful. Here, we wish to thank Hans-Joachim Braczyk, Nicola Bellini, Rick Delbridge, Christopher Harvie, Juan Marie Iraeta, Mikel Landabaso, Anders Malmberg, Andrew Sayer, Paul Stewart, Roland Sturm, and David Wolfe.

Finally we wish to express thanks to our research assistant on the Wales–Baden-Württemberg project, Adam Price, to our research sponsors, the Economic and Social Research Council (Grant No. R000232962), the British Council, the Department for Trade and Industry, the Welsh Office, Welsh Development Agency, and Cardiff City Council, to our long-suffering editor at Oxford University Press, David Musson, and to Jean Rees and Diane Tustin for their secretarial skills. None bears any responsibility for the outcome of what we, nevertheless, like to think of as a truly associational process.

Phil Cooke

1 May 1997

Kevin Morgan

CONTENTS

LIST OF FIGURES AND TABLES

The Associational Economy: Introduction

INTRODUCTION

This book represents the fruits of some ten years' research into processes of regional economic development. Every journey begins with a first step and ours was taken in Wales where, in the early 1980s, an economic crisis of major proportions had been set in motion by the neo-liberal policies of the Thatcher government. The older industrial areas of the UK were similarly afflicted by being exposed to world market prices in the coal and steel industries in particular. Mass redundancy and long-term unemployment were the results as privatization and the injunction to compete, compete became the mantras of the day (K. Morgan, 1983). Unlike some similarly afflicted regions of the UK, Wales (and Scotland) were, arguably, fortunate to have in place devolved economic development authorities in the form of their territorial government offices and development agencies. These were charged partly or wholly with promoting economic regeneration, albeit as agents of state intervention in a political regime which conceived of such an approach as inimical to the free play of market forces. Worse, state intervention was officially perceived to be the source of the UK's economic malaise.

Tensions were present in the governance of regional economic restructuring from the outset and, in the case of Wales, these were made apparent in the travails of the Welsh Development Agency in the latter part of the 1980s and early 1990s. Much of Chapter 6 is given over to an analysis of the difficulties of squaring the circle of adapting a public policy delivery mechanism to the exigencies of a free market ideology. During this period, the opportunity arose to conduct comparative research on a region with many similarities to Wales in terms of scale and economic difficulties, albeit in a different European country unencumbered by an avowedly neo-liberal government. The Basque Country had emerged from the grip of Francoist dictatorship and had voted for regional autonomy in the same year, 1979, that Wales had voted against it. With our colleagues in the University of the Basque Country's department of Applied Economics, we began a British Council-funded *Acciones Integradas* project to analyse the comparative responses of the economic development authorities in the Basque Country and Wales in 1988. There were three key differences for the Basque case compared to that of Wales. First, the precipitous speed of restructuring and plant closure in steel and shipbuilding was initiated through Spain's accession to the European Community in 1986 and the associated tapering of subsidy to these industries under competition rules. Secondly, the Basque government had developed a regional innovation strategy centred on five key technology centres in aspects of engineering, machine tools, and new materials. Thirdly, because inward investment was not a strong option, partly due to political troubles, the Basque government had adopted a strategy of developing, upgrading, and promoting the small and medium-sized enterprise (SMEs) sector, supported by the technology centres. Partnership and co-operation among the diverse actors, including the European Community, were thus most pronounced (Cooke *et al.*, 1989). The progress of Basque restructuring is recounted in Chapter 7 of this book.

Shortly after embarking upon this comparison, a form of co-operation suddenly rose to the top of the agenda in Wales with the announcement that Wales had, through the Welsh Office, been invited to become an economic partner of the economically powerful German *Land* of Baden-Wüttemberg, itself the initiator of the 'Four Motors for Europe' interregional partnership with Catalonia, Lombardy, and Rhône-Alpes. These events were taking place against the back-cloth of the Single European Market legislation due to take effect at the end of 1992 and signalled the onset of what Christopher Harvie later termed 'bourgeois regionalism' (Harvie, 1994). In contrast to the more traditional 'ethnic regionalism', this new variant revealed leading economic regions forming partnerships to enhance access to each other's markets, promote inter-firm collaboration, and encourage technology transfer to take advantage of the lowering of trade barriers, without waiting for initiatives from what were commonly perceived to be dilatory or otherwise unhelpful national or federal state administrations. Mindful of the need for research on this new partner-region for policy as well as intellectual reasons, we received seedcorn funding from the Welsh Office, British Council, and Cardiff City Council (twinned since the 1940s with Stuttgart) to begin comparative research on Wales and Baden-Württemberg.

The results of this foray, published in Cooke and Morgan (1990; 1991*a*; 1994*a*), revealed a number of major differences between the regions in question and raised many further research questions. First, Baden-Württemberg's prosperity was associated with much higher levels of linkage between sectors and firms, on the one hand, and interaction by firms with governmental and non-governmental agencies, on the other. Secondly, *innovation* was an important focus for much of this interaction, with Baden-Württemberg firms making fuller use of the rich infrastructure of research institutes, universities, higher education institutions, and technology-transfer agencies than seemed possible in the UK, let alone Wales. Thirdly, large firms like Daimler-Benz, Robert Bosch, and Standard Elektrik Lorenz (a subsidiary of Alcatel) were major animators of the regional economy and they, along with the leaders of business associations representing the *Mittelstand* (SMEs), were in very close contact on a regular basis with the regional political élite who, in turn, designed customized industry and innovation policies to coincide with their expressed needs. Bestriding this process at the time was Minister-President Lothar Späth, author, political visionary, main challenger for a time to Helmut Kohl as leader of Germany's Christian Democratic Union, and arch-political fixer before his downfall for politically dubious practices in 1992.

Among the questions our first visit provoked were: precisely how did large firm–SME interactions work, were they merely sub-contracting or more far-reaching, and to what extent were they collaborative as distinct from arm's-length market exchange in nature? Were SMEs collaborative or not and did they operate in industrial districts such as had been argued by Charles Sabel (1989) and his colleague Gary Herrigel and others (Sabel *et al.*, 1989*a*; Herrigel, 1989)? What was the nature of the public–private interface and what special role, if any, did it play in the receptivity to innovation of firms in the region? Finally, what, if anything, could be learned from this high-skill, high-income, high value-adding economy that might, with adjustment, be transferred to less accomplished regional policy settings such as those of Wales or the Basque Country? These questions became the basis for a successful bid to the Economic and Social Research Council which funded a two-year project entitled 'Regional Innovation in Europe: Networking, Training and Technology Transfer in Wales and Baden-Württemberg' in 1991. This enabled us to benefit greatly from links we had developed earlier with researchers, policy-makers, and business figures in the region. The fruits of this research are contained in Chapter 4.

The scepticism engendered in aspects of the 'flexible specialization' thesis from our initial studies in Germany led us to revive an interest in the industrial districts of Italy, particularly Emilia-Romagna, subject of one of our earlier publications (Cooke and da Rosa Pires, 1985). First, we organized two visits to the region in 1991 and 1992, funded by a grant from the Department of Trade and Industry. There we renewed or developed afresh valuable research contacts who helped us conduct detailed research, much of which is reported in Chapter 5 (see also Cooke and Morgan, 1991*b*; 1993). Our interest in Emilia-Romagna lay in the apparent paradox that the regional government had, since its inception in 1974, been a fiefdom of the Italian Communist Party, yet the economy was overwhelmingly composed of SMEs and the society was one of the most prosperous in Europe. While we were not naïve enough to anticipate Bollinger Bolshevism we were, nevertheless, intrigued to know more about the, then, unexplored policy-dimension of the districts and to examine the claims that their labour processes heralded a new, co-operative, craft-based type of capitalism potentially capable of out-performing competition based on mass production. Importantly, the inclusion of Emilia-Romagna balanced our case studies neatly since we were now comparing two less-favoured regional economies, one, the Basque Country, pursuing a small-firm-led regeneration strategy, the other, Wales, pursuing a large-firm inward-investment-led policy, with two successful and prosperous economies. Emilia-Romagna had been successfully developed through the promotion of small firms and Baden-Württemberg had become so through its globally competitive large firms and niche-focused SMEs. Moreover, each had some form of regional state apparatus with responsibilities for economic development, but each had very different political regimes—mainly Christian Democrat in Baden-Württemberg; neo-conservative in Wales; nationalist, in the main, in the Basque Country; and Communist in Emilia-Romagna. None could be called 'high-tech' economies, all had a substantial existing or historic base in industry; coal, steel, and shipbuilding being replaced by mechanical, automotive, and electronic engineering in Wales and the Basque Country, mechanical, automotive, and electronic engineering in Baden-Württemberg and mechanical, automotive, clothing, ceramics, furniture, and leather in Emilia-Romagna.

Despite their historical, cultural, economic, and political differences these regions have been exposed to comparable macroeconomic effects during the decade we have been studying them. Globalization had forced all economies to become more competitive, European Monetary Union has hung spectre-like over the fiscal and budgetary policies of all member states, and innovation has become a major instrument of competitive strategy for firms of all sizes.

Since our focus is on regions we dwell less on the macroeconomic and more on the microeconomic issues affecting these regions. We have relatively little to say about European Union policies generally because in our accomplished regions actual Structural Fund transfers are negligible, and, in respect of Framework Funding of science and technology, this is dwarfed by other sources in Germany and scarcely accessed in Italy, other than by a few large firms, none of which has significant laboratories in Emilia-Romagna. Structural Funds have been important in Wales and the Basque Country but these have mainly been invested in traditional transportation infrastructure until recently. It is only very recently, with the growing emphasis on *innovation* in aspects of Structural Fund programmes and a growing awareness of the importance of Framework Funds for research and technology development, that our less accomplished regions have begun to initiate and access less prosaic funding opportunities. We think this is important for regional economic development and we offer extended commentary on the implications of this for policy in Chapter 8.

ISSUES EXPLORED

The new economic order, based on free trade within and between large trade blocs such as the EU, NAFTA, and ASEAN, presided over by the World Trade Organization, has accompanied a changed role for the member states of these organizations. Gone are the days when national administrations could easily protect their ailing industries, promote their 'national champion' firms and pursue self-contained industrial policies. The role of the state with respect to economic management is more circumscribed by international agreements, most evidently in the case of the European Union. States with a lengthy history of strong intervention in economic affairs are, in many cases, sacrificing the goal of low unemployment to that of maintaining balanced budgets. Yet those economies in which full play has been given to the power of market forces cannot be said to have resolved the problems of the social economy, such as economic marginalization and social exclusion, by virtue of their pursuit of neo-liberal political agendas. In Chapter 1, we explore the emergence of a third way between state and market-led development, namely the associational model, based on a more social and collaborative mode of economic organization. We find that economic activity is increasingly based on notions of collective learning and that competition increasingly involves partnership and interactive innovation. This occurs between management and workforce, between firms in respect of pre-competitive collaboration, and between firms, large and small, and their governance systems at national and regional levels. We find, particularly, that local and regional milieux have risen in importance as mediators of economic co-ordination, joining the historically crucial nation states and the newer supranational blocs in this process. High trust, learning capacity, and networking competence are now widely perceived to be associated with relative economic and social success. Each of these is founded upon high capability in social interaction and communication rather than either individualistic competition or strong state-led economic development programmes.

Globalization is the overweening process that is commonly thought to underpin the changing behaviour of corporate and small firm practices in the new economic order. While recognizing the importance of the globalization of financial markets and the obvious effects of international trade in consumer markets, we, like others, remain unconvinced of the totalizing nature of globalization. It is clear from, for example, OECD data that major trade flows remain resolutely transatlantic and directed from South-East Asia into the EU and NAFTA far more than towards Japan and the other Asian 'tiger' economies. Moreover, trade within the blocs predominates and will continue so to do. The export of capital is dominated by the UK, the USA, and Japan, while Japan imports little. So, while there undoubtedly is more international business activity of various kinds, for most firms much of their associational activity is relatively confined nationally and, in many cases, is surprisingly focused in respect of the sourcing of inputs upon the regional level. In Chapter 2, we explore the ways in which the corporate governance structures of large firms is being rethought to give greater consideration to a community of stakeholders that is less rootless than that of shareholders and note the ways in which leading corporations are seeking to break down the walls inside their own organizations to reintegrate, for example, research and production. We argue that, in leading cases, a laboratory-like mentality is imbuing the atmosphere of production as firms recognize the imperative of involving the competences of the workforce in general in the pursuit of better quality, more innovative output. We show as well how the involvement of supplier firms in co-makership is now a far more pronounced practice than hitherto. Thus we would wish to qualify the somewhat deterministic view of globalization as a hegemonic economic process, by drawing attention to important ways in which firms are becoming increasingly embedded in more localized business settings for many of their most important functions.

This leads us in Chapter 3 and the regional case-study chapters which follow, into an extended theoretical and empirical investigation as to the reasons for the increased decentralization of corporate functions to relatively specialized regionalized locations. As with our discussion of changes in state and corporate predispositions towards economic co-ordination, we see regionalization as an evolutionary process, and we are assisted in this understanding by the insights offered of late by proponents of evolutionary economic theory, particularly that version which finds common cause with neo-Schumpeterian analyses of processes of innovation (Freeman, 1987; Lundvall, 1992; Nelson, 1993; Hodgson, 1993; Edquist, 1997*b*). Given our observations on the growing importance of associational activity, learning capability, and networking practices among firms and governance organizations, we find the arena within which important aspects of such activities are played out to be regional for three key reasons. First, the processes involved in a more decentralized, less hierarchical corporate stance involve greater reliance upon others outside the ultimate control of corporate management. Regions, or localities within them, displaying characteristics of industrial agglomeration or 'clustering' to use Porter's (1990) description, offer advantages to firms seeking enhanced external economies from geographical proximity. The elaboration of, for example, supply-chain hierarchies does not imply that all supply-chain transactions have to be confined regionally. But for those involving knowledge transfer of a non-codified or only partially codified type, of which innovation activities are the most obvious, the existence of localized knowledge pools, a specific kind of industry culture, and, increasingly, the availability of high-quality knowledge centres such as universities, are externalities of tremendous importance. Secondly, we show by reference to the work of others and our own case analyses, that where such regional clusters exist they tend to become more specialized, technologically and in terms of product focus, and that trade may well be increasingly characterized in terms of intra-industry trade. Specializing locations may thus attract foreign direct investment seeking such expertise, thereby strengthening the agglomeration, but, of course, running the future risk of path-dependence and industrial 'lock-in' (Grabher, 1993*b*). Finally, with the relative decline in national economic sovereignty, regional administrations, often possessing strategic enterprise support functions, adjust or design support policies for 'their' industry, encouraging inter-firm interaction, evaluating and monitoring cluster 'performance', and promoting the region and its economic expertise abroad. In these ways, we argue, the regional level becomes more important to the process of embedding economic co-ordination for larger and smaller firms alike.

In our empirical studies (Chapters 4 to 7) we delve into the processes by means of which the four regions have evolved economically, paying special attention to four key dimensions in each. The first of these is the governance system, including relationships between the multiple levels of governance involved in economic affairs, special attention being devoted to the system of innovation and interactions between national and regional characteristics. Secondly, considerable attention is devoted to corporate restructuring and the ways in which large firms interact with smaller ones within and beyond the region. Thirdly, we seek to tease out the specific role of intermediary organizations involved in the process of enterprise support for regional industry, giving accounts of the evolution of functions as new challenges are faced in the context of new production organization and globalization tendencies. Finally, a special focus is given to the experiences of smaller and indigenous firms as recipients of policy support and corporate injunctions to become more quality-conscious, innovative, learning organizations. It is from these analyses that we derive confidence to argue, strongly, that the trend in all cases is towards a more associational mode of economic organization in which the regional governance and enterprise support system plays an increasingly active role in the pursuit of economic development.

What emerges from the regional analyses is a clear picture of the role of 'social capital' (i.e. norms and networks of trust and reciprocity) as a valuable economic externality. Interestingly, there is evidence, in all cases, of this intangible commodity being made and re-made. There is evidence, too, that moderates the possible interpretation of Robert Putnam's (1993) work on social capital to the effect that it is a question of centuries (or even millenia) rather than decades in its formation. Both of our now-prosperous regions were, at the turn of the nineteenth century, poor regions suffering from economic backwardness and out-migration. At approximately the same time, the Basque Country and Wales were amongst Europe's strongest regional economies in the heyday of their heavy industries of coal, steel, and shipbuilding. The social capital of strong communities, industrial cultures, and civic responsibility was inevitably weakened during the lengthy periods of economic decline and restructuring which the Basque and Welsh economies experienced during the twentieth century and it is only in the relatively recent past that institutional form has been given—through the development of localized and regionalized governance systems—to their ambitions for recovery.

In Baden-Württemberg and Emilia-Romagna, significant political and economic convulsions seriously undermined traditional socio-economic structures during their periods of national dictatorship. Both, in different ways, rediscovered, or developed anew, associational modes of civic and economic organization, Emilia-Romagna in a highly localist, community-based form of specialized industrial economy, Baden-Württemberg through the institutionalization of mutual support under the aegis of a strong, federalized governance system. In both cases, robust institutional structures, animated not only by public authorities, take care to monitor, evaluate, and learn ways of maintaining and improving their economies in the clear realization that this is the cornerstone of their recent success.

Hence, in the final chapter, this book seeks both to chart the evolutionary processes of economic restructuring and change at the regional level and to offer the outline of a mode of civic, political, and economic action which is polarized by an emphasis neither on state nor market as the ultimate arbiter of economic fortunes. Without confining the analysis solely to the regional level we seek to make the case that this may be the most appropriate, most manageable, strategic, yet locally-sensitive level of social organization at which future economic development policy should be pitched to secure significant economic gains.

However, we also argue that the most effective regional strategies will be those that engage with multi-level governance involving regional, national, and supra-national centres of political power. If it is the case that the dawning of a new millennium sees us operating fundamentally in an 'Information Society', though we think 'knowledge society' might be a better term, then the capacities to learn and communicate usable knowledge are crucial assets. Learning and com-munication are profoundly collaborative, socially interactive processes and, in our judgement, the 'associational economy' best captures this central idea with respect to economic evolution.

1

The Institutions of Innovation

INTRODUCTION

Throughout this book we use the term innovation in a decidedly broad sense to include both *technological* innovation in firms and industries and *institutional* innovation in regions and countries. Such a definition obviously carries the risk that it is too broad and thus too imprecise to be meaningful, since just about anything could be included. While this is a plausible objection we nevertheless believe that the benefits of such a broad understanding outweigh the costs because, as we shall see, the factors which foster or frustrate technological innovation are not confined to the internal jurisdiction of the firm. On the contrary, we shall argue that successful innovation is becoming ever more dependent on the *associational* capacity of the firm—that is its capacity for forging co-operation between managers and workers within the firm, for securing co-operation between firms in the supply chain, and for crafting co-operative interfaces between firms and the wider institutional milieu, be it local, regional, or national. This institutional milieu is to be understood in a dual sense, consisting of both 'hard' institutions (the ensemble of organizations, like government agencies, banks, universities, training institutes, trade associations, etc., which have a bearing on economic development) and 'soft' institutions (the social norms, habits, and conventions which influence the ways in which people and organizations interact).

Broad as it is we believe that this conception of innovation is at one with the theoretical tradition of evolutionary political economy which informs our work (Dosi *et al.*, 1988; Hodgson, 1988; Lundvall, 1992). Unlike the more static and equilibrium-oriented approach of neoclassical economic theory, evolutionary political economy is concerned not with a supposedly optimal allocation of resources at a given point in time but with how firms and industries mobilize, deploy, and develop their resources over time. It is thus a dynamic approach in which the key question is how agents learn in a world of uncertainty. The evolutionary approach recognizes, in a way that neoclassical theory does not, that learning is something to be explained rather than assumed, that learning is guided and constrained by a wide array of social norms and cultural conventions, and that prices and markets are not the only mechanisms for transmitting information and co-ordinating resources in capitalist economies (Nelson, 1996).

Our aim in this chapter is to elaborate on these theoretical insights by focusing on some key aspects of the innovation process. First, we argue that innovation needs to be recognized for what it really is, namely a collective and iterative endeavour rather than an act of heroic individualism, a point which we illustrate by reference to the interactive model of innovation. To develop this argument we examine three institutional 'carriers' of innovation—firms, states, and sys-tems—where we argue that the capacity to promote associational behaviour is one of the most important ingredients in the recipe for successful corporate strategy and more effective public policy. Finally, we identify some of the intan-gible factors—like trust, voice, and loyalty—which underpin associational action in firms, countries, and regions.

MODELS OF INNOVATION: THE SCHUMPETERIAN LEGACY

In a justly famous passage of *The German Ideology* Marx and Engels criticized the idealist conception of history for seeing only 'the political actions of princes and states' and for ignoring 'real individuals, their activity and the material con-ditions under which they live' (Marx and Engels, 1970). Much the same could be said of countless histories of business and technology which abstract the role of key individuals from the unsung heroes on whom they relied for their breakthroughs, be they enterprises or technical discoveries. While the 'heroic individual' model of innovation may have had some foundation in earlier phases of capitalist development, the twentieth century has witnessed a progressive socialization of the innovation process, such that the role of the individual, while certainly not insignificant, is nowadays highly circumscribed. Paradoxically, we find both models—the individualist and the socialized—in the work of Schumpeter, one of the founding fathers of evolutionary political economy. This has led some commentators to speak of two Schumpeters, the early Schumpeter surveying the world of owner-managed firms in turn-of-the-century Vienna and the later Schumpeter who acknowledged the advent of the large corporation in the USA in the 1940s (Freeman, 1982), while others argue that there is an unre-solved tension, between the individual and the social, running throughout his work (Langlois, 1991).

While his *agents* of innovation do indeed shift over time Schumpeter con-sistently defined innovation in a broad sense to mean 'the carrying out of new combinations', a definition which embraced much more than just technological innovation because it included (1) the introduction of a new good; (2) the intro-duction of a new method of production; (3) the opening of a new market; (4) the conquest of a new source of supply; and (5) the development of a new form of industrial organization (Schumpeter, 1934). One of the reasons why Schumpeter resonates so much today is because he was the first twentieth-century economist to fully grasp that capitalism was essentially a process of cre-ative destruction and that innovation was what fuelled it. While his neoclassical peers were transfixed with price competition, Schumpeter forcefully argued that

it is not that kind of competition which counts but the competition from the new com-modity, the new technology, the new source of supply, the new type of organization—competition which commands a decisive cost or quality advantage and which strikes not at the margins of the profits and the outputs of the existing firms but at their foundations and their very lives. (Schumpeter, 1943)

Innovation, or 'quality competition', was the driving force of economic development in Schumpeter's schema, not price competition.

. In the early Schumpeter the key agent of innovation is the individual entrepreneur (not to be confused with the 'mere manager'), a figure akin to a charismatic leader bent on breaking routines, uprooting conventions, and capable of charting a new course for the means of production. The will and the vision are as important as rationality in this conception because:

Here the success of everything depends upon intuition, the capacity of seeing things in a way which afterwards proves to be true, even though it cannot be established at the moment, and of grasping the essential fact, discarding the unessential, even though one can give no account of the principles by which this is done . . . In the breast of one who wishes to do something new, the forces of habit rise up and bear witness against the embryonic project. A new and another kind of effort of will is therefore necessary in order to wrest, amidst the work and care of the daily round, scope and time for conceiving and working out the new combination . . . This mental freedom presupposes a great surplus force over the everyday demand and is something peculiar and by nature rare. (Schumpeter, 1934)

Although this passage from the early Schumpeter is often held to contradict the later Schumpeter, it is worth noting that the former already contains the seeds of the latter. Anticipating his later argument that the mechanization of progress would lead to the obsolescence of the entrepreneur, the early Schumpeter was already arguing that the 'entrepreneur type must diminish' with the socialization of the innovation process (Schumpeter, 1934). In other words the early Schumpeter was keenly aware that with the growth of trustified capitalism 'the carrying out of new combinations' would become internalized within large firms.

If there is greater continuity in Schumpeter's work than is often realized it is certainly in the later Schumpeter that we find the most developed model of innovation as a socialized process. In the panorama of *Capitalism, Socialism and Democracy* he laments that 'innovation itself is being reduced to routine' because technological progress:

is increasingly becoming the business of teams of trained specialists who turn out what is required and make it work in predictable ways. The romance of earlier commercial adventure is rapidly wearing away, because so many things can be strictly calculated that had of old to be visualized in a flash of genius. (Schumpeter, 1943)

Schumpeter was manifestly wrong in thinking that innovation was being reduced to routine, still less to a process which could be strictly calculated, as we shall see when we discuss corporate R&D strategies in Chapter 2. Another major problem is the way that Schumpeter extolled innovation over the related processes of invention and diffusion, to the point where the latter are portrayed as somewhat prosaic activities compared to the heroic act of innovation, which was deemed to be the truly creative act. This distinction is clearly overdone because a good deal of creativity is involved not just at the inventive stage but also in the process of diffusion as producers and users reconfigure the original innovation to their evolving requirements. The most cogent critic of this conception has argued that 'it is economically absurd to consider the innovation of the automobile as having been accomplished when there were a few buffs riding around the countryside terrifying horses' (Rosenberg, 1976). In other words, innovation is not a well-defined act but a series of iterative steps which are often—but not always—linked to the inventive process. The caveat is in order because, as we show later, inventors and innovators need not be the same party.

Although Schumpeter recognized that innovation was becoming more formalized and indeed more bureaucratized, he could not have foreseen the extent to which it was to become even more socialized through the spread of R&D laboratories within firms, technology alliances between firms, the growth of state-sponsored science programmes, and university-based research efforts (Nelson, 1990). For much of the postwar period, the *linear* model was the dominant model of innovation, a model so heavily influenced by the rise of the scientific community that it was sometimes called the 'science-push' model of innovation. Whereas Schumpeter thought scientific inventions of secondary importance, the linear model overcompensated by conceiving innovation as a linear-like process which followed a well-defined sequence: from basic scientific research at one end, through product development and production, to marketing at the other end. In other words, technological innovation was essentially conceived as the application of 'upstream' scientific knowledge to the 'downstream' activities of product design, production, and marketing. This linear model suffers from at least three fatal weaknesses: it exaggerates the role of basic science, it invokes an unwarranted hierarchy of knowledge, in which 'pure' scientific knowledge is ranked above 'applied' technical and engineering knowledge, and it fails to appreciate the need for continuous interaction and feedback (Kline and Rosenberg, 1986; Aoki and Rosenberg, 1987).

Critics of the linear model have convincingly argued that the primary sources of innovation originate farther 'downstream', without any initial dependence upon, or stimulus from, frontier scientific research:

These sources involve the perception of new possibilities or options for efficiency improvements that originate with working participants of all sorts at, or adjacent to, the factory level. These participants include professional staff, such as engineers, but especially those who have responsibilities for new product design or product improvement. But they also include . . . a wide variety of blue collar workers. Such knowledge typically has no specific antecedents in organized scientific research. (Aoki and Rosenberg, 1987)

In place of the linear model these and other critics posit an *interactive* model because they argue that innovation is first and foremost:

a continual, interactive process in which success requires an ongoing synthesis of changing information from a variety of sources, including potential buyers. Terms such as 'feedback', 'upstream' and 'downstream' carry heavy overtones of a rigid temporal sequence of events, and of a hierarchical ranking of significance of different information sources (with basic research at the top, technological and engineering toward the middle, and marketing at the bottom) which is quite irrelevant for the innovation process. (Aoki and Rosenberg, 1987; see also Rothwell and Zegveld, 1985; Kline and Rosenberg, 1986; Lundvall, 1988; OECD, 1992)

If the linear model of innovation is (theoretically) dead, it continues to exert a perverse influence from beyond the grave. Indeed, its spirit informs those state-sponsored strategies which privilege 'upstream' research activity over 'downstream' development and diffusion activities, even though the latter are far more important to innovation and economic development (Rosenberg, 1991). It is also apparent, as we argue in Chapter 2, in the deep divisions—functional, cognitive, and spatial divisions—which separate R&D, production, and marketing in many large firms today, and which constitute formidable barriers to interactive learning and innovation.

The interactive model which informs this book carries radical implications not just for firms but for a wide array of public and private institutions. In particular, the interactive character of the innovation process means that to be effective, firms, regions, and nations need to develop organizational structures and mechanisms which promote continuous interaction and feedback within and between firms and among the various institutions which constitute the national system of innovation. Most important of all, the interactive model 'underscores the importance of *cooperation* between firms and institutions and, thus, the role played by links and networks involving different organizations' (OECD, 1992). In the following three sections we examine the implications of the interactive model for firms, states, and systems.

THE FIRM AS A REPOSITORY OF KNOWLEDGE

Our understanding of the firm as an innovating institution has been greatly enriched by evolutionary political economy. To a large extent, evolutionary theory developed out of a profound dissatisfaction with neoclassical economics, a theoretical approach which has three key attributes: (1) it assumes rational, maximizing behaviour by agents with given and stable preferences; (2) it focuses on attained (or movements towards) equilibrium states; and (3) it severely underestimates chronic information problems on the part of economic agents (Hodgson, 1996). From an evolutionary perspective the key assumptions of neoclassical theory are not merely unhelpful, they are positively dangerous if used as a guide to the way in which firms behave in the real world. To assume, for example, that firms possess near perfect information, that they are objectively rational, and that they optimize their utility means that neoclassical theory credits firms with a capacity for action which is as staggering as it is unrealistic. What this means is that neoclassical theory takes as resolved some of the largest and most pressing questions in economic development, like how firms come to know what they know, that is, how they learn.

A somewhat more tenable theory of the firm has been developed under the rubric of transaction cost economics, an approach which has its origins in the work of Commons (1934) and Coase (1937) and which more recently has been elaborated by Williamson (1985), who refers to it as 'a contractual approach to the study of economic organization'. This approach is predicated on two key behavioural assumptions: *bounded rationality* (that there are limits to what agents can know) and *opportunism* (that agents engage in self-interest-seeking with guile, i.e. they may lie, cheat, and steal). The key argument in this approach is that when exchanges between firms involve uncertainty, when they occur frequently, and when they require large transaction-specific investments—that is, when transaction costs are high—such exchanges will be transferred from markets to alternative governance structures, principally to hierarchies (vertical integration) or to hybrid contracting (long-term contracting).

Although transaction cost theory helps to underscore the significance of the organizational form of the firm, it sees the firm as nothing more than a vehicle for reducing transaction costs, which is static optimization theory applied to a new realm (Sayer and Walker, 1992). The central problem of the firm in transaction cost theory is how to find the optimal governance structure for transactions under the assumption that inputs, outputs, and technology are given, a problematic which focuses on the allocation of existing resources in an equilibrium state rather than the creation of new resources in a dynamic setting. Hence one of the key weaknesses of this contractual approach is that dynamic evolution, learning, and innovation—the hallmarks of the Schumpeterian firm—are virtually ruled out in favour of an exercise in comparative statics (Foss, 1993).

To appreciate the firm as a dynamic institution we must turn to theories of the firm which put learning, knowledge-creation, and innovation at the centre of the analysis, which is precisely what evolutionary theories seek to do. Indeed, as one of the pioneers of the evolutionary approach argues, understanding 'the ongoing, interrelated processes of *change* in technology and organization is the central intellectual problem to be confronted by a theory of the firm' (Winter, 1988). In evolutionary political economy, the firm is understood first and foremost as a repository of productive knowledge, a vehicle for continuous learning and knowledge-creation. In a radical departure from neoclassical assumptions about firms as rational, perfectly endowed, and optimizing agents, the evolutionary approach builds upon the basic premiss of bounded rationality (namely, that the economic world is far too complex for a firm to understand perfectly), a position which emphasizes 'the inevitability of mistaken decisions in an uncertain world' (Winter, 1988).

In mainstream neoclassical theory all agents are assumed to be equally capable of optimizing because economic competence (broadly defined to mean problem-solving skills) is assumed to be relatively abundant, when in fact it is scarce and uneven as between both individuals and firms (Pelikan, 1988). In contrast, the evolutionary approach recognizes in theory what we know to be true in practice, that there are significant variations in firms' knowledge bases and major differences in their capacity for creating knowledge from within and absorbing it from without the firm. The uneven distribution of economic competence, which is firm-specific and partly tacit, helps to explain the wide variations in corporate behaviour and performance and why apparently superior organizational forms diffuse slowly, if at all, within and between sectors, regions, and countries (Dosi and Coriat, 1994; Nelson, 1991). While all capitalist firms share the same profit-seeking goals, what differentiates them—in terms of competence, organization, technology, and culture—seems so much more striking than what they have in common.

The argument thus far owes much to the seminal study of Nelson and Winter (1982), which was the first systematic attempt to construct an evolutionary theory of the firm, a theory which revolves around three basic concepts. The first is *organizational routine*, a term which covers all regular and predictable behaviour patterns inside the firm, the ways of doing things and the ways of determining what to do with respect to investment, production, R&D, and so on. It is here, in its routines, that the firm stores its operational knowledge. Routines are the economic analogue of genes in biological organisms in the sense that they determine the firms' possible behaviour, but whereas organisms are stuck with their genes, firms are not stuck with their routines. Indeed, they have built-in mechanisms for changing them. Secondly, they use the concept of *search* to denote all those organizational activities which are associated with the evaluation of current routines and which may lead to the modification, or more radically, to the replacement of these routines. Where routines in general play the role of genes, search routines stochastically generate mutation. Thirdly, the *selection environment* of a firm is the ensemble of factors which affects its well-being and this is partly determined by conditions outside the firm (like product demand for example) and by the behaviour of other firms in the sector. In this approach, market competition is the economic analogue of 'natural selection', the mechanism through which firms grow and expand, decline and perish (Nelson and Winter, 1982).

The evolutionary metaphor should not be taken too far: routines are likened to genes because they appear so durable; but they are clearly not immutable because, through searching, they can be changed. Furthermore, while market competition may be analogous to 'natural selection', this does not mean that the market is a natural artefact (Hodgson, 1996). More generally, these three concepts should be understood as an attempt to develop Schumpeter's key insights: that capitalism was essentially an evolutionary process rather than a system in equilibrium, a process of creative destruction which produced winners and losers, a process in which price competition was trivial compared to quality competition (i.e. innovation).

From an evolutionary perspective, the key challenge for firms is how to strike a balance between routines on the one hand and creativity on the other because, as Schumpeter put it, 'all knowledge and habit once acquired become as firmly rooted in ourselves as a railway embankment in the earth' (Schumpeter, 1934). The durability of routines helps to explain why so much technological and organizational change tends to be path-dependent: in other words what a firm can do in the future is heavily constrained by what it has been doing in the past (Dosi, 1988*b*). Learning is what helps the firm to strike a balance between routines and creativity and the capacity to learn depends in no small way on its *absorptive capacity*: that is to say the firm's ability to recognize, assimilate, and exploit knowledge, from within and without, is largely a function of the level of prior-related knowledge (Cohen and Levinthal, 1990). This critically important concept of absorptive capacity refers to much more than technical skills. Indeed, it underscores the need for a shared cognitive framework within the firm and the ability to transfer knowledge across functions throughout the firm, a point we illustrate more concretely in Chapter 2.

The concept of absorptive capacity highlights the significance of *organizational* learning, which is much more than the sum of individual learning, as Japanese firms know so well (Cole, 1994). It is perhaps no coincidence that, as the pressures to innovate have increased, there has been a burgeoning interest in organizational learning (Senge, 1990; Lundvall, 1992; Nonaka and Takeuchi, 1995). In this literature we find distinctions like that between first and second-order learning. First-order learning refers to the refinement of existing practices —doing things better; while second-order learning refers to the production of novel practices—doing better things (Nooteboom, 1996).

While first-order learning can be achieved through better use of codified (tradable) knowledge, second-order learning is more difficult for firms, not least because novelty involves a greater degree of tacit knowledge, which has been defined simply but effectively as 'we can know more than we can tell' (Polanyi, 1966). Because tacit knowledge is personal and context-dependent, it is difficult if not impossible to communicate other than through personal interaction in a context of shared experiences. The ability to share tacit knowledge through intensive interaction is said to be the key to organizational knowledge-creation in Japanese firms, a competitive asset which is not easily emulated (Nonaka and Takeuchi, 1995).

Sharing knowledge—be it tacit, codified, or both—is a crucial aspect of organizational learning, but the capacity to share requires more than robust communication channels in the firm. What is also required is a high degree of trust and commitment among members of the organization because, as theorists like Polanyi (1958) and practitioners like Deming (1986) knew only too well, these are key conditions of successful learning and knowledge-creation. In other words, opportunistic behaviour, as defined by Williamson (1985), is highly unlikely to foster such intangible assets as trust and commitment. For this reason we argue later that voice and loyalty have much more potential for promoting learning within and between organizations than exit and opportunism.

There is no single form of economic organization which is, in principle, superior to others for promoting learning, knov̶̶̶̶
and Langlois, 1995). Indeed, the organ
not hierarchies or networks *per se* that
forms operate given the nature of the
logical change, the presence of econoi
small firms producing memory chips, a
Allowing for these environmental fact
but the capacity to create and sustain
using knowledge from a wide variety of
customers, and public bodies—which i
city. From this perspective there is no sl
networks because the former (i.e. verti
themselves in a wide array of inter-org

With the advent of the new competi
erating technological change, shorter pi
tougher environmental standards, and
services—it is not surprising to hear
resource and learning the most importan
this view seriously, it implies the need for organizational forms, within and
between firms, which are more readily attuned to learning than to power and
status. Since learning is an interactive and socially embedded process, which
cannot be understood outside its cultural and institutional context, this view also
implies that the wider environment of the firm—the social and political system
in which it is embedded and with which it interacts—can play a vital role in
facilitating (or frustrating) its learning capacity.

THE STATE AS ANIMATEUR: CREATING A MILIEU FOR INNOVATION

If the firm is the main repository of productive knowledge in capitalist economies, and hence the key agent of innovation, the state is the main regulatory
mechanism, at the national level at least, of the environment in which innovation takes place. Most theories would accept that the state has a legitimate duty
to set the basic framework conditions—law, security, social and economic infrastructure, and so on—without which economic development as we normally
understand it would be impossible. Over and above this basic framework, however, there is little or no political agreement as to what role the state should
play in economic development. Over the past fifty years the prevalent conception of the state's developmental role has changed dramatically, in part because
of shifting ideological waves.

In the first wave, which spanned the twenty-five years following the Second
World War, the Keynesian state was widely perceived to be part of the solution, a benign force in promoting and regulating economic development. As

new economic problems emerged in the 1970s and 1980s, like the combination of inflation, unemployment, and slower growth, a second ideological wave emerged, in the form of neo-liberalism, in which the state was portrayed as part of the problem, a malign force which had to be rolled back because it was ill-equipped to steer and regulate the market. More recently, a third wave has tentatively begun to emerge which eschews the first wave's heroic assumptions about state power and rejects as dogma the second wave conception that the state should be rolled back to the limited nightwatchman functions it performed in the nineteenth century. The common thread running through many third wave conceptions is the idea that to be an effective animateur of development the state must be reconstructed rather than dismantled and this means enhancing its capacity rather than its size (Evans, 1992).

As opposed as they seem in principle, these first and second wave conceptions—the classical repertoires—are paradoxically at one in regarding the *scale* of state intervention as the key issue, an index which tells us nothing about the efficacy of such intervention. As we shall see, the efficacy of state intervention depends not just on the internal resources of the state as an independent actor, but on the capacity of its interlocutors to engage in interactive learning among themselves and with the state, and this broader, associational capacity is partly conditioned by the *national system* of innovation of which the state is but one element. In other words, we see no value in the distinction which is sometimes found in the political science literature between 'strong' states (e.g. France and Japan) and 'weak' states (e.g. the USA and the UK) when this is predicated on such questionable indicators as the scale or regularity of intervention (Katzenstein, 1978). A far more fruitful theoretical approach is to focus attention on the concept of state capacity, which refers to 'a combination of internal coherence and external connectedness which can be called embedded autonomy' (Evans, 1992).

But before we look at the role of national systems of innovation, we propose to examine the scope and limits of the state in the two classical repertoires before considering some third wave conceptions of the state.

The State-Centred Repertoire

First wave conceptions of the state are basically variants of the Keynesian state, an interventionist state which drew its political support from the popular backlash against the stubbornly high levels of unemployment that had scarred many countries in the inter-war period. In varying degrees across advanced capitalist countries, the Keynesian state assumed three key economic roles over and above basic infrastructure provision, understood here in a broad sense to include such public goods as education, training, and basic research. These were the roles of regulator, entrepreneur, and animateur. In the role of *regulator* the state performed a wide array of functions, the most important being macroeconomic demand management and the containment of anti-competitive practices. In countries where key or ailing industries were nationalized—as in the UK, Spain,

France, and Italy—the state became a *de facto* public *entrepreneur*, a role which was often associated with high levels of industrial subsidy. Finally, in its role as *animateur*, the state sponsored a raft of spatial and sectoral programmes to promote the competitive position of regions, firms, and entire industries.

Although we are primarily concerned with the state's role as animateur of innovation, this does not mean that its other roles, with respect to infrastructure, regulation, and public ownership, are unimportant. Indeed, the provision of innovation-related infrastructure (in education, training, and research) was perhaps the state's most important role in facilitating postwar economic growth. Similarly, its regulatory role helped to create a more stable macroeconomic environment than would have ensued otherwise, though the scope for unilateral demand management has been steadily eroded by the forces of economic globalization.

The state's role as a public entrepreneur is more difficult to assess, not least because public enterprise has laboured under too many structural constraints— stifling bureaucracy, political interference, and ideological opposition—for it to establish a secure position for itself as a successful form of enterprise in capitalist society. In European terms, France is perhaps the best example of a country which has consciously sought to use public enterprise as an instrument of national innovation policy and we draw on this experience to illustrate both the scope and the limits of the state as a public entrepreneur.

The most successful industrial strategies in France have been in sectors deemed to be critical either to national security (e.g. defence and energy) or to national economic development (e.g. mass transport and telecommunications). In all these cases the state itself constitutes much of the market, hence these sectors lend themselves to the *'grand projet'* type of intervention. In other words, the state has displayed a remarkable capacity to marshal large resources so as to accomplish a national mission (OECD, 1986). This mode of intervention was less successful where markets were open to strong international competition and where the state was less of a force with respect to public procurement. Of the former sectors, the modernization of the telecommunications network in the 1970s is the outstanding example of innovative public enterprise at work (Morgan, 1989; Cawson *et al.*, 1990).

At the heart of the modernization effort was the Direction Générale des Telecommunications (the DGT, now called France Telecom), the public agency responsible for telecommunication services. Under the seventh plan (1976–80), telecommunications was defined as a national priority and a budget of over 100 billion francs was dedicated to the modernization of the network. What was equally important was a series of internal reforms which transformed the DGT from a traditional civil service bureaucracy into a more commercially minded public agency. The key reforms were the substitution of a five-year financial plan for annually controlled budgets; breaking the power of the R&D centre, which had extolled technical over commercial considerations; a decentralization of managerial responsibility to regional directors, who were obliged to submit *monthly* progress reports; the recruitment of a new breed of commercial manager;

and the introduction of financial incentives to engineers. These organizational innovations were rendered possible by a close political relationship between the head of the DGT and the French president. Such was the success of the modernization programme, which transformed the network from a laggard into a leader in less than a decade, that the DGT was described as 'an enterprise disguised as an administration' (Cohen and Bauer, 1985).

With its newly acquired status dependent on a large, but diminishing, investment programme, the DGT sought to develop a new vocation for itself in telematics, a new generation of electronic services based on the convergence of telecommunications and computing. In contrast to the basic network, where demand and technology were fairly well defined, and where the DGT had a clear mandate, the emerging telematics market exhibited none of these propitious features. In short, the DGT paid too little attention to these commercial and technical differences, so much so that while some initiatives were successful (like videotext for example), many others had to be abandoned, with the result that the DGT began to attract criticisms instead of plaudits for usurping its basic mandate and for entering markets where its network-based knowledge was less relevant (Cawson *et al.*, 1990).

The DGT's experience highlights the scope of, as well as the limits to, the state's role as a public entrepreneur. Where the circumstances are conducive—for example, where there is a strong public procurement dimension and where there is not too much uncertainty as regards demand and technology—public enterprise can indeed play a highly innovative role, though even under these favourable conditions success if far from assured, as the UK's tortured experience with network modernization testifies (Morgan, 1989).

While the public entrepreneur role varies in scale from country to country, the state's role as an animateur is common to all countries. The most visible instruments for prosecuting this role during the Keynesian era were industrial and regional policies, the results of which promised far more than they delivered even on a charitable assessment (Wilkes and Wright, 1987). The reasons why the practice fell short of the promise are complex and varied but, generally speaking, they stem from the way in which these enterprise support programmes were designed and delivered. All too often these programmes were designed with too little consultation with or knowledge of the targeted sectors and, equally debilitating, recipient firms were rarely obliged to demonstrate that state aid had been used to enhance their absorptive capacity (Morgan, 1996).

This criticism is less applicable to the developmental state strategies practised by 'latecomers' like Japan and other East Asian countries (Johnson, 1982; White, 1988; Amsden, 1989; Wade, 1990; Hobday, 1995). What needs to be emphasized here is that the 'strong' state explanation for these developmental success stories often obscures more than it reveals. The key point about Japan, for example, is that it is not the scale, but the *mode*, of state intervention that is most significant. Here we concur with the argument that 'wherever the Japanese state has intervened in the economy it has done so in collaboration with private-sector interlocutors, and it is this collaboration that explains why these interventions have on balance been beneficial' (Sabel, 1994). This argument does not presume that the state is more knowledgeable about markets than firms themselves—a key weakness of the 'strong' state thesis—and, with its emphasis on conjoint intervention, it lays the basis for third wave repertoires of state intervention.

The Neo-Liberal Repertoire

As the political analogue of neoclassical economics, the neo-liberal repertoire privileges the market over the state because firms are deemed to be rational, optimizing agents with few if any informational problems, while the state is perceived to be an incompetent economic agent because it has 'low tacit knowledge of business, few specific business skills and a very weak capacity for learning by doing' (Bennett, 1995). If the neo-liberal conception of firms cannot be sustained, its criticism of state competence is not without substance and needs to be taken seriously. Although the neo-liberal repertoire is mainly associated with the USA and the UK, the ideology of neo-liberalism is far more pervasive since it informs the deregulation currents in Europe today. Here we wish to focus on the neo-liberal critique of the state as an economic agent before considering the limits of neo-liberalism itself.

The neo-liberal critique of the state owes much to Hayek, perhaps the most sophisticated exponent of the merits of the market even though he was not part of the neoclassical fraternity. The key problem of a 'rational economic order', in Hayek's view, lay in the fact that 'the knowledge of the circumstances of which we must make use never exists in concentrated or integrated form but solely as the dispersed bits of incomplete and frequently contradictory knowledge which all the separate individuals possess' (Hayek, 1945). In contrast to the neoclassical view that knowledge is readily accessible, Hayek wanted to highlight the significance of tacit knowledge when he drew attention to that 'body of very important but unorganised knowledge which cannot possibly be called scientific in the sense of knowledge of general rules: the knowledge of the particular circumstances of time and place' (Hayek, 1945). The fact that knowledge is not given to any single agent in its totality, plus the fact that the tacit element could never be codified let alone centralized, informed his critique of central planning and his defence of the market, which he saw as a form of 'decentralized planning by many separate persons'. In this view, it is a 'fatal conceit' to imagine that central planning, in the form of the state, can substitute for the market because the latter, being a decentralized discovery mechanism, is the best way to ensure that knowledge of the particular circumstances of time and place is promptly exploited (Hayek, 1945; 1988).

Powerful as it is as a critique of the 'strong' state this view has some major flaws: it crudely juxtaposes central planning (the state) with decentralized planning (the market) as though these were the only mechanisms for co-ordinating economic activity; it views the market as the only discovery mechanism, when this is just one among many mechanisms; and, by reducing knowledge to an attribute of atomistic individuals, it neglects the much more important form of organizational knowledge, which is created and diffused through social interaction.

Some of these theoretical problems assume concrete form in countries which have vigorously embraced the neo-liberal repertoire, the UK in particular. As we show in more detail in Chapter 6, the neo-liberal strategy in the UK, which was initially consumed with the idea of extending the market through deregulation and privatization, was forced to accommodate more pro-active enterprise support policies. Recognizing the limits of the market as a discovery process, the Conservative government felt obliged to reform, rather than dismantle, the business support infrastructure; significantly, many of these reforms were predicated on the principle of collaboration: between firms (e.g. supply chains), between firms, government, and scientific establishments (technology foresight), and between the public and private sectors more generally.

In this case, a whole series of non-market mechanisms was deemed necessary to overcome the limits of the market as an animateur of innovation. In other words, beneath its ideological apotheosis of the market, this neo-liberal repertoire reluctantly conceded that, in practice, the market is far from being the only mechanism for conveying information, for disseminating knowledge, and for nurturing the norms of trust and reciprocity which underpin successful collaboration.

The Associational Repertoire

In the associational repertoire, the key issue is not the scale of intervention but its mode, not the boundary between state and market but the framework for effective interaction. In contrast to the classical repertoires, which seek to privilege either the state or the market, the associational repertoire seeks instead to empower intermediate associations which lie between state and market, be they groups of firms, trade associations, chambers of commerce, labour unions, or civic associations. Elements of this approach can be found in those countries— like Germany, Sweden, and Switzerland—where the state–market antinomy tends to have been more muted, and where the principle of self-organization plays an important role in fostering social and economic development on the one hand and political stability on the other. This is because:

Institutions of this kind, in addition to mediating between the state and the market, seem to limit the extent to which the two can invade each other and enlarge their domain at each other's expense. In this way, they seem to inject an element of stability in their respective polities which makes them less subject to changing political fashions. Also, an elaborate intermediary associational structure seems to enlarge a country's repertoire of policy alternatives—its 'requisite variety'—and this may enable such countires to respond to new problems without having to undergo dramatic internal realignments. (Streek and Schmitter, 1985)

In this perspective one of the key developmental roles of the state is to create the conditions—the formal framework as well as the informal norms of trust and reciprocity—whereby firms, intermediate associations, and public agencies can engage in a self-organized process of interactive learning (Lundvall, 1992; Sabel, 1994; Hausner, 1994; Amin and Thrift, 1995). Although some variants of associational theory would have the state almost 'wither away' as public functions are progressively devolved to self-organized intermediate associations, such views have been rightly criticized for ignoring the strategic significance of the state (Amin, 1996). While the associational repertoire sets a high premium on pluralism and subsidiarity (i.e. the devolution of responsibility to the lowest levels of competence), the state does not lose its unique status as an institution; on the contrary, it remains the only institution to have overall responsibility for social cohesion and the integrity of the national system of innovation.

However, the associational repertoire involves two institutional innovations which the more centralized political systems may be reluctant to sanction. First, it involves the devolution of power within the state system, from remote central departments to local and regional tiers which are better placed to forge durable and interactive relations with firms, their associations, and other cognate bodies. Secondly, it involves delegating certain tasks, like enterprise support services, for example, to business-led associations because the latter have far more knowledge of, and credibility with, their members than a state agency. A state that withdraws from direct intervention to indirect animation need not be a weak or ineffective state; if its policy goals are more effectively met through regulated delegation, it can actually become stronger by doing less and enabling more.

This is somewhat similar to what Sabel (1994) is trying to suggest when he argues that the effectiveness of the state in Japan stems not from the scale but the mode of its intervention, a mode in which the state works in and through developmental associations of firms in an interactive process of 'learning by monitoring'. The challenge here is to create institutions which can transform transactions into discussions because 'discussion is precisely the process by which parties come to reinterpret themselves and their relation to each other by elaborating a common understanding of the world' (Sabel, 1994). This view has strong affinities with the 'interactive' mode of intervention, whereby the state 'takes on the role of participant and treats the other participants as independent agents, whose behaviour can only change as a consequence of mutual interaction' (Hausner, 1994).

While the state is just one among many institutions in the developmental process it alone has the capacity to influence the (national) conditions under which others interact and, for good or ill, this power is unique to the state. While associational theory recognizes this distinctive capability, it also insists that to be effective, this power needs to be used in such a way that it empowers others, that it is used to build 'capacities for collective action', where this is understood to mean 'mutually coherent sets of expectations, built into conventions, which underlie technological-economic spaces, permitting the actors involved to develop and co-ordinate necessary resources' (Storper, 1995). While the state is indeed a unique institution, the effective use of state power is contingent on the active co-operation of others, hence it needs to collaborate with and work through the institutions which collectively constitute the national system of innovation.

NATIONAL SYSTEMS OF INNOVATION

Having looked at the role of firms and states we now turn to consider the role of *national systems* of innovation (NSI), a concept which is attracting growing interest (Freeman, 1987; Lundvall, 1992; Nelson, 1993; Patel and Pavitt, 1994; Freeman, 1995; Edquist, 1997*b*). The NSI concept, which stresses the continuing significance of nationally structured institutions and conventions, is a useful and necessary antidote to the more exaggerated claims made on behalf of globalization (Ohmae, 1990; 1996). In this respect the NSI is just one example of the seemingly paradoxical point that globalization, which exerts a 'convergence' effect between countries, coexists with 'diversity' because nationally based patterns of economic behaviour have proved to be stubbornly persistent; this is not merely because they are deeply embedded in custom and practice, they also signal different ways of organizing economic activity and, no less important, they reflect the fact that countries still exhibit significant levels of technological specialization. In short, 'convergence' is just one among a number of possible evolutions, alongside 'catching-up', 'forging ahead', and 'falling behind' (Dosi *et al.*, 1994; Boyer, 1996). To be more specific, the continuing significance of national borders is suggested by the following stylized facts:

- in the main industrial economies, some 90 per cent of production is for the domestic market;
- domestic investment by domestic capital far exceeds direct investment overseas plus foreign investment at home;
- world stock markets are far from fully integrated because few companies have a sufficiently global reputation for their stock to be actively traded beyond their home base;
- multinational companies are more accurately called national firms with international operations because, as we shall see, the bulk of their high value-added activities is confined to their home base;
- firms in many industries, other than those involved in simple assembly operations, are far from fully footloose once they have invested;
- OECD countries have demonstrated persistent, not converging, differences in the rate and pattern of technological activities since the 1960s, which suggests that national systems are robust and tend to determine the technological activities of large firms rather than vice versa, which would be the globalization thesis;

- in 1960, when most of the globalization literature starts the clock, national economies were surprisingly closed entities, since when we have witnessed dramatic increases in internationalization, but from a low base;
- the notion of a 'national system' rests on the assumption that technology continues, even after big improvements in computer-based codification, to have a large element of tacit knowledge, that tacit knowledge is costly to acquire, and that it is cumulative and path-dependent in its development;
- national boundaries are proxies for physical, cultural, political, and linguistic nearness and sameness, which continue to affect the transfer of tacit knowledge from person to person and from organization to organization (Wade, 1996).

It is against this background that evolutionary theorists have developed the NSI concept, which admits to both a narrow and a broad interpretation. Narrowly, the concept refers to 'the network of institutions in the public and private sectors whose activities and interactions initiate, import, modify and diffuse new technologies' (Freeman, 1987). On a broader definition, the NSI includes 'all parts and aspects of the economic structure and the institutional set-up affecting learning as well as searching and exploring' (Lundvall, 1992). In this broader definition, the national system is understood to mean a nationally structured system of interactive learning.

This broader definition is also consistent with the view that institutions—understood in the dual sense to mean organizations and social norms—are both the medium for and the result of social action: they enable as well as constrain social action (Giddens, 1984). This is important because while the NSI concept thoroughly disavows any notion of 'one best way' for organizing resources, it nevertheless recognizes that some systems are far more effective than others in fostering learning and innovation. Let us address this issue directly by examining six elements of these systems.

The role of R&D is clearly of crucial importance to any national system of innovation since this is what gives firms and countries the capacity to generate, absorb, and diffuse technology. Although governments play an important role here, particularly in the funding of basic research, large firms are the key players in this field. Contrary to fashionable notions about 'techno-globalism', the technological activities of large firms remain overwhelmingly biased towards their home countries. For example, a study of patenting data for 587 of the world's largest firms found that 89 per cent of their technological activities in the second half of the 1980s continued to be performed in their home country, a 1 per cent decrease over the previous five-year period (Patel and Pavitt, 1994). Moreover, the technological activities of large firms are strongly correlated with those of their home countries, which suggests that multinationals are not as 'stateless' as the globalization literature sometimes implies. The degree of national technological specialization remains significant and seems to be increasing, confirming the localized and path-dependent nature of technological learning. Between 1963–90, for example, the USA enhanced its technological position in weapons, raw materials, and telecommunications, and suffered rapid decline in consumer electronics and motor vehicles, while almost the opposite occurred in Japan. In Western Europe the pattern was different again, and very close to that of its dominant country, Germany, namely continuing strength in chemicals, growing strength in weapons, declining strength in motor vehicles, and weakness in electronics (Patel and Pavitt, 1994; Archibugi and Pianta, 1992).

The technology performance indicators of national systems show a remarkably similar picture whether measured by inputs, like R&D as a percentage of GDP, or outputs, like patents. The general picture is of a certain stability in the rankings from the mid 1960s to the early 1990s, the major exceptions being the declining position of the UK and the USA and the improved position of Japan, Germany, Sweden, Finland, and Switzerland (Patel and Pavitt, 1994).

The ensemble of education and training institutions constitutes another core element of all national systems of innovation, furnishing the technical skills to exploit existing knowledge and generate new knowledge. While most OECD countries have a similar proportion of their workforces with graduate degrees, between 7 per cent and 11 per cent, there are still significant differences with respect to the composition of these qualifications. For example, Germany and Switzerland have nearly 60 per cent more home graduates in engineering and technology than the UK, while the latter has proportionately more graduates in arts and pure science. However, it is at the level of intermediate vocational qualifications that we see the most striking differences. In this sphere the UK is doubly distinctive: just 25 per cent of its workforce had intermediate vocational qualifications in 1989, compared to 63 per cent in Germany, and 64 per cent had no such qualifications at all, compared to just 26 per cent in Germany (Prais, 1993). The availability of workforce skills is clearly a major factor in deciding which quality segment of a market a firm is able to target. More significant is the way these skills are valued and organized *within* the firm: for example, low level technical skills, combined with Taylorist methods of work organization, render it difficult for UK firms to secure the kinds of incremental innovation we see in Japan and Germany. Moreover, as we argue in Chapter 6, these data help to explain why the UK is able to mount a strong challenge in pharmaceuticals and military electronics, sectors which depend on élite science, and why it is unable to do so in many manufacturing sectors, which depend on engineering and vocational skills.

A third element is the financial system. While this is probably the most globalized segment of the economy, it continues to display strong national characteristics with respect to the interface with industry, the price and time-frame of borrowing, financial regulations, accounting practices, and corporate ownership rules (Wade, 1996). Much of the research in this field suggests a strong contrast between Anglo-Saxon countries, where the links between finance and industry are loose, short-termist, and exit-based, and European and Asian countries, where the links are closer, longer-term, and voice-based (Hutton, 1996). According to this argument, it is much easier to raise 'patient capital' for innovation in the latter, not least because banks and industry tend to have more of a shared destiny, most notably in Germany, where the likes of Deutsche Bank have a major ownership stake in many firms.

Fourthly, the network of user–producer relationships is another significant element because this is an important conduit through which learning and innovation occurs between firms. The idea that advanced domestic users can play a major role in explaining the innovative capacity and competitiveness of their fellow national producers has been around for some time (Hirschman, 1958) and recent evidence confirms this view (Porter, 1990; Lundvall, 1992). In particular, a study of sixteen countries over the period 1965–87 found that there was a positive link between the existence of advanced domestic users and the competitiveness of their domestic producers in most of these countries, with the UK being one of the notable exceptions (Fagerberg, 1995). While the intensity and stability of user-producer relations will vary by sector within each country—with a tendency for more complex products to be associated with more intense, stable relationships because of the need for close co-operation—there are also important national differences in the character of these relations. For example, user-producer relations in Japan and Germany are said to be closer, more stable, and longer term, marked by a higher degree of trust, voice, and loyalty, than they are in the UK and the USA (Dore, 1986; Dertoutzos *et al.*, 1989; Sako, 1992; Lane and Bachmann, 1996).

The mainstream literature on national systems has little room for what we might call intermediate institutions, be they sectoral organizations (like trade associations) or territorial bodies (like local chambers and regional technology transfer centres). But we believe that these intermediate institutions, our fifth element, constitute an important but hitherto neglected part of a country's infrastructure for diffusing knowledge and keeping sectors and regions abreast of advanced practices. These sectoral and territorial institutions tend to be weaker in the UK and the USA than they are in Japan, Germany, and Scandanavia, with the result that the latter are better equipped to diffuse new practices to a wider population of firms (Cooke and Morgan, 1994c).

The final element we wish to mention differs from the others because it is an intangible asset, namely social capital, which refers to features of social organization—such as networks, norms, and trust—that facilitate co-ordination and co-operation for mutual benefit (Putnam, 1993; Sabel, 1993). Because we shall say more about this in the following section on trust, voice, and loyalty, here we merely want to highlight the point that social capital helps to lubricate associational action within the firm, in inter-firm networks, and between firms and their institutional milieu. If social capital is a proxy for the disposition to collaborate for mutually beneficial ends, then we can say that it is more prevalent in 'organized capitalism' (e.g. Japan and Germany) than in 'liberal capitalism' (e.g. the USA and the UK).

To summarize these differences we might draw a more analytical distinction between *myopic* and *dynamic* national systems of innovation (Patel and Pavitt,

1994). In myopic systems, like the UK and the USA, investments in technological activities are treated just like any other investment: they are undertaken
in response to a well-defined market demand and include a strong discount for
risk and time and, all too often, these activities do not compare favourably with
conventional investments. Dynamic systems, like Japan and Germany, recognize that technological activities are not the same as other forms of investment:
in addition to tangible outcomes in the form of products, processes, and profits,
they also entail the accumulation of important but intangible assets, in the form
of irreversible processes of technological, organizational, and market learning.

Thus far we have argued that national systems continue to be of significance
for an understanding of innovation and economic development. Even so, the
stark national character of these systems is being attenuated, and possibly compromised, by the twin processes of globalization and regionalization. This is
sometimes interpreted as part of the 'hollowing out' of the nation state, a process in which the latter progressively loses functions 'upwards' to supranational
bodies like the EU, and 'downwards' to regional and local states (Jessop, 1994).
Although the nation state is far from finished as a political entity, its power
and authority have been circumscribed by the trends towards globalization and
regionalization. Let us briefly illustrate each of these trends.

If the extent of globalization has been greatly exaggerated, it is nevertheless
a powerful influence in reshaping economies, polities, and societies in and beyond the OECD bloc of countries (Berger and Dore, 1996). Its most visible
effects are inscribed in the strategies and structures of transnational firms, which
collectively have global sales in excess of $4.8 trillion, a larger volume than
total world trade (UNCTAD, 1994). Although their markets are much more
globalized than their R&D activities, the latter are not as spatially immobile
as they once were. Between 1985–91, for example, overseas R&D investment
by US firms increased ninefold, while the amount spent at home stagnated; but,
to put this into perspective, the total spent abroad in 1991 was $8.7 billion, com-
pared to some $65 billion spent at home (National Science Foundation (NSF),
1994). The R&D activities of European and Japanese firms are also becoming less domestically skewed, though this is also a fairly recent phenomenon
(Granstrand *et al.*, 1993). Two of the main motives for the 'globalization' of
R&D are: first, to provide higher levels of technical service in foreign markets,
including more customized products and, secondly, to create 'listening posts'
to tap into foreign sources of knowledge. This trend suggests that the traditional product-cycle model needs to be amended because that model recognized
just one pre-eminent location for innovation, the home base, whereas now there
is a growing tendency for the most advanced firms to develop multiple locations for innovation, even if the home base remains the most important site
(Cantwell, 1995).

The growing globalization of markets, finance, and production is beginning
to compromise the hitherto dynamic national systems of 'organized capitalism'.
The German system, for example, was based on a highly regulated institutional

compromise, between capital and labour on the one hand and finance and industry on the other, buttressed by public and quasi-public intervention. This is now beginning to unravel. The larger industrial firms are beginning to substitute foreign for domestic production to improve market access and to escape high domestic labour costs, fuelling new conflicts with their employees. The intimate bonds between finance and industry are also mutating: banks are becoming more cosmopolitan, and looking to trim their industrial stakes, while large industrial firms are beginning to adopt more liberal accounting practices as their credit needs outgrow the domestic market. In short, the deregulatory bias of globalization means that global competition may produce 'the perverse outcome of the less well-performing Anglo-American model of capitalism outcompeting the better performing Rhine model' (Streek, 1995; Albert, 1993).

At a lower level we are witnessing a growing regionalization of national state structures as regions strive for more cultural identity on the one hand and more locally attuned development strategies on the other (Sharpe, 1993; Keating and Loughlin, 1997). As we shall see, some systems are national in name only because, in Italy and Spain for example, the most important systems are based on sub-national processes, even if these are formally nested in national regulatory regimes. Moreover, since globalization seems to be proceeding in parallel with a growing regionalization of economic activity, it appears that regions are (once again) becoming important arenas of development (Sabel, 1989; Storper and Scott, 1995; Scott, 1996). Indeed, the hitherto most dynamic national systems contain highly developed technology transfer mechanisms at the regional level, like the Fraunhofer Institutes in Germany and the Kohsetsushi Centres in Japan, which help to keep smaller firms on an innovative footing (Cooke and Morgan, 1993). More generally, it may be that regionalized networks, which can sustain close and regular interactions between public and private sectors, are the most effective scale at which to nurture the high-trust relations that are essential for learning and innovation. While this remains to be seen, the more pro-active regions in Europe and North America, no longer content to work within a nationally defined policy template, are crafting ever more customized development strategies. What this means is that national systems are becoming more variegated, as they are reshaped from 'above' by globalization and from 'below' by regionalization.

TRUST, VOICE, AND LOYALTY

Recent theories of innovation and economic development maintain that intangible factors can be every bit as important as tangible factors like fixed investment in explaining the success of firms, regions, and countries (Doeringer and Terkla, 1990; Freeman, 1994a; Storper, 1995). In this final section, we shall develop this point by focusing on the potential benefits (and costs) of trust, voice, and loyalty, factors which are often associated with the broader concept of social capital. We begin by looking at trust, a subject which has attracted enormous interest in recent years (Arrow, 1974; Luhmann, 1979; Sabel, 1992; Sako, 1992; Powell, 1996; Humphrey and Schmitz, 1996; Lane and Bachmann, 1996).

Trust—the confidence that parties will work for mutual gain and refrain from opportunistic behaviour—can be an important economic asset *if* it can be secured. Unlike most other economic assets, however, trust cannot be bought; rather it has to be earned by discharging one's obligations or by eschewing opportunities to exploit short-term advantages. In other words, trust is one of those rare assets, like loyalty and goodwill, which have a value but no price.

Because so few social settings are wholly devoid of trust it is, strictly speaking, best to speak of high-trust and low-trust relationships, the latter being close to the opportunistic behaviour which is assumed to be prevalent in transaction cost economic theory. In stylized terms the high-trust relationship can be characterized as one in which:

the participants share certain ends or values; bear towards each other a diffuse sense of long-term obligations; offer each other spontaneous support without narrowly calculating the cost or anticipating any equivalent short-term reciprocation; communicate freely and honestly; are ready to repose their fortunes in each other's hands; and give each other the benefit of any doubt that may arise with respect to goodwill or motivation. (Fox, 1974)

Conversely, in a low-trust relationship:

the participants have divergent ends or values; entertain specific expectations which have to be reciprocated through a precisely balanced exchange in the short-term; calculate carefully the costs and anticipated benefits of any concession; restrict and screen communications in their own separate interests; seek to minimise dependence on each other's discretion; and are quick to suspect, and invoke sanctions against, illwill or default on obligations. (Fox, 1974)

Alan Fox's outstanding analysis of work, power, and trust comes to the conclusion that the low-trust syndrome imposes severe limitations on human collaboration. While the severity of this problem varies with the task, the technology, and the aspirations of the participants, Fox argues that no system of interdependence can be other than impeded by the 'wary arm's length relations' which characterize the low-trust syndrome. Even so, we should remember that many arm's-length relationships exist not because of low trust, but because only simple tasks or transactions are involved, for which high trust is not so much unavailable as not required. Theories of trust sometimes forget that, in these cases, trust-building can be both costly and unnecessary.

The burgeoning literature on trust claims that a number of important benefits can flow from high-trust relationships. To summarize, trust-based relationships are said to confer at least three major benefits on participants who have taken the time and trouble to develop these relational assets: (1) they are able to economize on time and effort because it is extremely efficient to be able to rely on the word of one's partner; (2) they are better placed to cope with uncertainty because, while it does not eliminate risk, trust reduces risk and discloses possibilities for action which would have been unattractive otherwise; and (3) they have a greater capacity for learning because they are party to thicker and richer information flows (Arrow, 1974; Luhmann, 1979; Sabel, 1994; Sako and Helper, 1996).

If trust does indeed confer these benefits—as we believe it does—this raises the question as to how it evolves. Most of the literature on trust seems to fall into two, equally inadequate, schools of thought. The existence of trust-based relationships is either attributed to 'cultural norms', which tend to assume what needs to be explained, or it is reduced to purely 'calculative action', which over-states the parties' capacity for gauging the precise benefits of co-operation in advance. A more productive approach begins by recognizing that trust is neither an outcome derived from calculation nor a norm traced to culture but a dispo-sition which is learned and reinforced through successful collaboration, such that trust is a by-product of success rather than a pre-condition for it (Powell, 1996). To be effective, trust-based relationships require rich consultative struc-tures which allow the participants to monitor their interactions; while such monitoring reduces the possibility of opportunism, its central function is 'to regularise consultation between the parties so as to minimise the cost of mistakes and maximise the possibility of introducing improvements that benefit both' (Sabel, 1993).

In other words, monitoring is a crucially important device for minimizing problems that may result not from a breakdown of trust but from a lack of com-petence, and the latter might be read as the former without close and effective monitoring. Far from being a sign of mistrust then, monitoring helps to ensure that what is being crafted is *studied* trust as opposed to *blind* trust.

In Chapter 2 we examine the ways in which innovative firms are trying to build high-trust relations between management and employees within the firm and between firms in the supply chain. The new forms of co-operation which are emerging in and between these firms may of course reflect not trust but fear because, given the enormous asymmetry of power involved here, employees and suppliers might feel compelled to co-operate in new working practices. Indeed, the rhetoric of 'partnership' is all too often a fig-leaf for more sophis-ticated forms of coercion, the iron fist in the velvet glove. If this is the case, then firms will have to forgo the benefits which are associated with high-trust relations. At bottom the potential for trust-building depends on the way in which power is exercised and this, in turn, is linked to the way in which self-interest is defined: if corporate power is deployed towards narrowly conceived, short-term interests, then it is difficult to see any basis for high-trust relations. But the evidence we present in Chapter 2 suggests that leading firms are beginning to recoil from exercising power in this way, not least because they recognize that their long-term interests are inextricably linked to the quality of their employees and the calibre of their suppliers.

Building trust requires a constant dialogue between the parties so that interests and perceptions can be better aligned. Here it is useful to revisit Hirschman's concept of voice, which he defined as any attempt 'to change, rather than to escape from, an objectionable state of affairs' (Hirschman, 1970). In his classic study of responses to decline in firms, organizations, and states, Hirschman argued that while exit and voice were equally important reaction mechanisms, there was an unwarranted bias towards the former in economic theory and corporate practice. This is because exit is perceived to be the 'economic' or 'market' mechanism, while voice is the 'political' or 'non-market' alternative. Exit, which is predicated on the availability of choice, tends to be seen as a less costly reaction compared to voice because the latter involves organizing and channelling opinion, criticism, or protest. The key point, however, is that voice can be a substitute for exit as well as a complement to it. But there is an important difference between the two mechanisms because 'once you have exited, you have lost the opportunity to use voice, but not vice versa; in some situations, exit will therefore be a reaction of last resort after voice has failed' (Hirschman, 1970).

Exit-centred corporate behaviour is not as costless as it appears. Hirschman recognized that the effect of exit decisions could indeed be harmful, not least because they are often made on the basis of a short-term, narrowly defined calculus of self-interest (Hirschman, 1986). For example, it is difficult to see how firms can develop interactive learning relationships in their supply chains if they are constantly switching suppliers for the sake of short-term cost savings. Where learning, innovation, and tacit knowledge are important, where technologies and markets are less stable and standardized, then voice would seem to have a significant role to play. Even so, we should not underestimate the difficulties of voice-formation; indeed, Hirschman's original formulation has been rightly criticized for assuming that voice is a ready alternative to exit. Far from being readily available, voice requires investment, of both time and resources, if it is to be a viable alternative to exit.

In Hirschman's conception, the likelihood of voice increases with the degree of loyalty because, for a certain period at least, loyalty tends to delay premature exit. The importance of loyalty is that it tempers the tendency for the most quality-conscious customers or members of a firm to be the first to exit. They delay exiting in the reasoned belief that, having some influence, reform 'from within' is possible. Rather than being irrational, then, loyalty 'can serve the socially useful purpose of preventing deterioration from becoming cumulative, as it so often does when there is no barrier to exit' (Hirschman, 1970).

Like trust, loyalty appears to be a superannuated pre-capitalist attribute, something totally alien to the calculus of advanced capitalist economies. However, the emergence of 'loyalty-based management' suggests that this attribute is neither of these things. A pioneering study in this vein found that raising customer retention rates by 5 per cent could increase the value of an average customer by 25 per cent to 100 per cent and it concluded that loyalty is far from dead because 'businesses that concentrate on finding and keeping good customers, productive employees and supportive investors continue to generate superior results' (Reichheld, 1996). The implication of this study is that firms need to build accounting systems that measure defections as well as defects.

If trust, voice, and loyalty have the potential to play a positive role in promoting learning and innovation in firms and regions, these non-market governance mechanisms carry their own problems, not least the problem of *lock-in*. If low-trust, exit-centred behaviour reduces the capacity for inter-organizational collaboration, which is vital for learning and innovation, we need to recognize that high-trust, voice-centred relationships can easily degenerate 'from ties that bind into ties that blind' (Grabher, 1993*b*). This problem, better known as 'the weakness of strong ties' in network analysis (Granovetter, 1973), emerges when collaborators are so deeply committed to, or embedded in, a given set of routines that they fail to keep abreast of new sources of information, new ways of working, and new learning opportunities. Perhaps the only sure way to secure the benefits of collaboration without the costs of lock-in is for the parties to be assiduous about monitoring, a practice which involves 'the deliberately trustful principle of testing the reliability of particular arrangements while relying on them' (Sabel, 1993).

Creating these intangible assets requires quite deliberate action on the part of firms and public agencies. To build high-trust supply chains, for example, requires 'trust enhancers' in the form of customers' technical assistance to suppliers, information sharing, and delivering on informal commitments (Sako and Helper, 1996). For their part, public agencies have an important role to play in voice-formation, for example by creating fora in which firms and their cognate organizations can explore joint solutions to common problems. In short, trust-building and voice-formation should be treated as investments in social capital, intangible assets which can enhance the effectiveness of tangible assets.

CONCLUSIONS

Most theories of innovation remain heavily focused on the firm because, in capitalist economies, the firm is the main repository of productive knowledge. What we have tried to do in this chapter, however, is to suggest that this focus is too narrow and too restrictive. In other words, if we are to develop a better understanding of innovation, we need to focus not on the individual firm but on the ensemble of relations in which firms, states, and systems interact.

While Schumpeter's 'heroic entrepreneur' still resonates in certain circles, the fact remains that innovation is a collective social endeavour. For this reason the capacity to collaborate—or what we refer to as associational capacity—is becoming an ever more important attribute when, as Lundvall (1992) reminds us, knowledge is the most important resource and learning the most important process. No organization, no matter how large, can hope to keep abreast of all the innovations which might possibly be relevant to it: hence the importance of having access to multiple channels of information and diverse methods of learning.

The generation and diffusion of knowledge appear to be more spatially bounded than the globalization thesis would have us believe, not least because tacit knowledge, which is not easily communicated, tends to be place-specific. The transfer of knowledge within and between organizations also seems to be more dependent on trust than is generally thought and, since trust is not widely accessible, this too tends to circumscribe the knowledge-transfer process. To illustrate these arguments, we now turn to consider how firms are seeking to build new forms of collaboration, internally and externally, with a view to becoming more innovative.

2

Firms as Laboratories: Re-inventing the Corporation

INTRODUCTION

In response to the challenges of the new competition (Best, 1990) leading-edge firms have embarked upon a process of experimentation which has few parallels in living memory. Although these experiments cover virtually every aspect of corporate life, four activities in particular have come under the spotlight, namely: corporate governance, R&D, production, and supply chains. Taken together, these four activities play a major, indeed seminal, role in determining the innovative capacity of the firm.

Experimentation, of course, is not a new phenomenon; on the contrary, it has been the hallmark of truly innovative firms since the birth of capitalism. What we believe is new, however, is the scale and intensity of corporate experimentation and the tendency for this state of affairs to be the 'normal' condition for firms which are, or aspire to be, at the frontier of their core markets and technologies. In other words we are *not* for a moment suggesting that this process of semi-permanent experimentation is typical of all, or even a majority, of the world's firms: just that it seems to be a characteristic of the more innovative firms.

We use the 'laboratory' metaphor for two reasons; first, to convey this sense of experimentation and, secondly, to emphasize that this is a process replete with uncertainties, imponderables, and contingencies, so much so that long-term corporate strategies are fraught with danger. Critics might argue that this process of experimentation is not as open-ended as we have suggested, that while such experiments may indeed be under way, they are really 'tinkering' exercises which never compromise the existing distribution of power within the firm, especially the distribution of power between capital and labour. It is certainly true that neither shareholders nor management want to initiate truly radical experiments, like worker control for example; even so, we should not belittle the pressures that are building up on firms in the Anglo-Saxon world which elevate dividend payments over R&D outlays, shareholders over other stakeholders. In general, however, we take the view that these experiments amount to something more significant than a mere 'tinkering' at the margin, that in many ways they signal a view of innovation as a collective social endeavour. What this view implies is that the dualisms of the Fordist era—between conception and execution and between centre and periphery—have to be transcended if the firm is to make the best use of *all* its capabilities.

Drawing on the notion of innovation as a collective social endeavour this chapter aims to show that, in each of the four spheres we have identified, leading firms are trying to develop deeper and more durable forms of co-operation. In the sphere of corporate governance, many firms are trying to strike a better balance between the interests of shareholders and stakeholders on the one hand and between their central and peripheral organizations on the other. In the R&D sphere, all firms are coming under intense pressure to forge better links between their laboratories and their factories, so much so that some technologists feel that their laboratories are being turned into factories. In the production sphere, the more innovative firms are trying to devolve responsibility to work teams who are supposedly empowered to use their local knowledge in the name of continuous improvement, with the result that the factory becomes more like a laboratory. The advent of more integrated supply chains suggests that innovative capacity rests not so much with the firm *per se* as with a network of firms in which formally independent firms become ever more functionally integrated. Throughout this chapter the focus is on what we consider to be *emergent* tendencies in the large-firm sector of the economy.

CORPORATE GOVERNANCE: RETHINKING OWNERSHIP AND CONTROL

Corporate governance is generally understood in a very narrow sense to mean the rules which govern the activities of company boards and the rights of shareholders. But here we use the term in a much broader sense to mean two things. First, it is used to refer to the legal and cultural arrangements which determine how publicly traded companies balance the interests of managers, shareholders, and stakeholders (e.g. employees, suppliers, and customers): the socio-legal dimension. Secondly, it is used to refer to the management structures through which intra-firm activities are organized (e.g. as between hierarchy and heterarchy): the organizational dimension.

From Shareholders to Stakeholders?

In the socio-legal sense of the term, corporate governance has become a burning issue in the Anglo-American world. A number of factors—like escalating corporate fraud, the spread of hostile takeovers, and levels of executive pay which seemed unrelated to company performance—all helped to bring this issue into the public domain in the 1980s. These anxieties fed into the wider concern noted in Chapter 1, namely, whether the shareholder-based systems in the USA and the UK were not partly to blame for the latter's poor economic performance relative to countries like Japan and Germany, which had more inclusive, stakeholder-based systems that allowed their firms to operate in a more stable and long-term environment (Blair, 1995; Hutton, 1995). To illustrate the problem,

and the experiments it has triggered, we shall focus on the corporate governance debate in Britain.

Ever since Berle and Means highlighted 'the separation of ownership and
control' within the large corporation, there has been a perennial debate about the
rights and duties of managers and shareholders (Berle and Means, 1933). The
conventional view, based on the principal-agent model, is that the company is
owned by its shareholders, that managers are their agents, and that corporate
governance is a question of making managers more accountable to shareholders.
But this view is now contested because:

The principal-agent model bears no relationship to the way large companies are actually
run . . . Corporate managers are not the agents of the shareholders, but the trustees of
the assets of the corporation, which include its reputation, its distinctive capabilities, and
the skills of the employees and suppliers. Their objective should not be to maximise
shareholder value but to further the interests of the business. (Kay and Silberston, 1995)

The RSA inquiry into Tomorrow's Company, the most searching examination
of corporate governance ever conducted in Britain, found that most company
boards thought it more important to satisfy the current body of shareholders
than to secure the long-term health of the enterprise. The main reason for this
corporate outlook was *not* due to any legal requirement but to the threat of
hostile takeover. In company law, directors' duties are owed to their company
rather than to any specific third party and, while they must have regard to the
interest of shareholders, that obligation is not related to the holders of shares
at one particular time, but to the general body of shareholders from time to
time. As the RSA put it:

for directors *not* to give appropriate weight to *all* the company's key relationships may
well be a breach of their fiduciary duty. That duty is to arrive at a balanced judgement
about maximising the company's value on a sustainable basis, and not necessarily to take
a short-term view of maximising returns for current shareholders. (RSA, 1995)

In other words, many directors simply do not understand their legal duties:
believing they have an obligation to put current shareholders first, they are constrained in their ability to strike a balance between the interests of all the stakeholders on whom the long-term health of the company depends. Critics argue
that this principal-agent model of corporate governance, which is prevalent in
Anglo-American circles, is inferior to the trusteeship model that is more common in continental Europe and Japan. The main reason is that the trusteeship
model allows more scope for developing the core skills of the company, including the skills of employees, suppliers, and customers, and these, rather than a set
of financial claims, are the essence of the company (Kay and Silberston, 1995).
This was also the view of the RSA inquiry, which was endorsed by executives
from twenty-five of Britain's top companies and, through the recently created
Centre for Tomorrow's Company, the RSA aims to promote what it calls 'the
inclusive approach', which is based on the trusteeship model.

Most public companies in Britain are still trying to digest the recommendations of the Cadbury Committee, which was set up in 1991 to examine 'the
perceived low confidence' in companies' financial reporting habits (Cadbury,
1992). One of the key recommendations of the Cadbury Report was that shareholders should be more actively involved in corporate decision-making, which
amounts to a belated attempt to try to breathe life into the principal-agent model
of corporate governance.

The reality of shareholding in Britain today, as we show in Chapter 6, is that
60 per cent of the shares on the London Stock Exchange are owned by institutional investors, with pension funds being the largest single group of shareholders. Yet less than 15 per cent of the votes of pension funds are actually
cast at company annual general meetings, a situation which has been likened
to 'a democracy where nobody votes' (TUC, 1996). With the growth of activist
shareholder groups, many of which seek to promote more accountable corporate governance, it will be less easy to sustain this practice.

The trusteeship model aims to promote the idea of the company as a 'community' in which risks and rewards are more evenly balanced among stakeholders than they are under the principal-agent model. The ultimate form of
trusteeship is for stakeholders to have a direct financial interest in the company.
For employees, this covers a wide range of options, like profit-related pay, individual share ownership, and employee share ownership plans (ESOPs). For trades
unions, the schemes which fit most closely into the stakeholding approach are
those, like ESOPs, which provide for some form of collective ownership and
which provide for employee influence in decision-making through the trustees
who administer the system (TUC, 1996). While employee-ownership is growing
in Britain, it is nowhere near as prevalent as in the USA, where nearly a third
of Fortune 500 companies are more than 10 per cent owned by employees and
where 'employee-held stock is starting to replace and restructure the system of
fixed wages and benefits that have dominated the wage economy since World
War II' (Blair, 1995).

The problem of corporate governance, in which one of the key issues is how
to strike a better balance between the interests of shareholders and stakeholders,
is not confined to Britain. We have focused on the British case because it is
here that the interests of shareholders have been so singularly stressed and so
highly extolled over other stakeholder interests. While this view has long been
contested by organized labour, what is new and potentially more subversive of
the corporate status quo is the fact that it no longer commands unanimous support within the British business establishment.

Paradoxically, while British firms are coming under pressure to consider
stakeholders' interests, leading German firms, like Daimler-Benz and Siemens
for example, are now under pressure to realize greater shareholder value. There
is no mystery in these seemingly contradictory tendencies: the common thread is
the attempt to strike a balance because, in Germany, where the cult of equity
is less pronounced than in the Anglo-American world, shareholders feel that
their interests have been subordinated to the wider purposes of the company

(Charkham, 1995). Far from being an arcane legal issue, these experiments in corporate governance will have a bearing on innovative capacity because they determine the extent to which employees, suppliers, and customers are integrated into the core competencies of the firm.

From Hierarchy to Heterarchy?

The organizational dimension of corporate governance has been a vibrant issue ever since multinational corporations (MNCs) were faced with the problem of how to co-ordinate their activities across national borders and whether this should be done principally on the basis of function, geography, or product market lines. Irrespective of how these organizing principles were blended together, they all shared one important characteristic: they were all variations on the more basic principle of *hierarchy*, which was thought to be the most efficient way of ordering 'complex systems' (Simon, 1962). Here we want to examine why this most basic of ordering principles is coming under attack, in both theory and practice, from other organizing principles, especially from *heterarchy*, which is heavily informed by network-based forms of organization. Although the corporate world contains an awesomely complex mix of organizational forms, often within the same firm, we offer here a stylized account of the problems of hierarchy and the potential of heterarchy, drawing on the seminal work of Gunnar Hedlund (1986; 1993; 1994).

Until the advent of the new competition, most large diversified firms in the West assumed that a strictly enforced hierarchy was the only way to co-ordinate their activities, and this gave rise to conceptions of the firm as a hierarchical, M-form structure in which the headquarters (HQ) was deemed to be the apex of knowledge, power, and authority and the role of subsidiaries was precisely that, subsidiary. But in the era of the new competition it is argued that the MNC is confronting a world which largely invalidates the fundamental assumptions of hierarchy and its supposed effects on efficiency. These assumptions include (1) the existence of pre-specified and stable tasks, which is difficult to sustain in the face of accelerating innovation and the constant re-ordering of tasks; (2) instrumentality, in which the subsidiary is seen simply as an instrument of the HQ, a conception which underestimates the learning capacity of the subsidiary; and (3) the coincidence of knowledge, action, and hierarchy, which assumes that expertise coincides with status in the hierarchy. While all these assumptions are difficult to sustain today, the third assumption, predicated on the social and spatial division between conception and execution, is especially at odds with a learning organization because:

Knowledge may be greater at the periphery and far 'down' the command chain. Instead new strategies are developed, or emerge in subunits. The locus of knowledge may not coincide with the locus of strategic initiative. In fact, managerial work consists largely of constantly rearranging structures and work processes so that knowledge and potential for action may meet. (Hedlund, 1993)

In a context where uncertainty is high, where the environment is unstable, and where the emphasis is on the creation and diffusion of knowledge, the most effective form of organization appears to be *not* the hierarchical M-form but the heterarchical N-form. The defining features of the N-form (i.e. network-form) corporation are as follows:

- it is geared to combining tasks rather than dividing them, it thus stresses the complementarity of corporate assets rather than their exclusivity at any one point in the organization;
- it involves temporary constellations from a pool of given people rather than permanent structures with a changing pool of people;
- it recognizes that knowledge must be elicited from many nodes, hence it does not deify the role of senior managers;
- it emphasizes lateral communication and dialogue rather than privileging the vertical dimension;
- the HQ is seen as the architect of communications rather than just being a monitoring and allocative device;
- heterarchy not hierarchy is the basic ordering principle: in this network-like organization several strategic apexes can emerge and these may shift over time depending on competence in the network rather than status in the hierarchy (Hedlund, 1994).

Recent work on MNCs confirms the growing significance of these N-form features. We need only think of the notion of 'the transnational organization', which seeks to combine three key features: multidimensional perspectives, distributed and interdependent capabilities, and flexible but integrative processes (Bartlett and Ghoshal, 1989). There is the conception of the firm as a federation of interdependent business units, in which competence is widely distributed in keeping with the principle of subsidiarity (Handy, 1994). There is the burgeoning literature on the changing form and function of the corporate HQ, where 'the head office becomes less a centre of control and more a means by which the constituent parts of the organisation make their own inputs into the decision-making process' (Dunning, 1993; Ferlie and Pettigrew, 1996). Finally, there is evidence that parent companies are increasingly tapping their foreign subsidiaries as sources of product, process, and organizational innovation (Bartlett and Ghoshal, 1986; Schoenberger, 1996; Zanfei, 1996).

The transition from hierarchy to heterarchy creates new problems and opportunities at all levels of the MNC, not least for managers who are charged with the task of effecting this transition. The international business literature is especially concerned with the new and challenging roles which managers will have to play in this emerging network-like environment because:

managers of the twenty-first century corporation will take the strategy-structure-systems doctrine that shaped corporate development for more than half a century and subsume it in a much richer, purpose-process-people-oriented management philosophy. Instead of concentrating on defining strategy designed to maximise economic returns to shareholders, they will focus on defining a corporate purpose that reflects the company's responsibility to and interdependence with a broader group of stakeholders. Instead of imposing a structure to define individual tasks, they will concentrate on building processes that enhance collective relationships aimed primarily at creating knowledge and leveraging learning. And instead of using systems as a way to control behaviour by minimising human idiosyncrasies, they will develop a perspective that treats people more as assets to be developed than as costs to be controlled. (Bartlett and Ghoshal, 1994)

Bartlett and Ghoshal argue that this is the emerging management model in companies which are gearing themselves for the twenty-first century, a model which is already visible, they claim, in some of today's most successful enterprises. For most companies, however, it is more a model for the future rather than a mirror of the present. Even so, it illustrates how the two dimensions of corporate governance discussed here—the socio-legal and the organizational—are deemed to be both interrelated and necessary to the development of innovative capacity in the broad sense of the term.

R&D: REINTEGRATING CONCEPTION AND EXECUTION

The advent of the in-house corporate R&D laboratory, which was pioneered in the late nineteenth century by German and US firms in the emerging chemical and electrical industries, signalled the growth of a professionally distinct group of technical specialists within firms whose job it was to put the commercial exploitation of science and technology onto a more formal footing (Freeman, 1982). This radical institutional innovation inspired Schumpeter to say that 'innovation itself is being reduced to a routine' and he bemoaned how 'the romance of earlier commercial adventure is rapidly wearing away, because so many things can be strictly calculated that had of old to be visualised in a flash of genius' (Schumpeter, 1943). Though manifestly wrong about R&D being something that could be strictly calculated, Schumpeter was clearly on to something when he spoke of innovation becoming dominated by 'teams of trained specialists' on the one hand and by 'bureau and committee work' on the other.

From the managerial standpoint, the specialized R&D laboratory is both a blessing and a curse. It is a blessing because it provides a critical mass of specialized skills through which firms develop their distinctive technological competencies and in this sense it constitutes 'the heart of the modern capitalist engine' (Nelson, 1990). Yet it is also something of a curse because, in contrast to what Schumpeter argued, R&D remains 'a groping, searching, uncertain process' (Freeman, 1982). Since the success of R&D activity in capitalist economies is established *ex post*, rather than *ex ante*, firms have more problems than they care to admit in cost-justifying their R&D spending. Indeed, this is often an act of faith in the future. The history of innovation is littered with examples of successful products which, at the R&D stage, were said to have little or no market value. For example, citing the five biggest classes of pharmaceutical products introduced in the past three decades, ranging from beta-blockers to recombinant vaccines, the R&D director of SmithKline Beecham said 'all of these have been phenomenally successful, but all were denied as having commercial potential' (Houlder, 1996). Much the same could be said of the telephone and the computer.

What compounds the problematical nature of R&D activity from a managerial standpoint is that there is no direct correlation between R&D spending and the financial performance of firms. The key factor is *not* the size of a company's R&D budget but how well it is organized and converted into successful products. To illustrate how organizational capabilities can triumph over resource commitments we need only recall how, in the race to develop a digital switch, ITT was outperformed by Ericsson even though its R&D budget was three times higher (Bartlett and Ghoshal, 1990).

This highlights the main theme we wish to explore here, namely the ways in which firms are trying to (re)integrate R&D with their other activities so as to render this function more commercially and less technologically driven. The significance of this issue was confirmed by a survey of R&D management trends since 1970, which found that two of the fastest growing concerns were organizational issues generally and the interface between R&D and production in particular (Allen and George, 1989).

Why should this be so? The answer lies partly in the professionalization of the R&D function, with its social exclusivity and its spatial separation: R&D labs seemed to acquire a life of their own, with their own agendas, cultures, and careers, and with technical directors acting as ambassadors for the political interests of R&D *vis-à-vis* other departments in the firm. The biggest laboratories —like GE's Schenectady Laboratory, Bell Labs, Dupont Central Labs, IBM Yorktown for example—set a high premium on fundamental research and have performed at and even above the level of top US universities, winning Nobel prizes in their fields (Noble, 1977; Rosenberg and Nelson, 1994).

The social and spatial separation of R&D labs from other corporate functions, like production and marketing, has a key part to play in explaining the problems of the linear model of innovation. These problems were fully exposed over thirty years ago in a sociological study of the management of innovation which was incredibly prescient for its time (Burns and Stalker, 1961). Here we are treated to the mulitiple problems which attend the '*one*-way traffic of designs from laboratories into production shops' (emphasis added), where many of the problems 'had characteristics in common which can best be called linguistic'. While the deepest divisions were found to lie between technology and sales staff, there was also a deep and debilitating division between technology and production staff. Development engineers freely conceded that, for them, the workshop was 'a terra incognita'. In one firm there was an actual brick wall between the laboratory and the rest of the concern, but in every other firm they found a 'brick wall' which was no less of a barrier even though it was metaphorical. Anticipating contemporary concerns they argued that 'as laboratories grow

larger, and specialist groups multiply, there is a danger of some essential channels of communication becoming attenuated or severed merely because of the
presence of so many channels of communication around the individual'. This
led them to conclude that 'the fewer the links in the chain from development
to production, the more, that is, development and production were forced to
learn each other's language, the more effective, speedy and trouble-free was
the passage through of designs' (Burns and Stalker, 1961).

Despite the privileged position of the high prestige research laboratory, the
latter is perhaps the least significant component of what we loosely call 'R&D'.
Indeed, according to one estimate, if R&D expenditure is broken down into its
component parts some 66 per cent might be devoted to development, 20 per cent
to applied research, and around 15 per cent to basic research (Rosenberg, 1976).
In other words, the social status of these functions is inversely related to their
real economic significance and this, together with the poor organizational interface between R&D, production, and marketing, helps to explain why the linear-
like product development process practised by most Western firms made them
so vulnerable to the more integrated approach to product development pioneered
by Japanese firms.

The significance which Burns and Stalker attached to a 'shared language'
resonates in recent thinking on product development, which is now seen to be
the most iterative part of the whole innovation process, involving a good deal
of tacit knowledge. Drawing on hermeneutics (the discipline of interpretation),
researchers at MIT have argued that meaning and meaningfulness are always
contextual, they are part of the situation, so much so that 'there can be no
understanding independent of a mutual set of experiences and interpretative
practices' (Piore *et al.*, 1994). This view is heavily influenced by the Japanese
approach to knowledge-creation, which sets a high premium on the acquisition
of tacit knowledge (through experience and close personal interaction), as opposed
to the Western emphasis on codified knowledge. Hence, in this approach, the
'mere transfer of information will often make little sense if it is abstracted from
associated emotions and specific contexts in which shared experiences are
embedded' (Nonaka and Takeuchi, 1995).

The scope for generating a 'shared language' has been so much greater in
the Japanese approach to product development because of the distinctive way
this process is organized. Summarizing, we might say that there are at least
three distinctive features to the Japanese approach:

- the importance of the engineering department: the engineering departments
  in large Japanese manufacturing firms have traditionally played a significant
  role in the R&D process. They tend to be physically located on the manufacturing site and their engineers have a good command of practical knowledge concerning the manufacturing process. Most important, this arrangement
  facilitates a close interchange of information between product design and
  manufacturing staff;

- transfers of researchers and engineers: when a research project is commissioned, engineers from the engineering department are normally dispatched to the central research laboratory to participate in the project research team and, when the project is transferred to the manufacturing division, the dispatched engineers return with it. This helps to ensure robust channels of communication between the research laboratory, the engineering department, and the manufacturing division;
- ranking hierarchy: under this hierarchy, researchers and engineers share the cost of human investment when they are young and they reap the returns when, and if, they are promoted to higher ranks. Quitting a firm in mid-career is therefore likely to carry serious financial penalties and this is a powerful incentive for them to contribute to company-specific projects rather than develop personally marketable research capabilities. This also reduces the free-rider problem (i.e. the mid-career departure of skilled researchers), which makes firms more likely to adopt a long-term perspective in investing in R&D staff (Aoki and Rosenberg, 1987).

Compared to the traditional, linear product development model which was common in Western firms, and which is far from dead today, the Japanese approach has been far more integrated, using cross-functional skills at each stage of the process. It is an approach predicated on the view that learning and knowledge-creation are 'not the responsibility of the selected few—a specialist in R&D, strategic planning or marketing—but that of everyone in the organisation' (Nonaka and Takeuchi, 1995).

This integrated approach has helped Japanese firms to set new standards in product development, with the result that the time and costs of development have been substantially lowered relative to most Western firms, especially in the car and electronics industries (Nonaka and Takeuchi, 1986; Womack *et al.*, 1990; Clark and Fujimoto, 1991; Wheelwright and Clark, 1992). As Western firms woke up to this new competition they naturally tried to emulate some of these practices and this is why, over the past decade in particular, strenuous efforts have been made to reintegrate R&D with production so as to accelerate product development. Let us take two examples—GE and BMW—to illustrate the kind of experiments we have in mind here.

General Electric (GE) has gone further than most large firms in trying to reintegrate its R&D activities. Formally established in 1900, GE's corporate R&D centre at Schenectady in New York state was the first corporate laboratory in US industry, today employing over 1,000 technical staff. The reorganization of R&D is part of a wider strategy designed to create a 'boundaryless organization', which means cutting hierarchies and reducing the barriers between individuals within the divisions, between the divisions, and between GE and the outside world, principally suppliers and customers. One of the key aims of this general strategy is to create new incentives for *sharing* ideas so that information and knowledge circulate more rapidly throughout the organization, instead of being horded for personal gain, which was common in the past. As part of this new strategy, GE has completely overhauled the way in which its central R&D activities are organized and funded (Dickson, 1992).

While each of GE's thirteen operating divisions has its own R&D facility, the Schenectady centre is the intellectual hub of the company: with an annual budget of some $400 million, it accounts for 30 per cent of GE's patents and 50 per cent of its technical papers. Prior to the reforms of the 1990s, Schenectady was akin to a campus-like laboratory in which scientists had very little incentive to translate their technical projects into commercially successful products: indeed, it was not uncommon for them to 'throw an idea over the wall to the business division, sit back and say my job is done' (Dickson, 1992). When exhortation had failed to make Schenectady more commercially conscious, GE decided, in 1991, to make two structural changes to the way central R&D operated.

First, it changed the way the central laboratory was funded. Under the old system, GE's operating divisions paid Schenectady a fixed annual tithe, this went into a central pool, and the central laboratory decided how it would be spent. This system was frustrating for both sides: the operating divisions saw no connection between what they paid and what the centre did, while the latter complained that the divisions were sitting on commercially applicable patents it had developed. To overcome this problem, the tithe was sharply reduced and applied to a smaller pool to fund exploratory research, and any work beyond this stage now has to be wholly funded by the operating divisions. The result is that the divisions have a strong vested interest in their R&D project, while scientists at the central laboratory are rewarded for the number of products they have transferred from the laboratory to the market, an incentive system which binds R&D and production like never before, giving priority to the needs of the divisions.

Secondly, GE changed the way the central laboratory communicated with the operating divisions. Hitherto, it had used a group of full-time liaison managers, each of which was responsible for several divisions. Now, however, GE has assigned senior Schenectady managers to spend part of their time being the laboratory's representative with a single division. In the new system the representative informs the division of relevant research at the laboratory and tries to get the division to commit itself to furthering some of this work. This organizational change reinforced the effects of the new funding regime, and together these two reforms have induced much more of a shared destiny between the laboratory and the divisions, with the result that GE's product development process is now much more effective.

Our second example is BMW, one of the world's leading luxury car producers. To ensure that the product development process is as integrated as possible, BMW has embarked upon a radical experiment in which some 6,000 engineers and support staff are co-located at its Research and Engineering Centre to the north of Munich in what is the largest single concentration of vehicle engineering expertise in Europe. In the belief that R&D staff are most productive when they can interact on a face-to-face basis, the architecture of this Centre has been designed in such a way that no one has to walk more than 50 metres to meet a colleague. Despite its name, the Centre is much more than a conventional R&D facility because it represents an unprecedented co-mingling of skills, including research, design, development, manufacturing, personnel, procurement, and patents. Such extreme co-location is designed to achieve one fundamental goal, namely to reduce the development cycle of new models by up to two years through the use of advanced simultaneous engineering techniques, in which manufacturing methods are developed in parallel with prototypes. And, in BMW's view, the production of prototypes is '*the* area where you lose or gain time' in the product development process (Griffiths, 1990). This is also the area where iteration between different disciplines is most exacting, where the use of tacit knowledge is most pronounced, and co-location is deemed to be the key mechanism for tapping these intangible assets.

Although these are just two examples, we believe they illustrate a more general trend in which Western firms are trying to reorganize their R&D functions so that the latter become more integrated with the wider activities of the firm, especially with production and marketing. The new emphasis on integration does not necessarily entail *physical* co-location of course. As we saw in Chapter 1, the R&D functions of leading multinationals are becoming more globalized, albeit from a low base, and digital technologies play a key role here by creating 'electronic communities' in which R&D staff enjoy the benefits of *virtual* co-location. While these two forms of co-location are complementary, most firms would probably concur with Ford's experience, which is that 'the quality of face-to-face interaction is higher than the electronic variety, even between people who know each other well' (Lorenz, 1995).

The new emphasis on integrating R&D *within* the firm is paralleled by renewed efforts to make R&D more interactive with the *outside* world, with customers, leading users, and other external sources of knowledge. All the evidence suggests that what distinguishes successful from unsuccessful R&D strategies is the degree to which they have understood 'user needs' (Freeman, 1982; von Hippel, 1988). On this view, cross-functional teams within the firm need to be sufficiently alive to evolving user needs and, because the latter are rarely fully articulated, these teams need to interact with users on a close and regular basis. Indeed, in the most advanced product development strategies, leading users are actually members of these cross-functional teams, as in Xerox's strategy of 'innovating with the customer' (Brown, 1991).

As well as having to interact more intensively with leading customers, R&D laboratories are having to engage with other external sources of expertise. Burgeoning strategic alliances, joint ventures, and R&D agreements attest to the fact that an in-house R&D capacity is no longer sufficient to keep firms abreast of what they (may) need to know. These collaborative arrangements, together with the growing trend towards outsourcing of R&D, have led some commentators to suggest that 'the importance of large in-house R&D laboratories is declining' (Archibugi and Pianta, 1996). While external sources of R&D are becoming more important, it is wholly wrong to counterpose internal and external R&D as mutually exclusive options because a firm's *absorptive capacity* is nowadays more significant than ever before.

As we saw in Chapter 1, absorptive capacity—the ability of a firm to recognize the value of external information, assimilate it, and apply it to commercial ends—is absolutely critical to a firm's innovative capability and this absorptive capacity is a function of a firm's level of prior related knowledge (Cohen and Levinthal, 1990). In other words, firms need to be actively involved in R&D to be able to evaluate and apply relevant information and knowledge. Proponents of 'virtual R&D', in which R&D is outsourced to external parties (Houlder, 1995), do not fully appreciate that firms need to be knowledgeable users if they want to benefit from external sources of R&D or, indeed, if they want to be treated as equal partners in strategic alliances with other firms. This is not to belittle the significance of inter-firm networks, but to say that outsourcing of R&D means that firms no longer have the same degree of control over a core competence.

BEYOND TAYLORISM? THE FACTORY AS A LABORATORY

Just as the laboratory is beginning to ape some of the features of the factory, on account of the new disciplines being imposed on R&D, so the factory is becoming something of a laboratory because it is nowadays the site of a great deal of experimentation with respect to 'new physical spaces on the shopfloor, new ways of calculating, new forms of work organization and new modes of economic citizenship' (Miller and O'Leary, 1994). The view of the factory as a site where knowledge can be created as well as applied, where production workers are deemed to be capable of thinking as well as doing, where quality is as important as cost, was born out of the crisis of Taylorism, otherwise known as the principles of 'scientific management' which were first published in 1911. At the heart of Taylorism was the separation of conception and control—the prerogatives of management—from execution. Under this strict and routinized division of labour, the duty of management was to accumulate the knowledge hitherto possessed by workers, especially craft workers, and to translate this knowledge into rules which specified 'not only what is to be done but how it is to be done and the exact time allowed for doing it' (Taylor, 1967). In short, Taylorism was a systematic attempt to denude workers of knowledge, initiative, and control by reducing the discretionary content of their work to the lowest possible level.

The principles of Taylorism formed the basis for the organization of factory work under the Fordist system of mass production, so much so that Taylorism

TABLE 2.1. Taylorist vs. post-Taylorist regulatory modes

Taylorist modes	Post-Taylorist modes
Standard product	Product variety
Assembly line	Module production/production islands
Single-purpose mechanization	Flexible mechanization
Unqualified mass worker	Qualified (skilled) worker
Low work motivation (indifference)	High work motivation (identification)
Conflictual labour relations	Co-operative labour relations
Hierarchical management	Participatory management
Vertical division of labour	Vertical job integration
Horizontal division of labour	Job rotation
Workers tied to specific jobs	Work pace independent from production
Machine/assembly line-determined	cycle
workplace	Group work
Individual work	Self-control of time and motion
External control of time and motion	

Source: Jurgens *et al.* (1993).

presupposes Fordism and Fordism implies Taylorism (Sabel, 1982). Since the concept of Fordism is much broader than a production system, we shall refer to traditional and emerging forms of work organization in the factory as Taylorist and post-Taylorist factory regimes, the main features of which are shown in Table 2.1. The problems associated with the Taylorist regime, including worker alienation, low motivation, high control costs, and poor quality, were symptoms of a much more fundamental problem, namely that Taylorism was the epitome of a 'low-trust' relationship (Fox, 1974).

The work of Alan Fox is of critical importance in understanding the problems of Taylorism. According to Fox, the low-trust relationship is most commonly found in the relations between managers and workers where the latter are 'the occupants of low-discretion roles', as they most certainly are under Taylorism. The main effects of a low-trust relationship are that bargaining relations between management and labour are reduced to a zero-sum game, the scope for co-operation is limited, workers tend to be indifferent to their performance, and suspicious of management's motives, with the result that they feel unable to participate in 'a fellowship of common purpose and shared endeavour'. Low-trust regimes tend to reproduce themselves because workers have 'reciprocated with minimum commitment, grudging calculation, and a measured contribution —thereby reinforcing management's preference for low-trust strategies' (Fox, 1974). In contrast, the 'high-trust relationship' is often associated with the more discretionary work of professionals and managers and, as we outlined in Chapter 1, it is one where 'the participants share certain ends or values' (Fox, 1974).

The history of management–labour relations in Western factories over the past twenty years can be read as an ever more desperate attempt on the part of management to overcome the debilitating effects of Taylorism and to experiment, however tentatively, with the post-Taylorist forms of work organization identified in Table 2.1 (Auer and Riegler, 1990; Jurgens *et al.*, 1993). These attempts to move beyond Taylorism are paradoxically 'inspired by the same motivations as led to its adoption—namely economic efficiency, growth or profit' (Fox, 1974). In other words, many firms are trying to build high-trust relationships with their production workers not for their own sake but because this is perceived to be the best way to secure a highly motivated workforce, the key to tapping the deep, but under-utilized, knowledge of the shopfloor.

Throughout the history of capitalism firms have been forced to innovate not just in technological terms but also in terms of their *social* organization, particularly in their management–labour relations (Morgan and Sayer, 1988). However, both radical and conservative-inclined studies of the labour process tend to underestimate the modalities of social organization that are possible under capitalism. Indeed, one of the seminal Marxist texts assumes Taylorism to be synonymous with 'the logic of the capitalist mode of production' (Braverman, 1974). More recent Marxist studies have tempered such stark reductionism and have begun to acknowledge that, for all the conflict and coercion inherent in the labour process, there is also co-operation and consent because workers cannot be indifferent to the fortunes of their employers (Burawoy, 1979). The key point is that the social organization of the labour process will depend on a whole series of micro and macro factors, ranging from the technical competence and product-market strategy of the individual firm to the national system of employment relations in which it is embedded, a combination of factors which can produce wide variations within and between countries (Sayer and Walker, 1992).

For their part, managers long ago came to the conclusion that naked coercion was a blunt and ineffective way to realize their goals. Indeed, in advanced management circles today there appears to be a strong ideological consensus in favour of post-Taylorist forms of social organization, though this does not mean that all elements of Taylorism have been abandoned in practice, not least because post-Taylorist social innovations threaten traditional patterns of power, status, and control within the factory.

Since nothing concentrates the corporate mind quite as much as the threat of extinction, Western firms feel obliged to experiment with some of these post-Taylorist social innovations in order to meet the new competition. The main challenge here is how to respond to the Japanese model of *lean production*, a model which has consciously eschewed classical Taylorism to set new international benchmarks for product, process, and organizational innovation in mass production industries. The key features of lean production are:

- integrated single-piece production flow, with low inventories and small batches made just-in-time;
- defect prevention rather than rectification;

- production is pulled by the customer and not pushed to suit machine loading;
- team-based work organization with flexible multi-skilled operators and few indirect staff;
- active involvement of shopfloor workers in root-cause problem-solving to eliminate all non-value-adding steps, interruptions, and variability;
- close integration of the whole value chain from raw material to finished customer, through partnerships with suppliers and dealers.

The ambassadors of lean production claim that it will supplant traditional mass production and craft production 'to become the standard global production system of the twenty-first century' (Womack *et al.*, 1990). Before we examine this bold assertion of convergence around 'one best way', it is worth noting what these authors consider to be the two key organizational features of the 'truly' lean factory in the car industry, where the model was first developed. First, it transfers the maximum number of tasks and responsibilities to those workers actually adding value to the car on the line and, secondly, it has in place a system for detecting defects that quickly traces every problem to its ultimate cause. Both these features are predicated on the dynamic work team, which is said to be 'the heart of the lean factory'. In this view, work teams need to embrace a wide variety of skills, including machine repair, quality-checking, and materials ordering; they need to be encouraged to act proactively, so that they can anticipate problems; and they need to think about continuous improvement (*kaizen*). What is equally important, they claim, is an ethos of reciprocal obligation, where workers have a sense 'that management actually values skilled workers, will make sacrifices to retain them, and is willing to delegate responsibility to the team' (Womack *et al.*, 1990).

To the extent that we can generalize, the leading Japanese firms have secured a degree of commitment and involvement from their direct production workers that most Western firms find difficult to understand let alone replicate, and this sense of 'common purpose' has proved to be an extremely effective source of competitive advantage. But such 'common purpose' can be explained in terms of the three pillars of the Japanese enterprise system: 'lifetime' employment contracts for core workers, seniority-based payment systems, and company unions (Inagami, 1988). As well as conferring benefits, the social commitment which large Japanese firms display towards their core production workers also imposes costs because, compared to Western firms, they are much more reluctant to close plants. For example, when Nissan finally decided to close its Zama factory outside Tokyo in 1995, because of over-capacity and the high yen, it felt obliged to find alternative employment for its 2,500 manufacturing workers and its president ruefully declared that 'were it not for the problem of people, I would close factories one after another' (Nakamoto, 1995). Whatever the benefits of classical lean production, the main costs are the extraordinary levels of stress on the shopfloor, a problem which Japanese unions believe threatens to undo the car industry 'from the inside' (JAW, 1992).

Despite these levels of stress, the relative security of employment for core workers not only helps to explain worker commitment, but also worker flexibility. Compared to Western firms, which tend to have highly precise job descriptions, the large Japanese firms have much more flexible and diffuse job descriptions. What this means is that work allocation is both easier and faster in Japan because a given 'job' is associated with a far wider array of tasks (Cole, 1979).

While Western car firms are still coming to terms with lean production, the Japanese producers are having to come to terms with a new set of problems at home, principally the longest downturn since the 1930s, a painful appreciation of the yen, and the advent of a new, more fastidious generation of workers. These pressures are reshaping the macro and micro foundations of lean production in Japan: the downturn has forced firms to question the pillars of the enterprise system; the exchange rate crisis has encouraged a new wave of offshore investment, and, despite the growth in unemployment, the leading firms are experimenting with 'post-lean' production concepts to make factory work more attractive and less stressful to attract new recruits. For example, at its new Tochigi plant, Honda felt obliged to introduce a production system which dispensed with the assembly line for the first time and this was influenced by the 'skilled worker orientation' found in Germany and Scandanavia. Even Toyota, the pioneer of lean production, is having to rethink its original approach: at its newest plant in Kyushu the key innovations are social rather than technical, like the introduction of buffers between work stations and other ergonomic improvements to meet workers' concerns about the level of stress (Nomura, 1993; Turner and Auer, 1994; Berggren, 1995; Shimizu, 1995).

Lean production concepts—like teamwork, *kaizen*, total quality management (TQM), and just-in-time (JIT) production—have been internationally disseminated both directly, through Japanese overseas investment, and indirectly, through the mimetic behaviour of Western firms. As the car industry has been the first to feel the brunt of lean production, we can use this sector to highlight the problems and prospects of the post-Taylorist approach to work organization, an approach which stresses the involvement and empowerment of workers and the substitution of commitment for control as the key motivational device (Walton, 1985). While lean production is currently the dominant model of new work concepts, there is also the more human-centred model of work organization, inspired by Volvo's Uddevalla plant, which closed in 1993 and reopened in 1995, a plant which seeks to develop a more socially enriching form of production based on 'self-regulating teams' (Sandberg, 1995).

In the USA and the UK, these new production concepts have been developed in a number of 'flagship' factories, like NUMMI in the USA and Nissan in the UK, thus demonstrating that these concepts, suitably modified for local conditions, are transferable beyond Japan. Beginning in 1984 as a joint venture between Toyota and GM, NUMMI has exerted a powerful ideological impact in and beyond the US car industry, not least because it took over, and radically improved upon, the GM-Fremont plant which was closed in 1982. While there are many reasons for NUMMI's success, one of the key reasons is the radical reorganization of the workforce into shopfloor production teams, fewer job classifications, and a more democratic governance system within the plant (Adler, 1993; Turner and Auer, 1994). Although NUMMI hired some 85 per cent of its workforce from the former Fremont plant, new managers and new work organization concepts have made a decisive difference. For example, teams assume responsibilities which are not normally the province of line workers in US car plants, especially for quality assurance, preventive maintenance, and internal job rotation schedules. This system has been christened a form of 'democratic Taylorism', so called because, while it breaks with Taylorism in its emphasis on worker involvement, jobs remain specialized and work processes are standardized (Adler, 1993). Even so, the NUMMI experience signals 'a gradual but profoundly important shift in the nature of hierarchy, away from its coercive form based on positional authority, and towards a form more rooted in technical expertise and more dependent on workers' consent and participation' (Adler, 1997).

If NUMMI is a flagship for new forms of work organization in the US car industry, much the same can be said of Nissan in the UK. Beginning in 1986, Nissan is widely acknowledged to have set new performance standards for productivity and quality which are unmatched in the European car industry and bear comparison with some of the best plants in Japan. Nissan's performance has been attributed to the tripod of teamworking, quality, and flexibility. As in NUMMI, the production team is regarded as the centre of the enterprise, with all other functions playing a supportive role. Through a highly fastidious recruitment process, Nissan ensured that it had a relatively young workforce which was not 'contaminated' by traditional car industry practices. To secure maximum flexibility, all manual tasks are covered by just two job titles—manufacturing staff and technicians—which was revolutionary compared to the 516 job titles for manual workers at Ford in 1985 (Wickens, 1987).

Whereas managers and the union jointly select team leaders at NUMMI, the supervisor is the team leader at Nissan and the company has devolved a great deal of responsibility for production, quality, and discipline to the team leader. However, such is the level of peer pressure within the teams that some critics argue that Nissan signals a new 'system of self-subordination' (Garrahan and Stewart, 1992). While this may be true, the fact remains that Nissan has created a degree of worker involvement and commitment which is unprecedented for mass producers in the UK, one reason perhaps why it is now the top industrial tourist site in the UK, with some 400 company visits a year (IFS, 1995).

The deployment of lean production concepts has been far more difficult in Germany than in the USA and the UK, not least because Germany, along with Sweden, has inclined towards 'human-centred' forms of work organization. Furthermore, the German conception of skill is portable and specialized (as opposed to company-specific and broad as in Japan) and worker participation takes the form not of teamwork but of co-determination, which involves a great deal of negotiation between management and unions. As German firms are subject to extensive social regulation, by law and industrial agreement, they have less scope to experiment with new forms of work organization than their counterparts in the USA and the UK (Streeck, 1996). IG Metall, the engineering workers' union, recognizes that lean production poses threats and opportunities: while it welcomes the fact that lean production signals a 'post-Taylorist paradigm', it also believes that, in its Japanese form, it threatens the German model of skilled work and industrial relations (Roth, 1992). The highly regulated nature of the German labour market is cited as one reason why VW feels obliged to use its foreign subsidiaries to pioneer new production concepts, in the hope that these can be introduced at a later date into home plants like Wolfsburg (Simonian, 1996).

Despite these institutional barriers, German car firms are beginning to experiment with lean production concepts. The first to do so was an 'outsider', the Opel Eisenach plant, which opened in 1993: in other words this was a *US*-owned company operating in *eastern* Germany with a *handpicked* workforce in a *greenfield* facility. Of the indigenous German car firms, Porsche is said to be the furthest along the road in implementing a German version of lean production (Womack and Jones, 1996). As we shall see in Chapter 4, the test bed for new work concepts at Mercedes-Benz is its new plant at Rastatt, which began production in 1992. Here we find an attempt to combine certain elements of the human-centred approach of the Uddevalla plant with elements of lean production, with the result that the reign of the assembly line has been considerably reduced, rather than abandoned, work cycles are much longer than in Japan, and teamwork is the principal form of work under *elected* team leaders (Jurgens, 1995).

What these vignettes demonstrate is that far from there being 'one best way' of organizing work within the emerging post-Taylorist paradigm, what we have instead is 'a diversity of new work organization' because of uneven combinations of micro and macro factors (Turner and Auer, 1994). The devolution of responsibility to production teams may be a key feature of this paradigm, but it is just one of the attributes of the high performance manufacturing plant. Indeed, in a study of manufacturing performance in nine OECD countries, the two most important attributes of the 'world class' plants were process control within the plant and co-ordination of the supply chain (Oliver *et al.*, 1994). This suggests that high performance plants need to have participatory problem-solving structures both within the plant and between the plant and its key suppliers.

CO-MAKERSHIP: BUILDING SUPPLY-CHAIN PARTNERSHIPS

In the era of the new competition the 'make or buy' decision is proving to be one of the most important, exacting, and indeed unnerving decisions a firm can make, not least because it defines the boundaries and core competencies of the firm. Time was when large firms saw just two options to this economic governance problem: either they produced their key parts in house through a process of vertical integration or they procured their parts through contracts with external suppliers, in other words the options of 'hierarchies' or 'markets' in the original language of transaction cost economics (Coase, 1937; Williamson, 1975). As we saw in Chapter 1, 'hierarchies' can be a costly and bureaucratic method of organizing transactions in an era of rapid technological change, while 'markets' can be a poor conduit for exchanging knowledge, especially *tacit* knowledge. In short, the limitations of 'markets' and 'hierarchies' have forced firms to explore the potential of a third option, namely, supply-chain partnerships, a variant of the networked form of organization (Powell, 1990; Cooke and Morgan, 1993).

Supply-chain partnerships are part of an emerging vocabulary to describe the high priority which large firms are beginning to accord (at least in principle) to their suppliers. The key words in this new vocabulary are 'co-makership', 'collaborative manufacturing', 'lean supply', and 'partnership sourcing' to name a few (Lascelles and Dale, 1989; Sabel *et al.*, 1989b; Lamming, 1993; Macbeth and Ferguson, 1994). Whatever the vocabulary, these terms all share one thing in common, namely the belief that traditional arm's-length contracting relationships are at best ineffective and at worse a liability if firms wish to develop and sustain a capacity for innovation, learning, and quality. Here it is useful to draw a distinction between two ideal types of contracting: arm's length and obligational. In the former, contracting relations tend to be characterized by low trust, short-term commitments, limited information exchange, and a concentration on price, while in the latter there tends to be high trust, long-term mutual dependence, and considerable sharing of information, technical know-how, and risk (Sako, 1992). In stylized terms, we might say that arm's-length contracting (which privileges exit over voice) has been typical in Western economies, the Anglo-Saxon ones in particular, while obligational contracting (which favours voice over exit) is more prevalent in Japan.

While arm's-length contracting remains prevalent in most Western economies, a number of factors are pushing firms to experiment with obligational contracting, or with what we have called supply-chain partnerships. First, there is a growing awareness that a hefty part of the cost and quality of a finished product is determined *before* the final producer has begun its work, hence the significance of the supply base. Secondly, accelerating technical change and intensified competition have persuaded many firms that they need to specialize to a greater extent than hitherto, that they cannot maintain, in house, the complete range of expertise needed to keep abreast of all the relevant technologies. Thirdly, the advent of lean production has fully exposed the weaknesses of arm's-length contracting, and this demonstration effect has been the decisive factor in persuading Western firms to re-think their approach to their suppliers.

At bottom, arm's-length contracting was based on the assumption that the two parties to the contract were adversaries: hence the limited information flows, the multiple sourcing from a large supply base, the frequent switching to keep suppliers 'on their toes', and the inordinate emphasis on price. The result was very often an amalgam of mistrust, fear, dishonesty, and mutual frustration, all of which conspired against continuous improvement. Supply-chain partnerships, by contrast, are based on the assumption that both parties can gain more through co-operation than by separately pursuing their own short-term interests (Lascelles and Dale, 1989).

But this is easier said than done, not least because Supply-chain partnerships presuppose a measure of 'goodwill trust', that is, the confidence that the other party will make an open-ended commitment to take initiatives for mutual benefit and refrain from opportunistic behaviour (Sako, 1992). But it is a fallacy to think that the high-trust, long-term supply-chain partnerships pioneered in Japan are based on trust alone. Equally important, they involve an agreed framework for jointly analysing costs, determining prices, and sharing the savings: in other words, an incentive structure which makes for collaborative rather than advers-arial contracting relations (Womack *et al.*, 1990). Even though the supply chain is not a relationship of equals, since the odds are manifestly stacked in the cus-tomer's favour, this does not mean that trust cannot be built into the relation-ship. Customers may be the dominant partners, but recent outsourcing trends suggest they are becoming more and more dependent on their key suppliers, so much so that the latter are far from powerless.

To examine these recent trends we shall once again focus on the car industry because, being the first to face the challenge of lean production, this sector is at the forefront of supply-chain restructuring. Such is the scale of these changes that the *Financial Times* was prompted to ask:

Do carmakers need to make cars? A look at the PC industry suggests today's giant motor manufacturers will be very different companies 10 years from now: flexible design houses, with strong control over how vehicles are branded and sold but very little, if any, involvement in building them. Cost-conscious carmakers are outsourcing ever more com-plex sub-assemblies to component suppliers and asking them to share risk by chipping in capital and sharing R&D spending. The Japanese are already almost pure assemblers. Only 15% of the value of a Toyota is added at the parent company's factory, against over 50% at US rivals. (*Financial Times*, 26 August 1996)

Supply-chain partnerships have enabled the Japanese car firms to reap the benefits of *de facto* vertical integration without bearing the costs. Having fewer suppliers than their Western rivals meant that they were able to devote more time to building the partnerships on which they are so heavily reliant. While the leading (customer) firms have clearly gained most from these partnerships, it is argued that 'both purchasers and suppliers benefited from the synergistic effects that accrued from joint problem solving and continuous improvement in price, product quality, delivery, design and engineering' (Nishiguchi, 1994). The norms of trust and reciprocity which inform these supply-chain partnerships were not the result of some pre-existing cultural disposition, indeed they hardly existed prior to the war economy. In fact, these norms were actively constructed through a combination of corporate necessity (as when large firms had to delegate tasks to suppliers to meet surging postwar demand) and government legislation which proscribed unfair sub-contracting practices (Nishiguchi, 1994).

The competitiveness of the big five car firms—Toyota, Nissan, Honda, Mitsubishi, and Mazda—has been underwritten by their supply-chain *keiretsu*, a corporate grouping which consists of up to five tiers of supplier. But such relationships are not cast in aspic: during the *endaka* of the 1990s, these partnerships have begun to unravel as the large firms transfer production abroad and enforce drastic cost-cutting measures at home, with the result that many smaller suppliers have had to merge or go to the wall. Such is the pressure on the big five to raise capacity utilization and preserve jobs for their core workers that they are reclaiming tasks from their suppliers, proving that outsourcing is not some ineluctable corporate trend (Terazono, 1993; Nakamoto, 1996).

Whatever the problems with supply-chain partnerships in Japan, the integrated supply chain has become something of a holy grail for Western car firms. Even in the USA, where the stereotyped climate seems so inhospitable to inter-firm collaboration, there are signs that supply-chain partnerships are beginning to emerge, and not just with the Japanese transplants. Of the indigenous car firms, perhaps Chrysler has made the most progress: stimulated by the example of Honda in the USA, it reduced its supplier base from 2,500 in 1989 to 1,140 in 1996 and radically changed its working relationship with those that remained, as we can see in Table 2.2. The new strategy is embodied in its Supplier Cost Reduction Effort (SCORE) programme, which was unveiled in 1990 and which aims to build high-trust relations with its suppliers so that they can share information more freely to reduce the time and costs of product development in what Chrysler calls its 'extended enterprise' (Dyer, 1996).

Supply-chain partnerships are also emerging in the UK, where the procurement strategies of Nissan, Honda, and Toyota have been the most powerful stimulus. Being the first to arrive, Nissan has had the biggest impact. In 1995, almost a decade after it began producing at Sunderland, Nissan had 204 European suppliers, of which 131 were based in the UK. Nearly 50 per cent of these 204 suppliers had achieved a quality standard of ten or fewer defective parts per million by 1995, up from a mere 17 per cent in 1993 but well below the 70 per cent figure for Nissan's Japanese suppliers (Griffiths, 1995). It is not too much to say that Nissan has wrought a cultural revolution in the quality consciousness of its suppliers, largely through the tutoring effect of its Supplier Development Team, an organizational innovation which was launched in the UK in 1988. In addition to quality standards, suppliers are also ranked on the basis of four other criteria: cost, delivery, product-development capacity, and management calibre (NEDO, 1991; Sadler, 1996). Although the Nissan effect is strongest where the contact is direct, there are signs that the company has indirectly triggered a more general shift towards the principle of supply-chain partnerships in the UK car industry, though these have yet to deliver practical

TABLE 2.2. Chrysler's extended enterprise

Process characteristics 1989	1994	Relational characteristics 1989	1994
Suppliers chosen by competitive bid • low price wins • selection after design	Suppliers presourced • cost targeted to a set price • selection before design, based on capabilities	Little recognition or credit for past performance (transaction orientation)	Recognition of past performance and track record (relationship orientation)
Split accountability for design, prototype, and production parts	Single supplier accountable for design, prototype, and production parts	No responsibility for suppliers' profit margins	Recognition of suppliers' need to make a fair profit
Minimal supplier investment in co-ordination mechanisms and dedicated assets	Substantial investments in co-ordination mechanisms and dedicated assets	Little support for feedback from suppliers	Feedback from suppliers encouraged
Discrete activity focus, no process for soliciting ideas or suggestions	Focus on total value-chain improvement, formal process for soliciting suppliers' suggestions	No guarantee of business relationship beyond the contract	Expectation of business relationship beyond the contract
Simple performance evaluation	Complex performance evaluation	No performance expectations beyond the contract	Considerable performance expectations beyond the contract
Short-term contracts	Long-term contracts	Adversarial, zero-sum game	Co-operative and trusting, positive-sum game

Source: Dyer (1996).

benefits (Sako *et al.*, 1995). One reason for this may be the low levels of inter-firm trust, which is 'the result of many years of broken promises, abuse of confidence and general acrimony within the industry' (Lamming, 1994). Even so, Nissan has demonstrated that it is possible for an innovative firm to develop long-term, high-trust partnerships in an otherwise hostile climate, even though the benefits do not extend much beyond the first tier of the supply chain.

One might think that the new supply-chain partnerships would have spread quickly in Germany, where buyer–supplier relations have been less adversarial and more co-operative than in the USA and the UK (Lane and Bachmann, 1996). However, German supply chains in the car industry were more problematical than they appeared, and these problems have been exposed in the 'lean supply' era. To illustrate some of these problems, we might consider Mercedes-Benz, the flagship of the German car industry. In 1993, the company freely conceded that its products were over-engineered and over-priced and that it had a significant productivity gap to bridge in the 1990s. Part of the answer was seen to lie in greater outsourcing because, during the 1980s, its internal procurement costs had increased three times faster than those of external suppliers. But outsourcing could exacerbate a more basic problem at Mercedes, namely poor cross-functional co-operation within the firm, especially as between the engineering and the procurement departments. According to one senior manager, 'the engineers prefer to phone a Swabian and they will often say why go to Lucas when we know Bosch'. Indeed, the engineers would even make their own deals with suppliers without the knowledge of the procurement department, making it difficult for the latter to co-ordinate the supply-chain. Although Mercedes is intent on increasing its outsourcing, in the face of opposition from both engineers and IG Metall, it will have to resolve the cross-functional problems in its engineering-driven culture if it is to develop more effective supply-chain partnerships (Morgan, 1994).

What these examples demonstrate is that firms are becoming ever more conscious of the fact that their capacity for innovation, learning, and quality depends on their ability to secure the active co-operation of their suppliers. For all the potential advantages of supply-chain partnerships, the greatest single barrier to the development of this concept is the divergence between rhetoric and reality. In many cases, partnerships are no more than a rhetorical screen to transfer costs from customer to supplier: in other words, the reality is more power play than a partnership (Kearney, 1994). To be effective, supply-chain partnerships have to be built on trust, where the benefits flow in both directions. Although trust-based partnerships can be exceedingly difficult to construct, not least because trust has to be earned rather than decreed, they constitute intangible assets which the more innovative firms recognize to be every bit as important as tangible assets.

CONCLUSIONS

Large firms, we have argued, are in the throes of a semi-permanent process of organizational innovation as they strive to keep abreast of the protean worlds of technology and markets. In this chapter we have focused on four areas— governance, R&D, production and supply chains—where organizational change has been most pronounced. The common thread running through these innovations is the attempt to create a more collaborative corporate culture, both within the firm and between the firm and its principal suppliers. Collaboration, however, is a means not an end, a means through which firms hope to become more productive, more innovative, and of course more profitable. At a time when governments throughout the OECD are prosecuting a de-regulatory agenda and extolling the benefits of the market mechanism, it is ironic that leading-edge firms are experimenting like never before with non-market mechanisms like network forms of organization.

The organizational innovations covered in this chapter clearly admit of different interpretations, especially those surrounding the reorganization of production and the supply-chain, the areas in which trust-building is most problematical. Post-Taylorist forms of work organization, for example, are clearly most appropriate for up-market, high-value-added products, while Taylorist forms tend to prevail at the lower end, where there is less scope for, and therefore less emphasis on, learning and innovation. Even so, the options available to Western firms at the lower end would seem to be to innovate, to liquidate, or to relocate to low-cost labour zones.

It is sometimes argued that genuine collaboration is impossible in production and supply chains because power relations are so asymmetrical between management and labour on the one hand and between customer and supplier on the other. While this is manifestly true, the important point is that asymmetry does not preclude collaboration, and we do not suggest that the benefits of collaboration are equally shared. In supply-chain partnerships, for example, the customer is clearly the dominant partner, getting the benefits of both markets and hierarchy without the costs. In other words, supply-chain partnerships are closer than markets but looser than hierarchies, allowing the use of voice without losing the option of exit, and also spreading the risks. But there is no contradiction between acknowledging asymmetry and suggesting that suppliers often do better within partnerships (through larger orders, tuition, enhanced reputation, etc.) than outside them.

Perhaps the key point to emphasize is that where collaboration is purely rhetorical, where it is merely a fig-leaf to conceal narrow self-interest in other words, then firms will quickly discover that neither employees nor suppliers can be trusted to commit themselves wholeheartedly to the goals of the enterprise.

3

The Region as a Nexus of Learning Processes

INTRODUCTION

Corporate reorganization and the renewed emphasis on innovation as firms position themselves for the 'new competition' (Best, 1990) have highly significant implications for regions. We would argue that new models of economic co-ordination are in process of being marked out that will transcend those established in most advanced economies by the end of the 1970s. Writers such as Lipietz (1977) and Massey (1984) identified a Fordist division of labour in which regions were inserted in functionally specific ways. With hindsight, it is evident that they perceived the shape of the extremely complex processes of Fordist economic co-ordination at or just after their apogee, for the 1980s were a period of severe crisis for three key structures upon which they rested.

First, as we have seen in Chapter 1, the national economy was never so pronounced an arena within which economic co-ordination was orchestrated, especially in Europe, after the 1970s. For, while manufacturing had been internationalizing to some degree after the Second World War, it was normally branch-plant in nature with little notion of integration into other than specific national economies. In a prime service activity with massive international purchase like banking, for example, there was a fourfold increase in foreign banks to 403 in London and 307 in New York between 1970 and 1984, the period to which we refer (Thrift, 1987). But these movements had been into what were, to all intents and purposes, sovereign national economies. Even in the European Economic Community of which Germany and Italy had been members since 1957 and to which the UK and Spain acceded in 1973 and 1986 respectively, most economic decision-making on monetary, fiscal, and budgetary, let alone industrial and regional, policies was framed with national boundaries to the forefront. While that remained the case, distinctive national spatial structures expressing the functional organization of multilocational business emerged. In brief, it involved geographical concentration of command functions in primate cities such as London, Paris, or Milan, routine assembly in peripheral regions such as Wales, Brittany, or the Mezzogiorno, and intermediate functions in more skills-intensive regions such as the English Midlands, Rhône-Alpes, or North Central Italy. Much of this locational movement and functional specialization in specific kinds of regions was orchestrated by large, often multinational firms working in a kind of Fordist compact with states seeking to promote economic efficiency and social equity through the regional redistribution of employment, with lower-order employment the most mobile.

That account of the role of regions in the division of labour is inevitably a caricature and was perceived to be something of an over-exaggeration by critics at the time (see e.g. Scott, 1988) for its emphasis on large-scale corporations, especially manufacturers, and its neglect of 'new industrial spaces'. Yet a caricature can capture essential elements of a complex profile and, to that extent, the 'spatial divisions of labour' thesis of the Fordist locational landscape served a useful purpose.

A second cornerstone of Fordism which shuddered in the 1970s and early 1980s was its hegemonic 'M-form' management structure which was discussed in Chapter 2 (Chandler, 1962). This was also presented in rather caricatured ways though perceptive analysts distinguished between the accountancy-driven variants such as IBM and the marketing-driven ones such as Ford or General Motors. Moreover, the distinctiveness of Ford's rather standardized and GM's more diversified organizational structures could also be delineated. Nevertheless the model to which corporate boards aspired was ultimately a linear, 'top-down', hierarchical, divisionalized, and bureaucratic one in which conceptual skill resided with the multiple layers of management and orders were transmitted vertically in the divisional chain of command. Shopfloor workers were not expected or required to demonstrate other than their capacity to follow orders and, in consequence, became less and less committed to the job, especially in an era of relatively abundant alternative employment opportunities, and productivity began to stagnate. These problems, which the 'neo-Fordist' introduction of more fully automated production machinery often only exacerbated, leading to serious machinery under-utilization, coincided with the rejection by consumers of the standardized products typical of such a 'military' model of production. The linear production model, founded on the assembly line manned by workers who had become appendages of the machine, thus came into serious question.

A third blow to the linear thinking that supported Fordist spatial structures in national economies, coincident with efforts to find new, less developed regions in which to practise 'peripheral Fordism' (Lipietz, 1987), was the beginning of the demise of 'top-down' industrial policy and its spatial correlate, regional policy in advanced economies. This gathered pace through the 1980s to the point where research conducted in the UK's foremost national economics research institute could, by the early 1990s, identify no recognizable industrial policy operating at national level in the EU and precious little regional policy that was not coincident with EU regional policy designated areas (Mayes, 1995). More to the point, in Europe, the exigencies of the Single Market Act and the Maastricht Treaty meant that government expenditure budgets had to be inspected carefully and pared to meet the criteria for competitiveness on the one hand and monetary union on the other. Given its mixed record in supporting 'lame ducks' and failing often when it came to 'picking winners', industrial policy became a prime casualty everywhere, at least at national and federal level. Comparable questions about the efficacy of regional subsidies to stimulate growth through direct national allocations to regions such as Italy's Mezzogiorno, in tandem with burgeoning complaints from receiver regions about the insensitivity or lack of consultation by central governments in the allocation of regional investments, led, in one way and another according to country, to smaller budgets but more regional responsibility for the content of industrial or enterprise support. This usually meant foreign multinationals engaging more and more in bidding wars between regions but they also had to fit in with, in some cases, a more targeted, less shotgun, attraction strategy. Among these might be home-grown policies to support smaller, local businesses to become or remain internationally competitive as, by choice, in Emilia-Romagna and Baden-Württemberg or, of necessity, in the Basque Country. Wales has ridden out the demise of traditional regional assistance, which has seen UK funding decimated from its figure of over £1 billion in 1980, by securing, through political means, its own development agency which now seeks to knit together opportunities for smaller and indigenous firms with those of sectorally appropriate multinationals.

It remains to be seen whether the authorities in Wales, or even Baden-Württemberg for that matter, would turn away what was deemed an inappropriate foreign investor. But this happens in Singapore, perhaps the most impressive growth economy of the recent past, where, because of a policy to advance knowledge-intensive economic activity, the government of that small island-state routinely refuses to take production jobs from would-be inward investors or investment-expanders such as Apple-Macintosh, insisting that only higher-order management and R&D jobs can be allowed in. The redirection of assembly work to Malaysia and Thailand at Singaporean behest is also politically astute in a context where the Singaporean authorities feel politically threatened by these larger neighbours (Hing, 1997; Ashton, 1996).

Little more will be said about the demise of the foundation stones of Fordist linearity in what follows. It remains an interesting product of modern times. What is now of more interest is a re-theorization of the region in the changed circumstances that have been described and an analysis of the ways in which the region, as a key dimension of socio-economic and politico-cultural organization, functions in the corporate and governance dimensions of economic co-ordination. Not least, some reflection on the abiding as well as changing relations of regions to the national and global levels is also called for.

THE REGION: FROM DEFENCE TO OFFENCE

Numerous authors such as de Vet (1993), Ohmae (1993), Florida (1995*a*), Cooke (1995), and, most recently, Storper and Scott (1995) make the case that the regional level of economic organization has become more rather than less important in the wake of the profound economic restructuring of the 1980s and 1990s. In simple terms, logic would dictate that a withdrawal of responsibility by national governments for economic well-being in the regions within the state would provoke some kind of awakening as sub-central political authorities realized the rules of the job-generation game had changed. This indeed happened as a whole raft of books and articles on local and regional development 'from below' testified (specimen contributions would include collections such as Boddy and Fudge, 1984; Tabb and Sawers, 1984; Campbell, 1990; Geddes and Benington, 1992). But most of these were what might be called 'defensive analyses', that is, regions and localities in difficulty need locally and regionally worked-out survival strategies and the accounts are of what responses could be or in fact were.

But now the debate has moved on to the terrain of what can be called 'offensive analyses' where it is often shown how rich and dynamic regional economies are, alternatively, successfully recovering from major deindustrialization (e.g. the US Midwest after Florida, 1995a; or Los Angeles after Storper and Scott, 1995), developing as significant players in a globalizing economy (de Vet, 1993; Ohmae, 1993) or in some sense a crucial arena in which the economic co-ordination of major industries is worked out in a post-Fordist era (Cooke, 1995; Storper and Scott, 1995; see also Sabel, 1995).

What are these arguments of the regional *offensive* actually constructed upon and, more to the point, what is this entity under discussion—*region*—actually like? How is it defined, what is it composed of, to whom or what does it refer and defer, and how does it function?

The first key point to emphasize is that in the new formulation the region is a process or, more accurately, a nexus of processes rather than a thing, especially a thing to which other things (usually bad, sometimes good) are done. To dwell on the 'thingness' perspective of regions, often portrayable as 'regions as victims', we need only think of classic regional policy, the essential elements, or what philosophy would call the ontology, of which still imbue contemporary European Union designations of regions into Objective 1, 2, 5b and so on. Thus, regions were defined by their degrees of 'distress' (UK *circa* 1937) or status as 'depressed' (UK *circa* 1944) or in need of 'assistance' (UK *circa* 1974). Nowadays they are defined more gently as 'less favoured', 'older industrial' or 'disadvantaged' (EU *circa* 1996). These are all definitions of condition resulting from, usually, economic blows of some kind. Although often specific areas delineated on maps, they can come to designate the administrative or cultural regions in which they exist. This results in labelling of a peculiarly hierarchical, not to say linear, kind whereby Mezzogiorno equals 'economic black hole' although this large 'region' and long-term recipient of 'regional policy' contains some regions which are performing relatively well, as well as some that are not. Nothing is said in such designations about the *processual* nature, the partly or wholly systemically linked nature, the barriers and blockages to or capacities for change that regions that are accomplished and dynamic or disadvantaged and stagnant possess.

One exception to this way of thinking which *is* incorporated in European Union discourse on regional policy and is processual in its designation of a regional category is the use of '*reconversion*' to denote regions in transition from older to newer industrial structures. A more diluted and neutral usage in the UK in the past is 'development' areas, which, in the sense of development as 'unfolding' implies process but in undefined directions. What the non-linear designation of regions implies is a dynamic rather than a static approach which captures the evolutionary processes that constitute the region.

We shall explore the question of differentiation of regions in terms of evolutionary processes, but first it is necessary to say a little more about what we now mean by the term *region*. Formalistically speaking, *region* is a territory less than its state(s) possessing significant supralocal administrative, cultural, political, or economic power and cohesiveness differentiating it from its state and other regions (for discussion, see Cooke, 1996*a*). But this definition, though generic, is also static. For, if we are to conceive of regions in terms of evolutionary processes involving emergence and transformation, we must think of them also in terms of the dynamic tensions that give rise to such processes. Here, we introduce two well-debated process concepts: *regionalization*; and *regionalism* (see Hadjimichalis, 1986; Paasi, 1986; Harvie, 1994; Aronsson, 1995). The first of these, *regionalization*, is the delimitation of a supralocal territory by a superordinate politico-administrative body, normally the state. It may, exceptionally, be delimited by economic processes (e.g. Ruhrgebiet in Germany) and politico-administrative delimitation may follow. Similarly, and more commonly, it may be a 'culture area'.

However, it is the other process term of *regionalism* that comes into play more as cultural processes, combining with political and economic ones on occasions, come into focus. For, while regionalization involves some form of devolved administration through, for example, a prefecture or delegated authority such as a *land*, regionalism involves political demands, 'from below', for often culturally defined territorial autonomy in the face of perceived neglect or discrimination by the superordinate authority. Hence the state of any region at any given time is the negotiated outcome of a process which produces a particular *collective social order* (Scott, 1996). Within this is a *microconstitutional regulation* process as described by Ostrom (1992) which establishes the institutional routines, norms, and values permeating the organizations that articulate them. This 'constitutional order' as Sabel (1993) calls it, is the basis for *trust* relations among firms, organizations, and individuals that both differ from region to region and may be projected from different functional bases—they may be culturally derived in one context, politically, economically, or administratively in another. These are the sources of Putnam's (1992) 'social capital', something we explore in detail in the chapter on Emilia-Romagna. Such *social capital*, the collective consciousness and practical action of the regional social order mediated through its microconstitutional organizations, determines defensive and offensive regional action and hence the evolutionary processes of the region. But this always occurs within the constraints and opportunities offered by the superordinate state and global parameters which contextuate regional capacity.

Let us take three examples to illustrate how this approach to theorization of regions as evolutionary processes works. Each is taken from our regional cases, dealt with in far more depth later. First, the Basque Country which has only existed in its current form since 1981. Hitherto Francoism had sought to consign it to two divided provinces as its form of *'regionalization'*, adding to its historic administrative disintegration between France and Spain. Economically, it was earmarked as Spain's centre for steel and shipbuilding and its culture was diluted by the encouragement of migrants from all over Spain into the industrial cities. Basque was in danger of becoming a residual culture even as its economy moved into dominance within Spain. However, the suppressed residual formed the basis for the emergence of the microconstitutional norms of political *regionalism* of a more powerful and relatively autonomous kind, while the economy has entered a weakened state and a process of reconversion.

The case of Baden-Württemberg is that of major chaos in 1945 with at least three separate proto-*länder*: Württemberg-Hohenzollern; Württemberg-Baden; and Baden emerging from the centralist Nazi interlude with a shattered economy and large-scale in-migration from East Germany. A process of 'bootstrapping' entrepreneurship by in-migrating and indigenous firms and the recovery of larger, more established engineering and textile industry markets contingent on the Erhard 'economic miracle', gave a politico-cultural impetus to the postwar generation to develop the Baden-Württemberg model of a network economy. This attracted but also gave strength to a proactive regional governance system based on high-trust linkages and what critics see as a 'neo-mercantilist' political culture and economic policy.

Lastly, Wales was 're-made' (K. O. Morgan, 1983) in the late nineteenth century as a key node in Britain's heavy industrial imperial economy. South Wales overshadowed the rest of Wales in this regard and its politics and culture became internationalist and socialist as its economy boomed. But it was re-made again as a new political culture which rejected imperialism sought to build new organizations to meet regional and national political, cultural, and economic aspirations. Thus a dominant institutional basis has evolved for the development of a modern, high-performance engineering economy while the culture and politics of coal, especially, became relegated to the role of residual. This, and other complex cultural and administrative processes have given rise to a new form of constitutional and social order or microconstitutional regulation totally distinct from that of a century ago. Much of this can be traced to the political and cultural expression of social capital, provoking a negotiated but qualitatively different order within the parameters of the UK state and, increasingly, European Union regulatory powers.

REGIONS AS LABORATORIES

The concrete processes described in the preceding sketches and the theorization that they were based on are living versions of what Sabel (1995) refers to as 'Experimental Regionalism'. He notes that:

regionalization has been encouraged by the urgent desire of higher level governments—the federal government in the US, the European Community and in turn its member states—to escape responsibility for outcomes they regard as beyond their control by delegating decision-making authority to lower-level jurisdictions. (Sabel, 1995: 3)

This is clearly not a new argument, a similar one was deployed by Clark and Dear (1984). The weakness of Sabel's argument is that he only recognizes, one-sidedly, the *regionalization* impulse and ignores more or less totally the *regionalism*, or bottom-up dimension which gives the dynamic tension necessary for a real understanding of regional *change*. Only belatedly does he even introduce *regionalism*, and then with no conceptual differentiation having been made, when he notes in passing that: 'the crucial assumption of regionalism—and of the decentralization in firms as well—is that the local actors are best placed to assess their particularity and hence what they can learn from comparing their experience with that' (Sabel, 1995: 21).

While obviously true, the utility of what Sabel says of this state of affairs is that it releases great possibilities for regions as organizational and institutional processes to engage in *learning* processes by means of which they evolve to a new stage of development.

Regions as Externalized Learning Institutions

In his book on learning systems, Schon (1973) adumbrated many of the concerns and interests that are the present focus, albeit half-caught in the linear, centre–periphery, diffusionist thinking of the day. Nevertheless, the interest in revisiting Schon's work and that of his collaborators (e.g. Argyris and Schon, 1978) lies in their attempts to escape from the iron cage of linear thinking and to explore the intricacies of interactive systems insights. At one point, this is expressed in a section on regional diversity:

Territories are different from one another and from central. Does the central message lend itself to modification to take account of regional differences? What are the limits of acceptable deviation? Does the feedback loop between central and the regions permit modification of the central message? (Schon, 1973: 88)

Tellingly, Schon is reflecting here not on business strategy, government diplomacy, or even regional policy but weaknesses in the Communist Internationale in the 1960s. He contrasts it with what he presents as the advanced learning system of 'the Movement', the loose coalition of radical organizations that flowered at the same time as part of the political counter-culture. The Movement had no clearly established centre nor a stable, centrally established message. It was a loosely connected, shifting, and evolving whole in which centres and messages were transient; its infrastructure technology meant it was 'possible to know at Berkeley tomorrow what happened at Cornell yesterday. Third world factions in Algeria maintain connections with American blacks in Cleveland and in Cuba' (Schon, 1973: 106). And like what he called the 'constellation firm', the Movement expressed a system of overlapping and evolving innovations, not a set of replications. There is a family rather than a clone-like resemblance to the accomplishments of a complex network capable of transforming itself through interactive innovation.

With remarkable prescience, Schon concludes his differentiation of classic models for the diffusion of innovations in politics, government, and business from the new wave as follows:

The principal problem of design shifts from the design of a product or technique to the design of a network. The person's principal allegiance shifts from membership in an organization to membership in a network. And the pattern of social learning shifts from succesive 'sweeps' of limited innovations from a centre throughout a periphery, to the formation of self-transforming networks. (Schon, 1973: 108)

As corporations have downsized, delayered, empowered, renewed, re-engineered, re-invented, and transformed to relatively little positive effect during the 1990s, the best that can be said according to Mintzberg (1994) is that 'some organizations were able to learn from their experience'. Mintzberg's approach bears faint echoes of the cultural analysis of the 1970s whereby, in a 'strategic learning' corporation what was the intended strategy becomes *residual* as it interacts with an unrealized strategy (derived from learning) to produce an *emergent* strategy that replaces the deliberate (or *dominant*) strategy to become a realized strategy. In other words, *system interactions produce learning gains from unanticipated sources and events* (i.e. innovations).

One final indicator of conceptual convergence in the present discussion concerns Schon's (*circa* 1960s) and Mintzberg's (*circa* 1990s) itemization of necessary conditions for successful systems of strategic learning to occur. In the latter author's approach three things are necessary:

- sensing—spotting signs of change external and internal to the organization;
- awareness—communicating those signs and explaining them so that others understand their implications;
- responsiveness—mobilizing resources to respond to emergent 'emergencies' while maintaining a steady course.

For Schon, learning systems create new 'network roles' of:

- systems negotiator—the middleman who sensitizes others to system-guidance issues;
- underground manager—maintains and operates informal personal networks to keep system coherence;
- manoeuvrer—mobilizes internal resources to shift projects in new directions;
- broker—mobilizes external resources to smooth transactions requiring trust;
- network manager—provides resources needed for such networks to function in the 'official' system;
- facilitator—provides interface relations with distinctive 'regional enterprises'.

The Schon analysis takes us outside the key firm or organization and into both the transactions environment of other supporting or competing organizations, firms, and the like, and the affiliate organizations or branches inside the extended host system. It thus sensitizes us, as the Mintzberg approach does for the internalized system of the corporation, to the externalized system of the region and beyond. This it does in both its market and non-market dimensions.

The most important insight that emerges from this discussion of learning systems is that *learning is to be defined as a change in a person's or organization's capability or understanding*. This is also a conclusion of Eraut (1996) who argues, convincingly, that learning in the organizational or social sense is not simply the acquisition of further information. One crucial reason for this is that we never ourselves encounter experiences exactly as we have before and even less do we encounter the experiences of others precisely as they experienced them. Thus we enter the Piagetian understanding of learning where learning takes place in the process of interaction between what we know and bring to a situation and what we perceive to be new about the situation (Piaget, 1971). Because of this, learning involves costs of transfer that are greater the less the level of previous knowledge. This is why, in some countries, notably the UK, vocational learning and knowlege are being classified in terms of *competence* (i.e. ability to conduct a specific task) rather than *capability* (i.e. understanding of the mechanisms underlying solution of the problem involved in the task). Competence is cheaper to provide than capability.

The accomplished learning system will be the one that inculcates capabilities, notably the capacity for understanding. The competent *regional learning system* will not be one which assists in the cheap and cheerful transfer of competences from elsewhere. As we have said, the other's experiences are not replicable and mere mimicking only reproduces the lag between where the emulated was when the mimicking took place and where it is now. Japan leapfrogged not by mimicking the West but by learning new capabilities the West did not have, from the failures and weaknesses of the West.

Regional Externalization and Specialization

But why *regional* learning and/or *regional* innovation systems? There are three key reasons for this new focus. They concern, respectively, the massive growth in *externalization* of production of goods and services by corporations (as noted in Chapter 2); the increasing *specialization*, or what economists refer to as 'stickiness', of regional economies in consequence of externalization; and the growing *regionalization* of industrial policy, enterprise support, and promotion for inward investment.

First, let as look at the *externalization* of production. This has been a growing trend in most industries through the 1980s and 1990s as firms have sought the holy grail of leanness, some would say to the point of experiencing corporate anorexia (Lash and Urry, 1994). Outsourcing of systems, components, and services through the *keiretsu* was one of the advantages that gave Japanese firms their competitive edge and Western firms have had to follow suit. Statistically, figures quoted by Cooke and Morgan (1994a) for German engineering in general, and automotives in particular, testify to this. Thus between 1968 and 1989 there was a decline of in-house production for mechanical engineering, optical engineering, steel production, automotive engineering, and office machinery ranging from 40 per cent for office machinery to 5 per cent for mechanical engineering, with automotive engineering at 15 per cent. Some of these sectors were already relatively strongly externalized at the beginning of that period. The German automotive industry, as a case in point, already put out 63 per cent of production in 1970, a figure which *declined* to 56 per cent in 1978, only to rise again to 64 per cent in 1987. By that year, companies like Volkswagen, Audi, and Opel produced only 30 per cent or less by value in house and all were seeking further reductions in the 1990s. Regions with local suppliers to important industry branches could, where there was co-location, offer competitive advantage, especially in design and innovation, where *tacit* rather than *codified* knowledge is often the most important transactional asset.

Secondly, as a consequence of the localized learning implied in tacit knowledge-exchange at the regional level or below, regional economies may become more specialized in those areas of expertise. Evidence for this is patchy but exists at three levels. At the macro-level the work of de Vet (1993) shows, for seven OECD countries, how the location of foreign direct investment has become more focused in specific kinds of networked regional economies in which enterprise support and regional industry promotion have given the region a specific image or identity which is then reinforced as foreign firms learn of the regional advantage of locating there too. Archibugi and Pianta (1992) demonstrate the increasing specialization of trade flows in high technology goods. At the micro-level, both Dalum (1992; 1995) and Malmberg and Maskell (1997) have shown that industry in Denmark is becoming more specialized both in terms of international exports and in terms of its localization specificities. Dalum (1995), in a study of twenty-three OECD countries involved in mobile phone production, showed that six countries, Finland, Sweden, Japan, USA, UK, and Denmark scored above average in terms of specialization (Finland and Sweden scored 5.4 and 3.9 compared to the OECD average Gini coefficient of 1.0) and that production sites were highly concentrated. In the Danish case, a cluster of firms in North Jutland (mainly Aalborg) accounted for 50 per cent of the Danish mobile phone industry. Thirdly, Malmberg and Maskell (1997) show that most Scandinavian industry is becoming increasingly specialized even down to the local level of the commune (for similar conclusions on Norway, see Isaksen, 1996).

Even if specialization is increasing, does it also have to be expressed spatially? We would argue that even in a relatively under-specialized spatial system such as the UK, which lost this characteristic as it developed 'spatial divisions of labour' (except for cases such as London for financial services), then where

regionalization is strong (as in Scotland and Wales), the emergence of regionally integrated supply chains in specialized industrial branches such as advanced
electronic components and computing in Scotland, and consumer electronics,
telecommunications, and automotive components in Wales is becoming pronounced. This is because these parts of the UK have many of the key elements of
a *regional* learning infrastructure, notably good *sensing*, *awareness*, and *response*
functions in the organizations (development agencies, training organizations,
territorial governance offices) that promote their regional economies. Moreover,
to the extent these are linked informally and formally with universities, research
institutions, vocational training agencies, technology transfer organizations, and
science parks as well as regional firms both large and small, such regions approach
what may be called a *regional innovation system*.

REGIONAL INNOVATION SYSTEMS

It is important to differentiate regional learning systems from regional innovation systems. In one sense, both are valid aspirations for all regions but learning—
on the Piagetian definition we are deploying—is a first step to innovation. This
is because of a crucial distinction seldom made in the literature on institutional
learning between 'tutoring' and 'learning'. Much of the best literature on institutional learning originates in small economies like Denmark and other Nordic
countries where magnitudes of expenditure on innovation (expecially that part
devoted to research) tend to be relatively small. Such economies have proved
to be highly *innovative* despite this, by learning from other countries where
innovation and R&D magnitudes are higher in expenditure terms. But, inevitably, companies in these small economies only find room to innovate in niches.
Moreover, it is not clear how long term a learning-by-using approach to innovation can be, as the following quote from Johnson *et al.* (1991) suggests:

There are also some strengths in the Danish national system of innovation, however. In
some respects it is characterised by communication and interaction economies both
within and between firms making interactive learning rather effective. It seems as if cultural distances between different kinds of people participating in innovation activities
are often quite short. The results indicate that there may be some possibilities in a
national innovation system to compensate for a relative lack of both large, research
based firms and government technology policy, through communication and interaction
economies in a system of small and medium-sized firms. *At least for a period of time.*
(Johnson *et al.*, 1991, emphasis added)

Interactive learning of this kind and under these conditions is a 'catch-up' strategy. Notions such as 'learning-by-searching' identified in another of Johnson's
(1992) papers as part of an interactive, institutional learning process, underlines
this. So, to return to our Piagetian theory of learning: on the one hand, innovations
may arise from unanticipated effects of system interactions around inventions

from elsewhere but by that time, on the other hand, the originator(s) will have moved into new fields. So 'leapfrogging' is difficult in a regional *learning* system. However, it should also be remembered that one of the firmest conclusions from empirical research on learning conducted from within the Piagetian tradition is that ability to learn is directly correlated with the level of learning accomplished at the outset. So 'learning-by-learning' is achievable and there is a point at which a regional *learning* system can develop towards a regional *innovation* system. This occurs as upstream and downstream or applied research is integrated into regional industry. Thus a developed regional innovation system is an arrangement in which *tutoring* functions are also present. Tutoring is rooted in the possession of understanding and the capability to initiate innovations based on *upstream* (i.e. close to the point of origination of the invention or idea) interactions as well as more *downstream* (i.e. near-market) linkages.

Regions which possess the full panoply of innovation organizations set in an institutional milieu (Johnson and Gregersen, 1996; Maillat, 1995) where systemic linkage and interactive communication among the innovation actors is normal, approach the designation of regional innovation system. The organizations can be expected to consist of universities, basic research laboratories, applied research laboratories, technology transfer agencies, regional public and private (e.g. trade associations, chambers of commerce) governance organizations, vocational training organizations, banks, venture capitalists, and interacting large and small firms. Moreover, they should demonstrate systemic linkages through concertation programmes, research partnership, value-adding information flow, and policy action lines from the governance organizations. These are systems that combine learning with upstream and downstream innovation capability and thus warrant the designation *regional innovation systems*. We think that Baden-Württemberg is a strong candidate for such a designation as it has evolved thus far. Whether it can continue as such remains an open question for reasons to be discussed in Chapter 4.

Two further points, one conceptual and one practical, need to be made to clarify this stage of the argument about the salience of regions to contemporary economic co-ordination, especially with respect to innovation. A conceptual distinction between 'organization' and 'institution' will have been noted in the discussion of innovation system-members. Many writers tend to use the terms interchangeably but Johnson and Gregersen (1996) make a compelling argument for greater precision in usage. They say:

We define *institutions* in the spirit of classical economic institutionalism as regularities and patterns of economic behaviour, or rather as the habits, norms, routines, established practices, and rules, which pattern behaviour. Concrete things like firms, banks, research organizations, state departments, etc., which are often referred to as institutions in everyday speech, we prefer to call *organizations*. (Johnson and Gregersen, 1996)

They do this because the two play different roles in innovation and much else in social science. Organizations can be conceived as embedded in institutions in a process view of socio-economic change. This rule–action distinction is important to an understanding of systemic innovation. An innovation previously unthinkable may become achievable by an institutional rule change such as the imposition of an environmental tax on polluting industries, as happened in Germany and, more specifically, in the regional economy of the Ruhrgebiet in the 1980s (see below and papers in Cooke, 1995).

A second, more pragmatic point, connected to the organization–institution issue, is that because of increased regional (and national) specialization, less and less of a country's and *a fortiori* a region's given *upstream* innovation capacity will be generic. Even the USA is unlikely to retain invention–innovation hegemony in all sectors: indeed, it has already lost it for wide areas of engineering. So, unless countries vacate technology areas, their innovation capability will tend, for more and more sectors, to be in downstream activities where regional *learning* systems will be extremely important. This will obviously be the case to the extent that the region in question has or seeks to develop a regional presence of some kind in the given field. Regional innovation systems of the upstream variety will approximate to Porterian (1990) 'clusters'. These are likely to have the full panoply of organizations necessary for leading-edge sectoral innovation in a region. One thinks of Silicon Valley, as described by Saxenian (1994) or Storper and Scott (1995). One thinks of the Glaxo-Wellcome axes in London for world-class pharmaceuticals, or the Silverstone epicentre of *grand prix* motor-racing engineering also in south-eastern England, as spaces of this kind. Here, Johnson and Gregersen (1996) speak of the distinctiveness of knowledge-production, knowledge-distribution, and knowledge-regulation organizations. For instance, they note standard-setting committees and patent-regulating organizations that function to create and maintain formal institutions, regulating creative paths and definitions of usable knowledge. Such institutions may have a global or merely national remit but their implications for knowledge production will be felt most sharply and increasingly in the specialized, externalized regions engaged in *tutoring* (knowledge production and distribution) and *learning* (knowledge using) for purposes of innovation.

INNOVATION, SYSTEMS, LOCK-IN, AND INDUSTRIAL DISTRICTS

There is an interesting tension, not to say contradiction, implied in the two concepts 'system' and 'innovation', the one emphasizing stability, the other change. The microconstitutional order, innovation institutions and regulations, learning, innovation and enterprise support organizations, and their upstream and downstream relations make, in a functioning system, a nexus of processes for many kinds of communication and knowledge transfer. Disruption to parts or totalities of some of the network relations embedded in the institutional milieu can, in principle, result in either positive effects where new opportunities are seized or rapid system-degradation. A process innovation such as 'lean production' with its protean implications can take a considerable time to become embedded as we show in Chapter 4 for Baden-Württemberg. The implications of that systems-adjustment process still resonate years after the systems-learning mechanisms sensitized the actors to the principles of lean production. They include major relocation decisions, global sourcing decisions, and even deliberations about the need to shift the economy away from its automotive 'monoculture', each having a potentially profound impact on the regional economy.

Most innovations are much less far reaching than this, for radical innovations (e.g. the personal computer) set the framework for incremental innovations (e.g. electronic mail) and fortunately radical innovations occur once or twice per half-century at best (Freeman, 1987). So most innovations, either process or product, are small in systems impact and contribute to the slow evolution of the system within the framework of shared understandings, institutions, and culture. The learning organizations in the regional system (the research laboratories and technology transfer agencies in particular) scan and sensitize the sources and users of innovation. But now a new function enters the scene and it is one that neither Schon nor Mintzberg anticipates, the *reflexivity* function (Lash and Urry, 1994; Cooke, 1995; Sabel, 1995). This is the process of monitoring and evaluating in complex ways the likely implications of the innovation—especially where it is radical—for the regional system. Reflexivity is a crucial dimension of 'intelligence' that is itself clearly a fundamental ingredient of learning capability. Intelligence (in the institutional and organizational senses) consists of at least three dimensions:

- information—the raw material which is the medium for learning in the sense of knowledge-building, the prelude to the achievement of competence and capability;
- monitoring—the capacity to make judgements regarding the impact of information on the pathway or trajectory upon which the regional economic system is set;
- evaluation—the capability to assess the extent to which trajectories or the ends to which they are aiming need to be marginally or significantly adjusted (or the monitored information to be rejected) (Cooke and Morgan, 1991*b*).

Reflexivity is the systemic process which combines learning and intelligence such that, in a number of feedback loops the system receives guidance.

Loop 1 Reflexivity involves the assessment of the extent to which the trajectory on which the system is evolving is appropriate. This entails consideration of whether ends or means need to be changed (e.g. is the regional system structured to meet declining markets: option 1, 'change the products'; option 2, 'change the markets' as the Japanese did in what the West saw as saturated markets. They developed the market for second and third TV sets, for example, and changed the rules on quality and reliability of consumer goods, thus creating markets.

Loop 2 Reflexivity concerns the performance of the system in comparison to that of peer-systems. 'Benchmarking' is a fad of the 1990s in which firms do this by examining good or 'best practice' of peers. They are often liable to the Piagetian dilemma of learning yesterday's tricks. Nevertheless, even learning yesterday's performance by the good or best performer has a value. Regional and local administrations engage in this reflexive process in abundance, sometimes to greater effect than firms because incremental innovation is more the norm.

Loop 3 Reflexivity focuses on the relationship of different elements within the same system with each other. For example, two real cases: first, in the 1980s the Irish government embarked on an ambitious vocational training programme to skill the workforce intensively in Information Technology. But this 'building for stock' strategy produced oversupply which reawoke the Irish bugbear of out-migration of its youngest and ablest people. In the mid-1990s a big push to attract American computing and software firms resulted in out-migration falling to zero. Secondly, Wales in the 1980s embarked upon a successful programme of attracting foreign electronics and engineering firms but by the 1990s these were complaining of shortages of multi-skilled craft and technical workers. Belatedly, efforts are being made to plug the gaps. Ideally, in both cases, the inward investment and vocational training strategies should have proceeded hand in hand. Or, with hindsight, the Irish and Welsh should have co-operated more!

Each of these forms of reflexivity operates in a well-integrated regional system as means of system-guidance. On a day-to-day basis, guidance relates to evolution in relation to incremental innovations. Critical points arise, however, when radical innovations cause more thoroughgoing reflexivity to be called upon. The crisis is usually one of perceived lock-in (cognitive, functional, and/or political: see Chapter 4, after Grabher, 1993*a*), or the aftermath of lock-in transcended. Wales and the Basque Country find themselves picking up the pieces after the cataclysmic decline of their basic industries. Baden-Württemberg and Emilia-Romagna find themselves faced with the question of whether and how to escape their often tightly circumscribed systemic lock-ins in engineering and craft goods.

Industrial Districts and Evolutionary Economics

We are, of course, always discussing systems as open systems rather than the closed systems (e.g. a central heating system) so beloved of engineers, when our concern is social systems. But even social systems have, at least analytically and conceptually if not in reality, system boundaries with their environment and the other systems with which they interact. A version of actually existing socio-economic systems with quite clear boundaries are industrial districts as found in many regional economies, most notably today in north-central Italy and, paradigmatically, in Emilia-Romagna. We do not wish to rehearse material about the origin and nature of industrial districts that will be discussed in Chapter 5 in much more depth. Rather, we wish to move towards a solution to the still unresolved question of reconciling systemness with (radical) innovation through the acoustic of recent work on this problem coming from Italy.

As we have seen in Chapter 1, in evolutionary economic theory, firms are theorized as repositories of knowledge with social capabilities of compromising, satisficing, learning, and resource-developing behaviour (Alchian, 1950; Simon, 1962; Arrow, 1962; Arthur, 1994). Innovative, imitative, unpredictable, and chance effects occur. Firms even engage in collaborative as well as competitive behaviours (Nelson, 1995). Most analyses point to these capabilities as being particularly characteristic of small firms in the tightly knit sub-contracting networks embedded in an institutional milieu that recognizes collaboration and competition as equally valid modes of economic co-ordination typical of industrial districts (Dei Ottati, 1994; 1996). They have systemic information and transaction flow processes which serve them well in periods of economic stability. But it is in periods of instability such as the recession of the early 1990s that they become especially interesting intellectually.

We can see two key system weaknesses in high-trust, intensely networked, relatively closed socio-economic arrangements such as these. First, long-term strategies of collaboration in an externalized, specialized, regionalized (even localized) industrial district demand common behavioural expectations and understandings amongst entrepreneurs. These institutional features are embedded (Granovetter, 1985) in forms such as institutional memory, insider-outsider practices, and obligations. Organizations such as firms, artisans' associations, trade unions, trade associations, and local chambers of commerce then tend to privilege consensus and denigrate dissonance. The absence of dissent delays 'creative destruction' processes and creates a barrier to innovation. Secondly, a point noted by both Belussi (1996) and Varaldo and Ferrucci (1996), this delayed response to shock may cause community-destroying panic actions such as a resort to cut-throat competition with associated erosion of investment capital, offshore sourcing, and even plant relocation unless there are system actors capable of plotting a new trajectory for traditional industry or a trajectory into a new industry. The current policy reflection on this from these authors is that the evolutionary way forward is to relax the tightly defined industrial districts into more 'loosely coupled' (Grabher, 1993*a*) production systems with some hierachical elements capable of integrating local with global networks, especially those involving university research, retail distribution corporations, and international supply chains (on this, see also Cooke, 1996*b*; Cossentino *et al.*, 1996).

Thus it is relatively easy to see that the tension between system and innovation, especially of the more radical kind, arises from the persistence of an over-enclosed system of collective social order in which microconstitutional regulation is too exclusive and localized learning is over-emphasized. While incremental innovation and learning can proceed constructively under relatively stable conditions of system evolution, even with an over-determined, locked-in set of arrangements, the latter become a major encumbrance when questions of trajectory or systemic path-dependence have to be confronted. The argument for regional (and local) innovation systems having the competences to maintain evolutionary stability during periods of reasonable economic calm, but the capabilities to deploy full intelligence, learning, and reflexivity capacities at or preferably well before points of disequilibrium, is overwhelming. The system-crisis position calls for recognition of what Granovetter (1985) and Grabher (1993*a*) refer to as 'the strength of weak ties' or loose-coupling of intra and extra-system organizations and actors to mitigate the problems arising from 'the weakness of strong ties' which can lead to cognitive, functional, and policy/political lock-ins that have to be transcended during periods of necessary economic restructuring. What must, of course, be guarded against in 'strength of weak ties' relationships is information overload.

BEYOND REGIONAL PATH-DEPENDENCE TO ECONOMIES
OF ASSOCIATION

We have seen how localized learning can lead to lock-in and the danger of network and system degradation. Too much communication about outmoded routines is fatal for innovation. Despite the inadequacy of relying simply upon learning alone in a global economy with a growing number of 'tutor economies', we nevertheless underline the sentiments expressed in the following

In the learning economy the organizational modes of firms are increasingly chosen in order to enhance learning capabilities: networking with other firms, horizontal communication patterns and frequent movements of people between posts and departments, are becoming more and more important. The firms of the learning economy are to a large extent 'learning organizations'. In a world of learning economies *the specialisation of firms and countries becomes increasingly important for economic performance.* (Lundvall and Johnson, 1994: 26, emphasis added)

The point about specialization has already been rehearsed in our discussion of reasons for 'the rise of the region state' (Ohmae, 1993). Here we want to explore some implications of this for regional development.

Learning regions are open, information-scanning, sensitizing, monitoring, and evaluating systems (Nonaka and Takeuchi, 1995) but learning economies are increasingly specialized and the firms within them more focused. This is a return to Andrew Carnegie's dictum for business success: 'put all the eggs in one basket *and watch the basket*'. It runs against the grain of the conventional wisdom regarding the importance of industrial diversification in regional economies. But it echoes the rediscovery of the desirability of 'core competences' and 'sticking to the knitting' as espoused by numerous business corporations. Nevertheless, the perils of being an outdated industrial 'monoculture', 'the Ruhr of the 1990s' clearly still animates industrialists and policy-makers in Baden-Württemberg, a regional economy that most outsiders still view with some admiration. Hence, contemporary trends and processes in regional development pose another potential dilemma. To what extent can industry and governance structures view with equanimity the prospect of all the eggs being put in a single basket?

Of course, it depends on the basket. Moreover, if, as seems increasingly indisputable, economies are becoming 'stickier', does that not in itself have implications for the security of the eggs? In other words, if each region were as specialized as possible economically, with the implication that the Porterian cluster in question was competitive, ideally globally so, would this fact in itself not further protect the firms in the regional cluster since, by definition, there would be few or maybe no competing clusters to worry about? Work conducted on the Dutch flower industry cluster strongly suggests *it* is in precisely this happy position, regional claims from potential 'competitors' in the Caribbean notwithstanding (Boekholt, 1994). The combination of world-class research, training, banking, marketing, and international logistics gives the fiercely competitive but in many respects also co-operative firms in the North Holland region a presently unassailable position.

North Holland is by no means monocultural, having the whole complex of financial, business, tourism, cultural, and transportation services associated with Amsterdam and various Randstad towns to call on as well. But, as the flower industry has succeeded, it has spawned, as Krugman (1991) and others going back at least as far as Stigler (1951), Marshall (1919), and Marx (1970) noted, supporting engineering industries in refrigeration, humidity control, glasshouse construction, and so on that have their own specialist role in the overall division of labour. In other words, a not insignificant part of the North Holland agricultural and manufacturing industry is path-dependent (Arthur, 1994) and as goes the industry, so goes the region and its enterprise support policies.

Regional path-dependence is by no means a new thing. In one sense that is how modern industrial capitalism began, but it has not been discussed to the same extent as industrial path-dependence, following the pioneering work of David (1985; Arthur, 1994; for a good review, see Freeman, 1994*a*). Their work has pointed, among other things, to the importance of institutional standards (e.g. FORTRAN) and resulting compatibilities and incompatibilities for the development trajectory of specific technologies, famously in David's (1985) case, including the QWERTY sequence on computer keyboards. Irreversibility sets in when it is cheaper and simpler than reversibility.

What, the question might be posed, is the QWERTY equivalent in regional development? That sequential structure was simply inherited from the typewriter keyboard of Sholes of Milwaukee, 1867, because it minimized type-bar clash, notably for the salesman who needed to type the words 'Type Writer' using only the top bar, to impress the would-be customer of the product's simplicity. The most obvious example, and one to which Arthur (1994) gives some attention, is the nineteeth-century city layout. It still, despite all its inefficiencies, produces increasing returns to scale from the function it plays in matching relative

efficiencies in market transactions to the value derived from 'untraded interdependencies' made possible by the face-to-face exchange of tacit knowledge
(Dosi, 1988*b*; Storper and Scott, 1995). The rent-capturing potential for property
developers from this process-nexus function of the city reinscribes its centrality
to the division of labour, journey to work, and associated transportation axes.
Little has fundamentally changed in this structure even though technologies
have been transformed.

Usually our path-dependence on nineteenth-century buildings and structures
is seen as a source of inefficiency owing to diseconomies appearing to outweigh economies of agglomeration. But in truth, such structures are only fully
abandonded when they have no apparent economic value. The case of Lowell
as described by Sabel *et al.* (1989*a*) is instructive here. The former heart of
the US textile and textile-machinery industry, its mill buildings were abandonded as production moved south and then offshore to retain competitiveness.
But Massachusetts and particularly the Boston area (see Saxenian, 1994) experienced an Arthurian (1994) 'switching' in its regional industrial path-dependence.
Defence contracts and critical research mass gave rise to the mini-computer,
the shortlived successor of the mainframe and ultimate harbinger of desktop
computing. Despite cognitive lock-in from state officials and policy lock-in from
the University of Lowell, the old mills ultimately became the refurbished hosts
for start-up microelectronics suppliers to the likes of Amdahl, Digital, Prime,
and Data General. Yet, as suggested, conditions in the mini-computer industry
changed dramatically in the 1990s and even leading firms such as Digital have
had a struggle to survive the personal computer onslaught, while others have
gone to the wall. Moreover, post-Cold War defence cuts have not helped, especially as, unlike southern California, the Boston area does not have a global
lead in the multimedia industry that software and computer firms located near
Hollywood enjoy.

There are not large numbers of cases of trajectory switching to a totally new
path-dependence in the recent history of regional development, although the
accounts of the progress of some former 'Rustbelt' regions given in Cooke (1995)
are relevant to this discussion of switching from one path-dependence to another.
The case of the Ruhrgebiet, Germany's traditional heavy industrial heartland,
is instructive in this connection. There, the crisis of coal and steel was met by
the emergence of what Schon (1973) refers to as 'self-transforming networks'.
Within large firms such as Krupp and Thyssen, co-determination meant that
managers and trade union leaders consulted on how to face change. Out of this
process emerged the possibility of using ventilation and water-purification technologies for new environmental clean-up products and processes. Concertation
with the *land* government in a context of early implementation of new environmental regulations by the federal government, anticipating new EU directives,
led to the establishment of environmental technology programmes and institutes.
Now North Rhine Westphalia has 47 per cent of Germany's burgeoning environmental technology industry with between 600 and 1,000 new or reconstituted

firms emerging from 1984 to 1994 (Rehfeld, 1995). Furthermore, this concertation process has been decentralized into fifteen 'regional conferences' which bring together representatives of local and regional community and business organizations to propose initiatives on environmental and other innovations which, within budget constraints, local administrations are obliged to implement on approval (Fürst and Kilper, 1995).

Economies of Association

The troubled exit from textiles' path-dependence in Massachusetts compared to the relatively smooth branching of Ruhr coal and steel path-dependence into environmental technologies has considerable relevance for the solution to a problem that economists have difficulty in identifying—the rarity or absence of what are referred to as *'annealing'* properties:

There is rarely in economics any mechanism corresponding to 'annealing' (injections of outside energy that 'shake' the system into new configurations so that it finds its way randomly into a lower cost one). Exit from an inferior equilibrium in economics depends very much on the source of the self-reinforcing mechanism . . . Where learning effects and specialized fixed costs are the source of reinforcement, usually advantages are not reversible and not transferable to an alternative equilibrium. (Arthur, 1994: 118)

However, where co-ordination is the problem, exit from lock-in is more tractable because, for example, users of a particular technology or citizens, employees, employers, and their representative bodies in governance and interest organizations may reach a consensus on the desirability of switching. As we shall see in Chapter 4, precisely this kind of co-ordinative 'annealing' process has been under way in Baden-Württemberg with the injection of associative energy represented by their Commission on the Future. In other words, accomplished regional systems are likely to display strong socio-cultural annealing mechanisms in their collective social order, institutions, and organizations.

In the case of Massachusetts, as described by Sabel *et al.* (1989*a*) and Saxenian (1994), poor co-ordination and a relatively hierarchical state, with many competing jurisdictions dominating the economic policy arena, itself riven by conflicts between high-tech industry and labour, lay close to the heart of the problem:

Massachusetts boasts a broad range of programmes and services to workers and firms that are aimed at increasing the competitiveness of the state's workforce and industrial firms. These programmes are not particularly well-coordinated and involve a variety of state agencies and departments. Some are targeted to the state's high-tech firms, some to the state's 'mature industries'. Some focus on financing assistance, some on education and training and some on the development of new co-operative research and development ventures. (Sabel *et al.*, 1989*a*: 398)

This is a familiar litany of fragmented policy instruments each expressing an abundance of energy and commitment but hampered by being delivered by what

Cram (1994) calls a 'multiorganization' rather than a set of interlinked policy networks, themselves capable of absorbing lay expertise (Marin and Mayntz, 1991; Windhoff-Héritier, 1993).

The policy network is an informal or semi-formal organizational mechanism consisting of public and private individuals, groups, organizations, and associations whose key discriminating factor is that they interact around specific policies and programmes. In this sense, it is the direct equivalent in the policy-development sphere of the post-linear, interactive model of innovation (also, for the development of an equivalent model in vocational training service delivery, see Dehnbostel, 1996). The key is that network participants are 'of consequence' to the policy field in question. Network stability derives from the establishment of trust and reliability, reputation and customary rules to which members adhere. The regional level may be the most significant context in which to develop these attributes because it is the lowest *strategic* level at which to sustain the *regular* interaction which is a key condition for building trust. Network maintenance is secured by the access members have to resources and influence in the pursuit of collectively agreed projects. Schon's (1973) network managers, brokers, and facilitators also come into play here. Network configuration will reflect the programme issue. If it is innovation and regional development, individuals and organizations of consequence to the task constitute the network. Finally, network actors need each other because within their own institutional setting they cannot create all the financial or intellectual resources they need to tackle the issue alone.

The evidence for the success of policy networks in tackling and dealing with issues that administrative hierarchy alone had failed to resolve is by now quite large. The German 'discourse' approach to resolving intractable 'bury or burn' conflicts over waste disposal between local authorities has a copious literature, some of which is represented in Aichholzer and Schienstock (1994). Windhoff-Héritier's work, in Keman (1993), on the development of Environmental Protection Acts in Britain, Germany, and the USA is another case in point, and on regional innovation, the study of PlaNet Ruhr by Körfer and Latniak (1994) is informative on the wavering and recovery of a policy network at the stage of policy implementation.

However, policy networks as flexible organizational forms must rest on an institutional base of norms, routines, regularities, and patterns of behaviour as described, perhaps idealistically in some respects, by Putnam (1993) as the active civil or civic society, the investment of whose 'social capital' underpins social and economic accomplishment. We have returned to our processual definition of region as a distinctive system of collective social order. But it is a limited social order which functions through negotiation rather than fixed rules (Amin and Thomas, 1996). Among other orders which must also be accommodated are the important ones operating at national, supranational, and global levels. This is by no means a re-hash of the rather simplistic notions of corporatism, or even meso-corporatism (Sharpe, 1993) with its continuing emphasis on the salience of master organizations and undervaluation of 'secondary associations' (Heinze and Schmid, 1996).

The negotiated order of peak and secondary associations which has given Denmark its innovative edge, relative social peace, and high, well-distributed prosperity is usefully summarized by Amin and Thomas (1996) as follows:

- a high level of interest representation and organization of public life across economy, politics and society;
- a considerable spread of decisional authority and autonomy across a system of plural interest representation;
- the state as arbitrator and facilitator among associations, as well as rule-maker and service-provider;
- the evolution of a dense network of vertical and horizontal policy channels for decision-making;
- iterative dialogue for conflict resolution and policy consensus via policy networks and co-representation.

Denmark, though small, is a nation state with all the advantages of sovereignty, legitimate authority, and administrative resourcing that accompanies that status. It is thus not entirely appropriate as a model of regional associationism, though most of its imputed qualities are highly relevant to active civil societies at whatever level.

So where, ultimately, do the economies of association derive from and why is this kind of system preferable as a 'third way' between, on the one hand, market societies and, on the other, those characterized by hierarchy of the statist kind? They lie in three principal dimensions. First, they lie in the enhanced efficiencies that arise from the generalization of a *learning* culture in the economy and wider society, overcoming, for example, the policy mismatches that can arise from lack of synchronization between efforts to generate new productive investment and the need for associated re-skilling of the workforce. They lie, secondly, in the advantages that firms and other organizations gain when *trust* is a fundamental element of the system of collective order. As Sabel (1992, 1993) argues, lack of trust or breaches of trust result, in the economic sphere, in the need for expensive, time-consuming, contractual transactions. They lie, finally, in the potential for conflict-minimization by encouraging a more *democratic* and inclusive, thus also more egalitarian, involvement by the widest range of interest associations in the decision-making processes in which, ultimately, all members of the collectivity have a direct or indirect investment and to which, as a consequence, it can give its commitment.

CONCLUSIONS

The new organization of production in the economy involves regions in a transformed way compared to their role in previous modes of economic co-ordination. From being spaces upon which resource-based staple or routine production functions were inscribed, they have moved in many cases to positions closer to that definable as laboratories in the learning economy. New kinds of policy involving experimentation, innovation, intelligence-building, and reflexivity are found in both economically accomplished and reconversion regions. The externalization and specialization now evident as firms seek efficiency gains for competitive advantage are met by a regionalization of innovation programmes as part of a wider decentralization of industrial policy. This is consequent on a degree of political withdrawal at the national level as economic manœuvrability is compromised by wider processes of globalization.

The adjustment processes involved, as regional organizations and institutions seek to accommodate these changes, are immense. By no means all regions warrant the designation regional-learning system let alone regional-innovation system, yet these are the challenges for all if they are to retain or develop more self-sustaining regional-development capacities. The emphasis on the region as a nexus of processes helps fix the idea of regional development as itself an evolutionary process. This process definition draws attention to the institutional and organizational means by which the region as a system of collective social order actually seeks to secure or switch its inherited regional path-dependencies by enhancing its capacity for learning. Of crucial importance to this is the elaboration of economies of association which, where achieved, further both economic efficiency and, potentially, social equity.

4

Baden-Württemberg: The Evolution of a 'Model Region'

INTRODUCTION

Baden-Württemberg has a well-earned reputation as one of Europe's most successful regional economies. This reputation has been built on technical excellence and quality products in the key engineering industries of automotive, electronic, machine-tool, and other mechanical engineering such as printing machinery. It is thus a case of a strongly manufacturing-led growth economy in which service industries such as banking and financial management have played a rather limited role. Among these successful industries are found a plethora of small and medium-sized enterprises, the *Mittelstand*, often intimately linked to large firms through elaborate supply-chain relationships with some degree of lateral networking linkage to other smaller enterprises complementing these vertical supplier relationships. There is, finally, a dense infrastructure of enterprise support organizations including the *Land* Ministry of Economics, the Chambers of Industry and Commerce, Regional Credit Banks, various government agencies such as those for foreign investment, export promotion, and inter-firm co-operation, technology-transfer organizations such as the Steinbeis Foundation, universities, polytechnics, and public and private research institutes and consultancies. The regional economy is thus well integrated and consensual, with trade unions also involved in economic co-ordination. It thus warrants study as an exemplar of a well-functioning regional economic and, indeed, innovation system. But, more particularly, it warrants study because the system has shown signs of malaise in the 1990s brought on by a combination of the effects of globalization, tight monetary and fiscal conditions, high overall wage costs, and underperformance in innovation. Baden-Württemberg is thus a test-case study in how a strong regional economy deals with these tensions and seeks to adjust to new economic realities.

Baden-Württemberg came into existence as a *Land* as recently as 1952 after a plebiscite of its citizens. Although the result of the plebiscite was not *formally* ratified by the Federal Constitutional court until 1970 (Schmidt, 1991), the *Land* functioned as a unity despite the historic differences between its two components, which had been further complicated by the existence of different Allied occupation zones after 1945. In the postwar period, the *Land* was economically transformed from an agricultural, engineering, and textile manufacturing base with a population of 6.8 million, to a booming automotive, machinery, and electronics powerhouse, attracting German and 'guestworker' migrants, to reach a

1996 population of 10.2 million. The *Land* also absorbed over one million new immigrants, mostly from former East Germany and ethnic Germans from the Soviet Union, between 1986 and 1996, mainly of course after 1990 (*Statistische Landesamt Baden-Württemberg*, February 1996).

Therein lies the Baden-Württemberg story in its broadest outlines. It is a 'sunbelt' region, sometimes referred to journalistically as 'Germany's California' (*Independent on Sunday*, 24 March 1996), and by Germans as *Musterländle* or 'model region'. What makes it peculiarly interesting is not the fact that it is one of the world's most prosperous economic regions but that it should once have been one of Europe's poorest. It was a region from which poor farmers migrated to Texas, Minnesota, Ohio, and the Missouri valley in their tens of thousands at the turn of the century. But it was also a region where, for those who stayed, new enterprises in the emergent engineering economy at the end of the nineteenth century were carved out by men such as Karl Benz, Gottlieb Daimler, Robert Bosch, Claudius Dornier, and Ferdinand Porsche, Swabian *tüftler* (tinkerers) who became classic *Mittelständler*. The *Mittelstand* or mid-sized company is the backbone of the German and Baden-Württemberg economies. A term which is said to have over two hundred definitions (Simon, 1992) the German mid-sized firm is as much a state of mind as a category of turnover or employment size. It is usually family owned and run, familial and co-operative in management culture, with high levels of craft skill and job rotation. Even Robert Bosch, one of the world's leading automotive, consumer, power-tool, and communications electronics companies, employing over 100,000 in Germany alone, claims to be a *Mittelstand* company. This is partly because its plants retain some of the features noted, but perhaps more because all its after-tax profits go into the Robert Bosch Foundation which builds and runs hospitals and other health and welfare facilities in Germany and elsewhere. By no means all firms in Baden-Württemberg behave like Bosch but the co-determination rules by which German firms are managed mean that the labour point of view is fully represented at works council and supervisory board level. Hence German capitalism is less uncaring of worker interests—as are its federal and regional states—than its Anglo-American variant.

Of course, German capitalism and that of Baden-Württemberg, one of its leading exponent economies, is not immune to the vagaries and fluctuations of the competitive world economic system. However, until 1993, it was generally in better shape to resist the worst effects of inflation, fuel price quadrupling, and industrial relations difficulties than most. It remains rather surprising to note that Baden-Württemberg's manufacturing employment share, which was 50 per cent in 1957 when agriculture was still 18 per cent, had only declined to 46 per cent in 1994 when agriculture was, at 2 per cent, a vestige of its former importance. Services employment grew, as it has everywhere, but from 15 per cent to 52 per cent over that thirty-seven-year period. The UK figure, for example, had reached 75 per cent even by 1993 (*Census of Employment*, 1993). Nevertheless, the 1993–4 recession in Germany underlined the need for a reappraisal of the relatively stable growth path that had been pursued, not least in *Musterländle*.

The corporate structure of Baden-Württemberg's main indigenous employers such as Mercedes-Benz, Robert Bosch, the aerospace conglomerate DASA (until 1996 part of Daimler-Benz), and Standard Elektrik Lorenz (part of the French multinational Alcatel) had developed very differently from that more typical of the USA or UK. There were, until the 1990s, relatively few major production (as distinct from kit-assembly) sites outside Germany, even outside Baden-Württemberg. Corporate hierarchies were manifold and well staffed, the two main Mercedes complexes at Untertürkheim and Sindelfingen employing 47,000 and 46,000 workers respectively in 1992 out of a German workforce of 173,000. Moreover, a high, though declining, proportion of systems and components were produced in house, especially in Mercedes where it was 46 per cent in 1987, though less in Audi, with a plant at Neckarsulm, at 30 per cent. Robert Bosch and SEL purchased some 50–60 per cent of systems, services, and components, while Porsche, another of the *Land's* leading brand-names, sourced 75 per cent of the value of its cars from suppliers, 57 per cent of which are located in Baden-Württemberg (Morgan *et al.*, 1992; Cooke and Morgan, 1994*a*).

Clearly, with a small number of very large employers and a very large number of smaller suppliers, the Baden-Württemberg economy needs to operate as a system in which there are high external economies of scale and scope to complement the high internal economies of the larger producers. To refer to its 'systemic' propensities should by no means be understood as meaning the economy is an exemplar of successfully equilibriating market clearance, uninhibited by state or intermediary intervention. The reverse is in fact the case. Baden-Württemberg is institutionally richly endowed. One commentator refers to the 'redundancy' (Herrigel, 1989) of this back-up, using the engineering failsafe metaphor. It has intermediary institutions in training, technology transfer, R&D/innovation, and business intelligence. Among the most visible of these intermediaries are the Chambers of Industry and Commerce (IHK), the various branches of the business associations (*Verbände*) in the key industries of automotives, electronics, and machinery, the large offices of key trade unions such as IG Metall and ÖTV, the public services union, and various para-government and private agencies for craft firms, small firm technology transfer, and so on, as well as banks, both public and private.

If it is the case that Baden-Württemberg's economic history is interesting because of the way the region rose from poverty, through enterprise, to prosperity, it is equally so in light of the new pressures to which the system that had successfully evolved over decades is being exposed as the twentieth century draws to a close. Throughout the century there has been a strong, autarchic strain in German political culture, the absolute nadir of which, for Germany and the world, was reached under Hitler. While the 'Germany can go it alone' disposition moderated after 1945, it remained a bedrock presumption during the period of postwar reconstruction, of necessity. Even in the 1980s and early

1990s (for example, with respect to reunification), it remains strong and when, at the more mundane level of the economy, the OECD statistics on foreign investment or patenting data are consulted, Germany is second only to Japan in its degree of relative introversion. Most German firms still sell to other German firms, even though the ultimate product is often exported. However, the pressures of competition on the global scale, from Asia and the Americas, not to mention inside the European Single Market, are pulling German firms outwards both in terms of production locations and for sourcing systems, services, and components. German, and especially Baden-Württemberg firms like Porsche and Mercedes, supported by the world-class capital equipment companies such as Heidelberg, Heller, and Trumpf, always sold on the technical excellence of their precision engineering; cost was a secondary consideration. Now, though, German labour costs are among the highest in the world and Japanese luxury cars and even Korean and Taiwanese machine tools are undercutting local prices while still offering acceptably high quality standards to German customers. This process risks the unravelling of the systemic features that evolved in the Baden-Württemberg economy after 1945. System-response to these serious institutional disturbances is a key theme of the rest of this chapter.

In what follows, the first area of focus will be upon the regional governance system of the *Land*, principally its relationship with the federal level of government. Thereafter, attention will be devoted to the changes in corporate organization, consequent upon the discovery by German business of the need for serious restructuring. The role of intermediary organizations in the animation of the regional production system will be examined as a prelude to considering the implications, both objectively and in terms expressed by official commissions and the like, regarding the future of Baden-Württemberg's historically dominant regional engineering economy, in the face of global competitive pressures.

THE REGIONAL GOVERNANCE SYSTEM

Germany has a federal system of government, one of the most devolved in the world, designed during and under the tutelage of the Allied forces of occupation. The Federal Republic was founded in 1949 and is thus younger than some *Länder* or states. These were already, in some cases, established and meeting formally in West Germany as standing conferences on education, science, and the like in 1948. Even in March 1949, the future Baden-Württemberg was represented at the Königstein Culture Ministers conference, which established the institutes of the Max Planck society for basic research, by Baden, Württemberg-Baden, and Württemberg-Hohenzollern (Götz, 1993). This apparently arcane historical point echoes down to the present day since it justifies the primacy that *Land* Ministers of Education, Science, and Culture have constitutionally *vis-à-vis* their Federal counterpart. Following Article 23 of the 1966 constitution, ratified in the Maastricht Treaty, European Union Council of Ministers meetings may have, as the representative of Germany, the agreed representative of the *Länder* culture ministries sent by the *Bundesrat* rather than the minister of the Federal Government. This was once a bone of contention, as the Treaty of Rome had been generally interpreted to mean only federal ministers should be present at Council meetings.

It is often thought that Germany's modern constitution, enshrined in its Basic Law plus amendments, helps understanding of Germany's successful postwar economic performance. To the extent that there is truth in this assumption, it may be that the contribution is really to reinforce the bonds of stability that are, in economic terms, provided fundamentally by the policies of the *Bundesbank*. As will become apparent, the processes and institutions, for example the Equalization Committees, German Unity Fund, Constitutional Court, and so on, by means of which Federal–*Land* relationships are mediated, make for slow, evolutionary change by absorption. This has even proved the case in connection with probably the greatest shift ever experienced by any European Union member up to the point when the Federal Republic reunified with the former Democratic Republic to create the new, united Germany.

This event re-opened and invigorated a long-standing debate among political scientists concerning the relationship between the federal level and the *Länder*, on the one hand, and, on the other, the degree to which the *Länder* could be seen to be developing their own *Land*-specific policies, especially regional economic policies. The absorption of the new *Länder* was seen by many experts as likely to entail a greater centralization, not least because of the associated costs of reunification. Sturm (1994) notes that even in 1993 only 26.8 per cent of the budgets of the former East German *Länder* were financed from their own income, the rest coming from transfers (54.4%) and credit (18.8%). Such extreme dependence on fiscal centralism draws attention to the fact that as he puts it: 'In comparative perspective the German case may be unique in the way it combines formal elements of federalism with the de facto centralism of unitary states. Many arguments have been made by academics in favour of a re-federalisation of Germany' (Sturm, 1994: 22). Financing lies at the heart of the present condition of 'formal federalism' but 'de facto centralism'. Weak states, not only in former East Germany, have benefited highly from fiscal transfers and valued federal backing. However, the demand from the new *Länder* means that not only have these transfers diminished, but even poorer states have had to.contribute, through the German Unity Fund, both to New *Länder* support and their own welfare spending because of federal expenditure cuts.

Although by no means as trenchant as the neo-liberal reforms on state expenditure and employment embarked upon in the UK and USA in the 1980s, the German Federal government has sought to cut expenditure, most severely in 1996, to try to kick-start the declining German economy (Karacs, 1996; Wolf, 1996). This has meant that those regional economies whose performance was the best in the 1980s and who remained comparatively wealthy in the 1990s, of which Baden-Württemberg is the exemplar, became disaffected. In particular, there has been more recourse to the Constitutional Court to resolve federal–*Land* transfers than hitherto in, for example, determining the terms and conditions of the Solidarity Pact for the Reconstruction of the New *Länder*, which replaced the original German Unity Fund effective from 1995.

The complexity of this apparent 'unitary federalism' is plain to see and gave rise to the *Politikverflechtung* debate, stimulated initially by the work of Fritz Scharpf (1976, 1988) who sought to transcend the 'centralization–decentralization' dichotomy hitherto conceptually dominant. 'Policy inter-weaving' is the literal meaning of Scharpf's term, though it can be presented relatively neutrally as a broader 'co-operative federalism' or narrower 'policy interlocking' as well as, more pejoratively, 'policy entanglement' or 'entanglement of the two levels of government' (Götz, 1993; Jeffery, 1996a). Whatever, Scharpf's concept referred to the ways in which decision-making as well as policy formulation and implementation were in the 1960s dispersed both vertically and horizontally in the German system. However, in an increasingly interdependent range of policy areas with high connectedness amongst ever more complex problems, issues of policy externalities, spillovers, and free-riding could more frequently arise, according to Scharpf's public choice theory approach. This would tend to lead to a politically undesirable centralization effect. So, intragovernmental negotiation and co-operation became more institutionalized as a way of reducing tensions of a territorial and functional kind.

Such intragovernmental, committee-based relations originated from three key sources according to Jeffery (1996a). Each derived from the constitutional relationship between levels of government. First, there is little clear division of responsibilities as neither level—but especially the *Länder*—has exclusive competence in given policy areas; most involve shared competences. In particular, the federal level tends to be legislative and the *Land* level executive. Secondly, the *Bundesrat*, as the second, federal chamber for legislative purposes, has absolute veto rights for some 60 per cent of federal laws with milder veto rights for the rest *and* the *Bundesrat* is exclusively representative of the *Länder*. This has obvious implications for the necessity of consensus as a condition for the success of any proposed legislative reform. Thirdly, where there are 'Joint Tasks', there are detailed joint legislative, planning, and financing procedures. Consensus also demands agreement amongst the *Länder* for their negotiating status towards the Federal Government to retain credibility. This is achieved through a panoply of policy co-ordinating committees focused upon the *Bundesrat* yet interacting with many others outside.

Scharpf criticized the 'cartel-like' nature of this relationship and the total interdependency between levels of government which tended to produce policy compromises 'converging on the lowest possible denominator' (Götz, 1993). Federal decisions produced inadequate problem solutions in a 'joint-decision trap' and blockage towards change. Even an increase in the scope of *Land* competences, which he advocated in his early work, he later thought unlikely to assist because their constitutional powers to initiate policies are comparatively limited. This legislative deficit expresses both a reality but also an emphasis in the *Politikver-flechtung* perspective. Much of the research which identifies the centralizing force of the Federal Government places too much emphasis on law-making and pays too little attention to other aspects of the policy development, interpretation, and implementation process, argue authors such as Benz (1989) and Fürst (see e.g. Fürst and Kilper, 1995).

These writers identify weaknesses in Scharpf's analysis. They demonstrate empirically that *Land* and even local governments have more discretion than the 'centralists' allow. For example, these governments possess substantial resources which allow them to pursue independent policy lines. Moreover, the blockages noted as endemic to the system are infrequent occurrences in what is actually a flexible and responsive policy system. City governments in Germany, though variably resourced, make many coherent and innovative policy impacts, especially where they are well endowed. Moreover, at *Land* level too, it is argued, there have been more independent policy-formulation instances since the late 1970s, not least because of subsequent changes in their economic condition. Not surprisingly, *Land* activities have become more important in terms of regional industrial and other economic development (Hesse, 1990).

So much had this become the case in the 1980s, argued Esser (1989), that distinctive regional development policies could be observed among North Rhine-Westphalia (Social Democratic Party-governed), Hessen (SPD–Green coalition), and Baden-Württemberg (Christian Democrat-governed). In North Rhine-Westphalia, the *Land* government had adopted a decentralist policy intervention stance based on encouraging co-operation and partnership between universities, science parks, and networks of publicly funded technology centres. These were aimed especially at helping regenerate older industrial areas such as the Ruhr. In Hessen, the SDP–Green coalition sought to enhance the status of Frankfurt while controlling the impact of its expansion upon the environment. In Baden-Württemberg, a more centralist, market-oriented technology policy was adopted based on the predominantly privately funded Steinbeis Foundation which arranged technology transfer to the *Mittelstand* via consultants based in the *Fachhochschulen* or local polytechnic colleges.

The character of regional economic development and enterprise support is the key interest of the remainder of this chapter. It will be shown that there have been and are distinctive policy developments for enterprise support, especially concerning innovation in Baden-Württemberg. But it would be misleading to conclude that these are because of significant or significantly different policy interventions from the *Land* government alone. Much of Baden-Württemberg's economic distinctiveness, to the extent it can be said to have it, derives from the concerns and actions of the *collectivity* of business and intermediary actors. These *associative* groupings are capable of taking initiatives to tackle collective business problems in concert with, in communication with, and in the absence of state intervention. To that extent we may see in Baden-Württemberg the emergence of a kind of 'self-regulation' of some economic issues as distinct

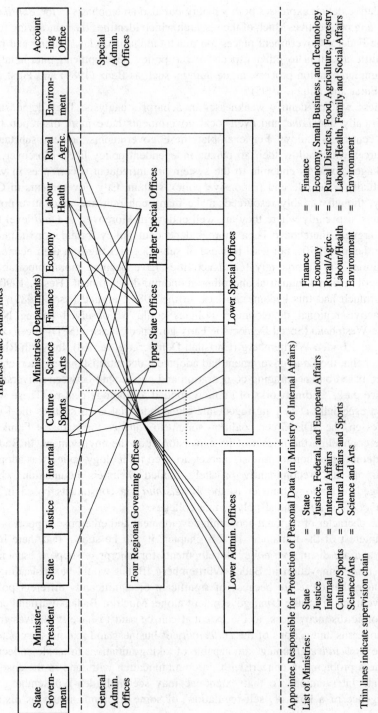

FIG. 4.1. Structure of the state administration in Baden-Württemberg

Highest State Authorities

State Govern-ment	Minister-President	Ministries (Departments)										Account-ing Office
		State	Justice	Internal	Culture Sports	Science Arts	Finance	Economy	Labour Health	Rural Agric.	Environ-ment	

General Admin. Offices

Special Admin. Offices

Four Regional Governing Offices

Upper State Offices

Higher Special Offices

Lower Admin. Offices

Lower Special Offices

Appointee Responsible for Protection of Personal Data (in Ministry of Internal Affairs)

List of Ministries:
State = Justice, Federal, and European Affairs
Justice = Justice, Federal, and European Affairs
Internal = Internal Affairs
Culture/Sports = Cultural Affairs and Sports
Science/Arts = Science and Arts
Finance = Finance
Economy = Economy, Small Business, and Technology
Rural/Agric. = Rural Districts, Food, Agriculture, Forestry
Labour/Health = Labour, Health, Family and Social Affairs
Environment = Environment

Thin lines indicate supervision chain

from its earlier neo-mercantilist approach or the more interventionary 'state regulation' of the problem-solving process more typical of problem regions. Having
said that, some authors claim to see comparable developments in North Rhine-
Westphalia consequent upon the decline in state (*Land*) budgets since 1990
(Körfer and Latniak, 1994; Latniak and Simonis, 1994; Fürst and Kilper, 1995).

Before investigating such claims for Baden-Württemberg further, it is important to clarify, as far as possible, the competences and responsibilities of the
Land level of government, taking Baden-Württemberg as the exemplar in order
to understand just how powerful, by comparison with most regional governments in other countries, the German *Länder* are. The structure of the Baden-
Württemberg government machine is given in Figure 4.1. It reveals many kinds
of ministry more typically found in unitary or federal state governance systems
including Ministries of State, Justice, Cultural Affairs, Finance, Health and
Social Affairs, Economics and Environment.

Beneath these are Regional Governing Offices, intermediate authorities responsible for a so-called 'focus effect'. They focus and act as a synthesizer of tasks
that are distributed among separate ministries unless these are already focused
in Upper State or Higher Special Offices. At the lowest *Land* level, these
powers are then redistributed to numerous authorities with their own regional
or technical capabilities. These are the *Kreise* (Districts), Counties, and Municipalities of local administration to which some *Land* functions are ultimately
delegated for implementation. The relationship of these to the four Regional
Governing Offices (RGOs) for Baden-Württemberg is that of seeking mediation
and balancing functions. Thus, the interrelated policies of different ministries
are assimilated and standardized by negotiation for implementation at local
level. RGOs are more administrative than political, though their presidents are
political officials. One especially interesting sector of public administration is
the previously alluded to sphere of *self-government*. It carries out tasks within
the legal framework through autonomous bodies at their own risk, with the state
merely supervising actions in respect of their legality. Social insurance, colleges,
media, savings banks, chambers of commerce, and administration unions (responsible for water supply and waste disposal) are examples of self-government
either on behalf of the state (e.g. chambers of commerce taking responsibility
for vocational training curricula and assessment) or in constitutional insulation
from it (media).

THE NATIONAL SYSTEM OF INNOVATION

Clearly, Baden-Württemberg operates within the German National System of
Innovation (NSI) and this colours the opportunities that exist for innovation in
particular directions since the Federal Ministry of Research and Technology
(BMFT) has its responsibilities and agreed agenda. Following Nelson (1993), we
can say that the Federal NSI is a strong and well-co-ordinated one, certainly

TABLE 4.1. Gross expenditure on R&D as a percentage of GDP

Country	1987	1990	1992	1993
France	2.27	2.42	2.36	2.41
Germany	2.88	2.75	2.53	2.48
Italy	1.19	1.30	1.31	1.30
Japan	2.82	3.08	2.99	–
UK	2.22	2.19	2.12	2.19
USA	2.84	2.74	2.68	2.79

Source: OECD.

by comparison with the increasingly market-pulled version operating in the UK. German R&D expenditure is marginally, though consistently, higher than that of most leading countries except that in the 1990s it has slipped against Japan and the USA, as Table 4.1 shows.

Furthermore, only some 5 per cent of German R&D expenditure is on military research compared to the situation in the UK where the figure is closer to 50 per cent (Cooke and Morgan, 1990). Moreover, industrial R&D is high at some 70 per cent and was rising, at least up to the 1993–4 recession. Finally, research funding is frequently collaborative in nature with proportions of up to 75 per cent of BMFT (Federal Ministry of Research and Technology) specific programme support having been allocated to collaborative programmes in Information Technology and Materials Research and 100 per cent in Production Engineering (Cooke and Morgan, 1991a). Small firms (SMEs) benefit from such programmes by being allowed to participate in advanced research with large firms and government support. SMEs thus account for some 15 per cent of private industry's total research expenditure. Special federal measures to promote R&D in SMEs numbered fifteen in the early 1990s, ranging from improving the rate of new technology development in industry to strengthening collaboration with the science base.

In line with the division of functions between federal legislation and *Land* implementation of policies, most of these programmes are implemented through Max Planck, Fraunhofer, or other kinds of research institute. A case in point would be the BMFT's Microsystems Technology programme which both led to the establishment of new laboratories within many existing institutes and also brought together SMEs that were not necessarily expert in microsystems research themselves but could adapt it to their specific expertise once they had learned sufficient about it over the course of a research programme which cost them little to join (Becker and Pfirmann, 1993). The advantages of collaborative research programmes at *Land* or even city level in the case of Bremen (which is both) are also spelled out for the pioneering case of Surface Treatment technologies by Häusler *et al.* (1993).

In accordance with the Federal Republic's traditionally close links between industry and finance, and the banks' tradition of supplying 'patient money' in the form of long-term credit, the supportive environment generated by collaborative government programmes has served industry comparatively well where change has been incremental. However, where step changes were sought, as in the 1970s with the federal Computer Industry and Data Processing (*Dataverarbeitung*) initiative, the results—as in many other countries—were a failure. Latniak and Simonis (1994) put this down to three weaknesses: too much (100%) subsidy and too little government influence over management deficiencies in firms; too large a share of resources given to large firms like Siemens and AEG; and a concentration on hardware to the detriment of software development. Technology-push strategies which seek to change German path-dependence too much may clearly come unstuck.

At *Land* level, initiatives are much more incremental, although the Baden-Württemberg Future Commission has advocated diversification into multimedia, photovoltaics, and biotechnology and, locally, these have been taken up in the *Solarinitiative Heilbronn* and *Multimedia Region Tübingen-Reutlingen*, though with what success remains to be seen. In Baden-Württemberg, there are three types of intermediary initiative in support of innovation or innovative organization that are more typical of the distinctive, but moulded, kind of incremental enterprise support that has served SMEs and, through them, larger enterprises, reasonably well in the past.

Co-operative Initiatives   These include the long-established work of the *Landesgewerbeamt*, the office for the Promotion of Trade and Industry, responsible for supporting co-operation networks among SMEs. An example of its involvement is represented by the case of twelve very small engineering firms that were helped to grow into an association of twenty-five important medium-sized suppliers in the automotive sector with *Landesgewerbeamt* assistance. A different case is that of the Gosheim Technology Centre, helped by the Steinbeis Foundation to become the centre of a co-operative network of 154 SMEs in metals, plastics, and electronics, starting with a group of lathe manufacturers afraid of going out of business due to the lack of an innovation support institution (Pyke, 1994). Finally, the AKZ consortium of engineering companies, a private co-operative association of firms in complementary products and industries, is an example of a self-induced intermediary institution capable of supplying 'club goods' to its members.

Associative Organizations   An institutional innovation originating in Baden-Württemberg within the interstices of Germany's 'formal federalism' (Sturm, 1994) are the *An-institutes*. Seven of the *Land's* universities have these intermediary organizations set up to bridge the university–industry innovation transfer gap. They are jointly funded by public and private sources and are meant to work as quickly as consultancies but as thoroughly as academic research organizations, meeting the transfer needs of, in particular, larger enterprises. They are, in a sense, modelled on the Steinbeis method of transfer through centres which are funded by public and private sources to enhance transfer to SMEs by using *Fachhochschule* professors as local technology consultants.

Taking technology transfer to an international scale, the *Land* Ministry of Economics established in 1987 the *Four Motors* programme in partnership with Lombardy, Catalonia, Rhône-Alpes, and subsequently Wales and Ontario. This economic, technological, and cultural partnership is responsible for numerous joint research projects between universities and institutes, technology transfer between SMEs, and trade fairs and exhibitions which combine commercial and cultural exchange.

Land Innovation Programmes   In support of the continuing need for innovation among *Mittelstand* firms, the *Land* Ministry of Economics promotes programmes, often themselves coming under the umbrella of BMFT programmes, to enable SMEs to take advantage of, on the one hand, the existing innovation infrastructure and, on the other, the financial resources of the regional banking system. Examples of such programmes in the past have been: the *CI Programme*, providing grants for SMEs to commission or conduct R&D into new products and processes; the *MT Programme*, providing grants for investment costs of new equipment in SMEs; and the *TOU Programme*, which provides loans for the founding of new technology-based firms. Other initiatives of a more ad hoc nature include the establishment of the Ulm Science City with support funding for research facilities from Mercedes and IBM, and the *model projects* for collaborative research among SMEs to meet large-firm innovation requirements.

It is relatively clear that the Baden-Württemberg enterprise and innovation support system is both comprehensive and multi-layered. The range and variety of public and private intermediaries and the emphasis that is not infrequently placed upon the co-operative dimension of economic co-ordination are testimony to the sense of a 'social economy' prevalent in the *Land's* self-image. This has served both economy and community well in the years of growth and stability. Whether this can be sustained for the future is a question receiving considerable attention as the twentieth century draws to a close.

CORPORATE RESTRUCTURING

Manufacturing is now, as it has traditionally been, Baden-Württemberg's leading economic activity. Some 43 per cent of Baden-Württemberg's employees were in production industries in 1995 even after job losses of 300,000 had been announced during the 1993–4 recession. The main employment sectors in manufacturing, which itself comprises over 80 per cent of industry, are automotive engineering (220,000), electronics (246,000), and machinery (245,000). The proportion of industrial employment is double that for the UK and USA and a third larger than that for Japan and the European Union. In an era when even service-sector growth may be beginning to cease for all but some business and financial services, this is a remarkable position and, given the fate of manufacturing employment elsewhere, one which makes the Baden-Württemberg labour market potentially very vulnerable.

Yet the leading firms in the *Land* have been slow to restructure and slow to raise their sights significantly beyond the *Land*, let alone Germany, either for production locations or sources of supply. For example, it was shown in Cooke and Morgan (1994*b*) that Daimler Automotive (i.e. Mercedes-Benz) not only kept the level of its in-house parts and components production as high as 47 per cent in 1986 when for Opel, Ford, and Audi the figures were as low as 30 per cent, it had actually increased it from 43 per cent in 1970, from which date all other German producers had been reducing the proportion of in-house production. Alternatively, Heidenreich and Krauss (1997) show that, in 1990, 60 per cent of automotive supplies in the automotive sector were sourced by Baden-Württemberg firms from other firms in the *Land*. They also show that machinery firms in Baden-Württemberg sourced some 45 per cent of their metal and mechanical parts from other firms in the *Land* and for electronics firms the figure was 45 per cent. In overall terms, these industries sourced 53 per cent of supplies from all industries from inside the *Land* and for industry-related services, the figure was over 90 per cent. It is clear that this has been, and still in the mid-1990s undoubtedly remained, an autocentric or relatively self-sufficient industrial economy. In that respect, it is the regional economist's ideal but in another respect it is their nightmare because of its monoindustrial culture and apparent lack of diversification. This problem has now begun seriously to concern industrialists and the wider economic policy community in the *Land*.

Already in the findings of the Baden-Württemberg Future Commission on *Economy 2000* (Future Commission, 1993), three key weaknesses were identified as contributing to the *Land's* economic malaise. The Future Commission was established as a consensus body representing the key business actors in the *Land* to monitor and reflect upon its present weaknesses and possible visions for the future. The primary problem the Commission identified was that *competition* was perceived to have reached the 'quality diversified production' markets that are the *Land's* speciality (Streeck, 1989; Semlinger, 1993). No longer could luxury cars and sophisticated machinery cushion the Baden-Württemberg economy from international competition. These and the electronics cluster faced increasing rivalry not only from Japan in automotive and machine-tool markets but from Korea and Taiwan in cheaper machine tools as well. With the establishment of the European Single Market and the liberalization of Central and Eastern European economies, Germany was expected to be assailed at both the higher and lower ends of its engineering product markets. The report revealed that Japanese imports had taken 25 per cent of the German market for CNC lathes while Germany only had 12 per cent of the whole Asia-Pacific machine-tool market, compared with Japan's 50 per cent share. The reason for this, it was concluded, was that Japanese firms had a 30 per cent advantage over German production costs, time to market, value for money, and after-sales service.

A second weakness, which came as a surprise to many given the apparent density of the Baden-Württemberg innovation infrastructure, lay in the sphere of *innovation deficits*. Baden-Württemberg's innovation posture was one which emphasized support for, usually incremental, technological and organizational change in *mature* industrial sectors, notably those involving mechanical engineering. But Baden-Württemberg firms were perceived to be weak in semiconductors, computers, and telecommunications technologies and these, along with new materials and biotechnology, were demonstrably the growth sectors of the future. The prescience of the report was shown by the initial effects of the German recession in 1993–4 which revealed a 15.9 per cent decline in automotive production, a 13.2 per cent fall in machine building and a 6.5 per cent decrease in electronics and telecommunications, the last named not exactly recession-proof but less vulnerable to recession than the more traditional sectors (Braczyk *et al.*, 1995).

The third weakness of the regional economy has revolved around *production costs* and *productivity*. The former have risen in comparative terms owing to a combination of the strong German currency (due to high interest rates to keep downward pressure on inflationary tendencies caused by the costs of German reunification) and high labour costs, especially in respect of the social wage (see Cooke and Morgan, 1994*b*). Productivity, once the source of Germany's competitive edge in spite of high production costs, has been rising more slowly since the onset of the 1980s. A gap opened up between labour productivity and GDP growth mainly because Baden-Württemberg firms, like their German peers, diminished the quantity and quality of capital investment. Herrigel (1996) disagrees with this, preferring to locate the problem in the *Land's* institutionalized model of production. But clearly the economic indicators point to weaknesses in firm performance at the same time as capital was flooding overseas. Managers ran their plants at near-full capacity, capturing further windfall profits from increased demand when former East German industry and then Central European industry began restructuring in the period from 1989–93. To the extent investment on any significant scale occurred, it was directed overseas. The OECD foreign direct investment statistics reveal a rise in German annual capital *outflows* to a peak of $23.2 billion in 1990 from $2.5 billion in 1982. Baden-Württemberg's *stocks* of capital invested overseas rose from 12 billion DM direct investment in 1982 to 30 billion DM by 1990 and 42 billion DM by 1993. The Baden-Württemberg *Landeskredietbank* (private communication, 1996) estimated that in the latter half of the 1980s and the first third of the 1990s Baden-Württemberg accounted for at least half of Germany's total foreign direct investment outflow. In light of these points it is worthwhile summarizing the main responses to this three-pronged crisis by the *Land's* larger corporate actors in the automotive and electronics industries.

Restructuring in the Automotive Industry

Three of Baden-Württemberg's six largest companies have a major presence in automotive production as Table 4.2 shows. This industry is dependent to a

TABLE 4.2. Baden-Württemberg's largest companies

Company	Sector	Employees (1994)	Change from 1993 (%)	Turnover 1994 (bn. DM)	Change from 1993 (%)
Daimler-Benz	Auto/Aerospace	330,551	−9.9	104.1	+5.6
Robert Bosch	Auto/Electronics	153,794	−1.8	34.5	+6.2
Bilfinger & Berger	Construction	47,071	+2.7	7.6	+13.5
Asea Brown Boveri	Engineering	35,120	−4.9	9.9	+4.4
Carl Zeiss	Optometry	32,781	−2.6	5.0	+6.1
ZF	Auto Systems	31,393	+9.4	6.4	+17.5

Source: Heidenreich (1996).

rather larger extent than the machinery or electronics industries on export orders. These dipped severely, by some 13 per cent in 1992–3. Added to export penetration and a weakening domestic demand, the industry is at something of a crossroads. There are even some suggestions in the final part of the Future Commission report (Emerging From the Crisis; Future Commission, 1993) that Baden-Württemberg should restructure its economy and the enterprise support infrastructure of R&D and vocational training away from automotive and towards newer multimedia and biotechnology industries. Even IG Metall's Walter Riester (1994) proposed that the automotive industry should diversify into new traffic systems technologies based on the excellence of innovation in sensors. Also environmental control technologies were, he thought, feasible future developments. However others, more soberly and undoubtedly realistically, question the *Land's* industrial capacity to catch up with, say, Hollywood in multimedia, Japan in advanced microelectronics, or the USA in biotechnology (Braczyk *et al.*, 1995).

So, how have the leading companies sought to retain a competitive, innovative edge within the path-dependence of the automotive industry? Three distinct but merging points can be made. First, under the co-determination system in German industry, discussions about alternatives to Fordist–Taylorist mass production methods and organization had been under way for more than a decade. The IG Metall position, shared by the trade union movement in general, favoured the 'Humanization of Work' approach. Programmes and initiatives, not least those promoted by the Federal as well as, in some cases, *Land* governments, were launched. Even in Baden-Württemberg, where employers displayed extreme scepticism as to the prospects for human-centred work organization such as that practised by Volvo at Kalmar and Udevalla in Sweden, IG Metall organized regional conferences for car assemblers and suppliers to discuss restructuring strategies 'with a human face'. An action group—the *Forum for Social Technology* —was also founded in support of such union initiative as late as 1992.

However, automotive industry employers, while willing to discuss these ideas, were committed to a much more radical step in the opposite direction. In the 1980s especially, they placed inordinate and, as it later proved, unfounded faith in a full-blooded *Computer-Integrated Manufacturing* (CIM) approach. The 'workerless factory' was a dream which could only make sense on such a widespread basis in an economy where labour had bargained for strong and permanent statutory representation in the corporate management process. Employers could see the reassertion of management prerogatives as well as the full and productive use of invested capital in a CIM-dominated production system. But union resistance and technical complexity meant that CIM remained, except on a small scale and in partial, piecemeal terms, a chimera. Attempts to develop a hybrid 'Humanized CIM' were doomed to the futility of their evident illogicalities and failed to get started in any serious way.

At this point, in late 1991–early 1992, Mercedes-Benz, in particular, became quite desperate faced with the Toyota luxury car, the Lexus. This new product brought competition to the highest end of their market but at a price affordable by mid-to-higher income brackets. Shortly before this, the Massachusetts Institute of Technology's International Motor Vehicle Program had reported (Womack *et al.*, 1990) on a new organizational concept they identified as underpinning the Toyota manufacturing method and dubbed it 'Lean Production'. Leading firms such as Mercedes and Robert Bosch purchased the book, a thousand copies at a time, for distribution among senior managers. Seminars, workshops, and presentations were made by the authors to main boards of key automotive and other companies.

The MIT report on the (un-named) Mercedes Sindelfingen assembly plant to the south-west of Stuttgart noted the plant was: 'expending more effort to fix the problems it had just created than the Japanese plant required to make a nearly perfect car the first time' (Womack *et al.*, 1990: 91). The Mercedes response, albeit belated, was to seek to introduce a threefold process. First, a new emphasis was to be placed on modular assembly and teamwork. Secondly, co-ordination between the company's Fordist design, development, production, and marketing divisions was to be improved by project-based 'simultaneous engineering'. Finally, new supply-chain management practices were intended to be installed with cost meant to take precedence over technology and greater collaboration with sub-contractors. New, more diversified models (including 'Swatch' cars) were envisaged as were new plants in Baden-Württemberg and elsewhere, notably in Alabama, USA. A new plant, based on lean-production principles, was constructed in Rastatt to act as a 'laboratory' of production methods following Japanese organizational concepts (Morgan, 1994).

Most of these innovations have been implemented, not without difficulties. As noted, putting out R&D intensive-supply work creates pressure for sub-contractors lacking a tradition of innovative thinking and expertise. IG Metall has, understandably, opposed sub-contracting to a supplier hierarchy feeding modular systems into the assembly plants through a supply chain because of the obvious job losses such a system implies as in-house production declines. And even in such brand new plants as Rastatt on the border with Alsace, France, old departmental divisions inbred in the Mercedes culture were transplanted via key workers from Sindelfingen and Untertürkheim who set up the plant; hence anticipated efficiences were not always achieved. Ironically, the automotive division was for a time effectively keeping Daimler-Benz afloat, given the vast losses in 1996 (5.7 billion DM) incurred by the parent company's troubled diversification into the aerospace industry (Münchau, 1996).

Audi and Porsche are the *Land*'s other two automotive assemblers. Audi has a small plant at Neckarsulm, Porsche at Zuffenhausen, north-west of Stuttgart. A vital part of Audi's strategy for the 1990s has been to develop new synergies inside the firm along the 'simultaneous engineering' lines Mercedes is also pursuing. There was an intention to reduce in-house production to below 30 per cent of value in 1995/6 and develop a supplier hierarchy, reducing its direct suppliers from 1,051 in 1991 to 650 in 1994. As with Mercedes, a premium is placed on first-tier modular or system-supply firms. These are expected to make a significant R&D contribution in their own right. Although only 16 per cent by value of Audi parts are sourced from outside Germany, the expectation is that this percentage will rise as global sourcing becomes more prevalent. Spain and the UK are anticipated beneficiaries of this process. Audi's logistics strategy eschews just-in-time delivery in favour of a 'consignment stocks' approach based on the construction of on-site warehouses at its plants in Neckarsulm and Ingolstadt on the Bavarian border.

Porsche was struck by the severest crisis in its postwar history in the early 1990s and it only began to return to profitability in the mid-to-late 1990s. As a luxury niche producer, its markets are particularly cyclical. Thus in 1986, worldwide sales peaked at 53,300 units of which 30,471 were sold in the USA. By 1990, US sales had slumped to 9,139 and worldwide sales to 26,000. Net income fell from 68.4 million DM in 1990 to 50.0 million DM in 1991 leading to a 6 per cent reduction in its 8,000 strong workforce. Porsche has traditionally put out 75 per cent of its value in sub-contracted supply. Engine, bodywork assembly, and testing are the main in-house functions, R&D employs 2,000 engineers, many also engaged in design consultancy for other customers. Japanese competition has become the main threat owing to the affordability of their rapidly changing model range. Porsche, too, expects to source globally to capture cost reductions; in the first half of the 1990s, 57 per cent of the company's 700 main suppliers were within a 100-kilometre radius of Zuffenhausen. Thus far, Porsche has resisted acquisition by an outside company though a similar fate to that of UK luxury producer Jaguar, acquired by Ford, was mooted at one time. Porsche's mid-1990s recovery with new, relatively downmarket models like the Boxster suggests that the company has survived the storm for the moment. The fact that Porsche invited a team of engineers formerly from Toyota to help achieve the turnaround created considerable tensions among the firm's 'proud engineers'.

Restructuring in Electronics

The other Baden-Württemberg industry with large, global firm presence is electronics. Apart from Robert Bosch and Standard Elektrik Lorenz (SEL), a subsidiary of Alcatel, there are firms such as Hewlett-Packard, IBM, and Sony. The corporate restructuring approach of Bosch is very similar to that of the automotive firms Mercedes and Audi. It involves more outsourcing, simultaneous engineering, and location of plants outside Germany. The UK and USA have been recent development locations for the company; the first, near Cardiff, aims to take advantage of the growing presence of Japanese assemblers in Britain while the second pursues new ventures by Mercedes and BMW as well as the Japanese in North America. SEL is probably the company that has had the hardest time in the 1990s, closing plants employing 10,000 people; defence cuts on the ending of the Cold War brought an end to SEL's military telephony division.

The overseas firms are more affected by their own internal strategies than specific conditions in the Baden-Württemberg economy. IBM's troubles in the 1990s have been legion as they sought to recover markets lost to imitators in personal computers while trying to come to terms with the demise of the main-frame market and develop a new, non-accountancy-driven corporate culture. The goals for IBM Germany are cost reduction, total quality control, and reduced development cycles. Outsourcing, including part of IBM's purchasing function, which is handled by media giant Bertelsmann's factoring arm, has long been part of IBM Germany's early adoption of a *lean enterprise* strategy. Sony's presence near Stuttgart (Fellbach) is as an R&D laboratory mainly specializing in factory automation, a product line it expects to be more in-volved in for the future and for which Baden-Württemberg offers an excellent learning environment.

THE *MITTLESTAND* SECTOR

We think it important to give priority to the large firms in discussing industrial change in Baden-Württemberg because there has been a tendency in previous literature to under-emphasize their role in animating the trajectory of the regional economy and to stress the role of the large number of smaller firms (see e.g. Sabel *et al.*, 1989a). Moreover, that emphasis has been further inclined to pre-sent the region as being characterized by a greater proportion of SMEs than the West German average and even, we think, to give undue weight to a presumed 'industrial district' nature to the inter-relationships among the *Land's Mittelstand* firms. While we do not wish to underplay the importance of SMEs in this eco-nomy, we think a corrective to the image of Baden-Württemberg as a region characterized by exceptional SME-led dynamism is overdue.

The first corrective is to point out that in general and with respect to man-ufacturing industry, Baden-Württemberg's SME profile is similar to that of West Germany. For example, data cited in an early report covering the period 1970 to 1987 (Cooke *et al.*, 1993) showed that Baden-Württemberg's share of firms employing less than 200 was 99.3 per cent in 1970 and 99.4 per cent in 1987. The West German share was, in 1987, 99.5 per cent. In manufacturing, Baden-Württemberg had exactly the same share (72% of companies) as West Germany in the 1–99 employee band in 1993 (Heidenreich and Krauss, 1997). So, we conclude, there is nothing exceptional about the density of small and medium-sized enterprises in the *Land*, rather Germany in general is an economy with a high overall proportion of smaller enterprises and Baden-Württemberg reflects that picture.

Where Baden-Württemberg's *Mittelstand* sector may be distinctive is in respect of its relative bias towards metal machining and working, mechanical engineering, electrical engineering, and automotive production. Some 62 per cent of manufacturing industry is concentrated in these four sectors (Heidenreich, 1996). This takes us back to a focus on large firms for, as we have seen, they too are concentrated in these sectors and, to the extent that there are distinctive inter-firm relationships of long standing, they are structured in *vertical* supply chains which often link the *Mittelstand* to large firms at the centre of elaborate inter-firm networks. This, it can be argued with reasonable confidence, is what differentiates the industrial fabric of Baden-Württemberg from that of Emilia-Romagna where lateral and vertical relationships among small firms in tightly defined industrial districts are quite commonly found.

Moreover, whereas in Emilia-Romagna inter-firm relationships can be based on *rapport* between members of a community interacting on an often informal but high-trust basis, those in Baden-Württemberg are also sustained by inter-mediary organizations such as the business associations, unions, technology-transfer agencies such as the Steinbeis Foundation, regional government offices, and regional banks, all of which operate on a large scale and in a more form-ally established manner. Interaction among firms in Baden-Württemberg is thus placed in an institutional setting where intermediation through formal organiza-tions is quite normal. This helps us understand, for example, the perceived need for the establishment of the Steinbeis Foundation. Given the relatively high density of *Fachhochschulen* or polytechnics even in rural areas, it might be expected that small business managers would feel able to make contact with local centres of technical expertise. However, this kind of interaction was mass-ively facilitated by the establishment of Steinbeis through which formal and legitimized introductions could be arranged between entrepreneur and local technical expert. This 'marriage-bureau' function of intermediary organizations should not be underestimated as a necessary phenomenon in the apparently smooth working of inter-firm and firm–agency relations in the regional economy.

This brings us to an assessment of the nature and extent of inter-firm inter-actions, given the support infrastructure of agencies, organizations, and the facil-itative role of large firms in sustaining supply chains. Clearly, it is no part of our argument to say that such inter-firm relations are non-existent. Rather we seek to understand the boundaries within which *Mittelstand* firms operate in respect of the all-important decision as to what constitutes a collaborative or co-operative relationship that can be engaged in without compromising competitive action. A case can be made for characterizing firms as belonging to one of three categories:

- stand-alone competitors;
- vertical collaborators;
- vertical and horizontal collaborators.

In carrying out firm interviews among *Mittelstand* companies we found numerous examples representative of each category.

Stand-Alone Competitors

These firms are not infrequently world leaders in specific niche markets. Even though their levels of employment, typically less than 500, put them squarely in the *Mittelstand* category, they have built a highly competitive position through technical excellence and high-quality products, sometimes based on long-established patents, which has enabled them to operate successfully, especially in customized markets. Some are classic examples of 'flexibly specialized' firms, making often highly expensive and complex products. Despite their relatively small size, such firms have remained relatively self-contained. Until recently, for example, *stand-alone* machine-tool manufacturers made much if not all of the components needed, including computer numerically controlled (CNC) equipment. However, the growing complexity and rate of change of such technologies has caused some to become less vertically integrated and source such key technologies from large-scale producers such as Siemens.

In general, firms in this category have resolutely eschewed collaboration with other firms, whether large customers or smaller niche firms operating in different market segments. This is even the case where such firms are highly conscious of the imprecations of 'lean production' which encourages 'co-makership'. The argument of a printed circuit board (PCB) manufacturer ranked second in Germany and third in Europe, as well as being rated by the Steinbeis Foundation as Baden-Württemberg's most innovative firm, was instructive. The chief executive perceived partnership with customers as a 'master–slave' relationship, in which the costs of testing and experimentation to meet the demands of quality enhancement and price reduction are loaded unfairly upon the supplier. The company would not engage in 'open-book accounting' with customers since negotiating from a position of strength would no longer be an option.

Other instances of *stand-alone* competitiveness, this time from the machine-tool industry, showed that apart from buying basic inputs such as steel from other, local machine-tool firms if a special need arose, there was little or no non-market interaction locally. Of course, it is not uncommon for *Mittelstand* capital-equipment firms who are users of machine tools to buy local products, but most of the producers rejected the feasibility of collaboration, claiming that as a world number one company there was nothing to be gained from it. More-over, they tend to require or expect little help from their industry association or the local chambers of commerce and pride themselves on never having had a bank loan or overdraft.

Nevertheless, the machine-building business association had been pressing its members to co-operate more, at least on marketing and, particularly, join-ing forces to penetrate Asian markets. But even this was only reluctantly being engaged in or rejected outright, these companies arguing that their name and their often excellent after-care, service, and spare-part delivery to as many as sixty countries to which they exported, did not warrant such action.

Vertical Collaborators

These firms tend to be more growth oriented than the *stand-aloners* and de-veloping a close supplier relation with one or more major customers is seen as a means of achieving growth. This does not necessarily mean they are not also world class in their specific market niche, but it may be that the niche itself is relatively circumscribed either in pure scale terms or because it may be vulnerable to scale fluctuations. In such cases, vertical collaboration is also a diversification strategy taking the firm into larger and more secure markets albeit at the risk of over-dependence on too few customers, something of which such firms and even their customers in many cases are clearly aware, some-times encouraging customer spread to mitigate this.

An interesting case of diversification from a restricted though global market niche is that of a manufacturer of circular jersey-knitting machines, the final market for which is the hosiery industry. There are only three such firms in Germany, of which the one in question has a 25 per cent world market share. In 1978 the firm was approached by IBM to become a sub-contracting pro-ducer of PCBs, training was provided by the customer, and the line was moved to the supplier. Ten years and five contracts later, the *Mittelstand* firm built a new factory to accommodate production. Eventually, as part of its 'lean enter-prise' strategy, IBM shifted all its German PCB production to this supplier which builds to IBM design but is expected to innovate to meet declining cost targets of up to 5 per cent per year. A key reason for IBM's outsourcing to this *Mittelstand* firm was to avoid difficulties concerning union agreement on overtime which had to be approved by the *Betriebsrat* or works council. As a 'family business', the supplier experienced no difficulty in achieving this as it was below the size required for it to have a *Betriebsrat*. By the early 1990s, the firm in question had also contracted to Daimler-Benz to make motor-block and diesel pre-chambers, a totally different set of products.

Other firms had gained preferred supplier status to Mercedes or to a range of large customers such as Bosch, Philips, and Hitachi, primarily as a growth or survival strategy. One, for example, a specialist programmable logic control (PLC) producer, hitherto producing turnkey solutions, had found difficulties in

surviving the 1993 recession and had, as a consequence, formed a close supplier relationship with Mercedes. As the latter developed its global production
strategy, so the pressure to follow as a supplier to Mercedes' American operation was felt. However, the firm lacked the capital so to do and, even though it
had been approached by a number of other *Mittelstand* firms to engage in collaboration agreements which would have eased its financial burden, the company
had resisted because of a fear of losing know-how to competitors and a belief
(shared also by *stand-aloners*) that co-operation agreements were unworkable
unless firms actually merged.

A third type of firm, set on a growth path involving close vertical collaboration, might typically have begun a supplier relationship with a large German
customer such as Bosch, itself conscious of the dangers of sole-supplier status
and so supportive of the case for risk-spreading among a number of customers.
Bosch actively supports such a strategy among its suppliers. The supplier might
then find other customers, enabling it to achieve high rates of growth during
the boom period of the 1980s and very early 1990s. In one case, precisely such
a firm was then approached by Hitachi, to supply presswork and connecting
systems, who asked it to 'open the books' which, to its surprise, the supplier
in question agreed to do. The reasoning for this was that the owner was strongly
disposed to high trust and understood the advantage of having as open and
transparent a relationship with his customer as possible. In consequence, the
firm had grown rapidly, had retained its *Mittelstand* character of low hierarchy,
practicality, and flexibility but had found it necessary to employ new quality
managers to meet the exacting total quality management (TQM) requirements
of, in particular, its Japanese customer. Having achieved the appropriate standards, the firm was thus set to continue its growth path serving a variety of customers rather than a single one.

Vertical and Horizontal Collaborators

There are a range of more horizontal collaborative relationship in which Baden-
Württemberg firms *are* happy to engage, a factor which underlines our general
point that while collaboration *per se* may have been overstated in some accounts,
it certainly exists in at least four specific forms. The first concerns the advanced
Mittelstand firm that is highly aware of, in particular, the organizational superiority, as many see it, of Japanese production methods. Some such firms have
even attracted the interest of Japanese firms in competition with them and, to
some extent, frightened them by their 'more Japanese than Toyota' management
style. There are probably not large numbers of such firms but where they exist
they have an egalitarian outlook, tending to treat their suppliers and customers
as partners, quoting cost savings through the supply chain of as much as 30
per cent in the medium term from such an open and collaborative disposition.
However, the direction of these linkages still tends to be more vertically than
horizontally inclined.

A second group of firms that, as a consequence of demands from a dominant supplier, becomes collaborative in the horizontal dimension—even with its competitors—is also interesting because it has overcome the fear of losing its know-how. A keyboard manufacturer from Weingarten exemplifies this type perfectly. As its key customer became a steel company that had diversified into car-door production, its basic switching technology needed to be significantly adjusted and next-generation innovation was being demanded. To tackle this, the firm in question proposed collaboration on switch manufacture to a competitor, dividing responsibility for different components equally between them. This was agreed and more efficient scale production resulted. Enthused by this, the two firms proposed an innovation network to five other competitors to work on next-generation innovation with the University of Munich electronics faculty. This model of innovation through co-operation was sufficiently successful to have become the basis for the Ministry of Economics' 'model projects' for SME innovation in the era of lean production. The *associative* mechanism here is that the chief executive of the lead firm was at the time *Mittelstand* representative on the board of the Steinbeis Foundation.

A third group of fundamentally horizontally collaborating firms are those which are members of a more-or-less formal 'club' type of arrangement. One such club is the AKZ (equipment, components, and sub-contractors) partnership founded in the 1970s by a group of *Mittelstand* firms who met at the Hanover trade fair and decided they could co-operate more fruitfully outside the large industry associations. Some twenty firms now belong to AKZ and exchange experience at regular monthly meetings identifying ways of co-operating more intensively with members having similar interests and *complementary* expertise. The club has 'groups within the group' focusing, for example, on electronic components and systems for the machine-tool industry. Another sub-group consists of firms making precision parts for hydraulic systems and a key aim of such firms is to upgrade themselves from parts to components or system suppliers, recognizing the threat to lower value-added production from Central and Eastern Europe and Asia. Horizontal collaboration between members on complementary parts and components, leading to systems-integration is seen as the way forward in AKZ.

A large 'tail' of *Mittelstand* firms in Baden-Württemberg are involved in groups which are dependent upon an *Industrievertretung,* an agent or middleman whose function is to interact with customer firms, bring a general idea of what they want to the suppliers, and leave them to decide if it is economical to meet the order together or individually. These are essentially jobbing subcontractors hoping for a large order but surviving on their ability to meet almost any demand. One such firm had specialized in the textile industry, making cloth-cutting machinery, but as the textile industry declined in the *Land* so did orders. Hence, a little like the jersey-knitting machine manufacturer described earlier, a contract was made with the Japanese firm Citizen to produce watch parts for a local firm Citizen had acquired to overcome European Union import restrictions by being able to use the 'Made in Germany' label. The link to Citizen was actually forged through GWZ, the Baden-Württemberg Agency for International Economic Co-operation, rather than the agent in this instance. When the contract finished, the company then relied on the agent for orders. In partnership with other small supplier firms, the company in question was, in the early 1990s, simultaneously producing central heating radiators and grape-harvesting equipment as well as machine-tool parts. Such agent-dependent groups were said to be very common at the end of the production chain, though we were unable to establish how many. They are clearly quite vulnerable to competitors from cheaper production locations since, by and large, they tend towards the lower value-added products and components in their production portfolios.

Hence, to conclude this analysis of competitive and co-operative postures of *Mittelstand* firms, it is clear that there exists a hierarchy ranging from those *'stand-aloners'* that are not significantly beholden to a single large customer but rather sell customized niche products of world-class quality and technical specifications, with good after-care, on the world market. They co-operate little and mainly through local market transactions, now involving purchasing of spe-cialized high-technology control equipment which was previously made in house. There are then often-excellent firms with preferred supplier status at or near the top of a specific supply chain to a large customer. These may engage in lateral co-operation with firms in complementary or even competitive niches in order to serve customers. Finally, there are firms who, for reasons of security and know-how transfer operate with complementary but not competitor firms in a co-operative club arrangement, gaining strength from so doing. By contrast, weaker *Mittelstand* firms are found in a dependent and precarious relationship with other firms and their agent, himself or herself dependent on getting orders from customers. In a context of recession and the rise of new competitors, especially in central and eastern Europe, these are in a particularly vulnerable market position.

THE *MITTELSTAND* AFTER THE RECESSION

The picture presented was that prevailing on the eve of the 1993–4 recession in Germany. The recession has had serious effects on the Baden-Württemberg economy in general and its engineering firms in particular. This has been ex-pressed in significant and extended processes of restructuring entailing serious job losses. The available statistics on production-firm size structure from the onset in September 1993 to the trough in September 1994 are indicative of this (Table 4.3).

The profile for Baden-Württemberg is a bi-polar decline of major propor-tions at the smallest (1–19 employees) and largest (>1,000 employees) scales.

TABLE 4.3. Production firm size structure, 1993–1994

Firm size (by employment)	1993 BW[a]	Germany[b]	1994 BW[a]	Germany[b]	% change 1993–4 BW[a]	Germany[b]
1–19	1,100	6,192	949	6,060	–13.7	–2.1
20–49	3,875	20,498	3,723	20,284	–3.9	–1.0
50–99	2,052	11,245	1,987	11,039	–3.1	–1.8
100–199	1,301	6,950	1,271	6,799	–2.3	–2.2
200–499	939	4,598	896	4,524	–4.6	–4.5
500–999	263	1,510	257	1,422	–2.3	–5.8
>1,000	174	969	157	878	–9.1	–9.4

Notes:
[a] BW = Baden-Württemberg.
[b] Includes East Germany.
Source: *Statistisches Bundesamt*, Bonn.

In between, most categories show a larger percentage decline than in Germany as a whole until the larger categories (>500 employees) are reached. It must be recalled that this was a major period of job loss in former East German firms which were strongly represented in the larger firm-size categories, although larger firms in former West Germany were also downsizing at this time. One fairly strong deduction that may be drawn from the data for Baden-Württemberg production industry during the 1993–4 period is that there was a downward cascading of firms into lower size categories and a sizeable loss altogether of those in the smallest category, despite some presumed entry of firms in the 1–19 employee category from firms in the next size category or categories. Research cited in Scott and Cockrill (1997) on engineering SMEs in Baden-Württemberg showed that 10 per cent of their sample, studied in 1996, were by then in the 200–499 category having been in the >1,000 category in 1993.

These data confirm an interpretation of the differential impact of recession on Baden-Württemberg manufacturers proposed by Sydow (1996). Arguing that this experience 'has not only taken some glamour away from the region but has also given rise to *doubts on the flexibility of flexible specialisation*' (ibid. 29, emphasis in original), he offers four reasons for this effect. First, Baden-Württemberg firms more than firms in other parts of Germany specialize in the manufacture of industrial goods such as machinery and automotive products that were most affected by the recession. Secondly, *Mittelstand* firms co-operating in regional networks are linked to strategic networks focused on large firms particularly affected by the recession. Thirdly, small-firm networks in the *Land* have little weight in the regional economy unlike, say, Italian industrial districts where such clusters have a greater economic importance. Finally, it is argued that organizational flexibility is no guarantee against economic downturns. This last point is asserted rather than demonstrated empirically. Research would be needed which compared matched pairs of firms in, say, the AKZ club and equivalents with those not in networks, for this to be accepted with confidence. As will be seen in the chapter on Emilia-Romagna, research of precisely that kind shows that firms in industrial districts survived the equivalent Italian recession better in employment, turnover, and average wage levels than equivalents outside such districts.

Evidence cited in Muzyka *et al.* (1997) suggests strongly that *Mittelstand* firms that have continued to perform well despite recession have demonstrated four key characteristics. First, they are *performance* focused at the organizational level, meaning the goals of the firm are openly communicated and understood at organizational, team, and individual levels throughout the firm. Secondly, they are *strategically* oriented to capture opportunity rather than to focus on financial health. They also have an iterative model of innovation based on value to the customer rather than on technology. Thirdly, they have become more network-based in *organizational* terms, overcoming the limitations of vertical information flow by working in teams, project groups, and maximizing horizontal information flows. Change is addressed by re-orientation and retraining of workers rather than job cuts, developing cross-functional skills to meet customer needs. Organizationally they are more open and transparent in their control structures than normal. Fourthly, they are *systemically* oriented, rationalizing their value chain and outsourcing to strong suppliers in preferred relationships, including suppliers located outside Germany.

At the specific firm level, examples such as those of Mettler-Toledo and Getrag (both Baden-Württemberg firms) have received attention (Cooke, 1996*a*; Herrigel, 1996). These firms epitomize the profile presented above and are used by the *Land* Ministry of Economics and the German engineering union IG Metall as exemplars of modern organizational practice. They are associated with successful restructuring involving reduction of management hierarchy, devolution of decision-making to work teams, and elaboration of customer and supplier networks, without inducing significant job loss. Such cases are used as demonstration projects of the government's 'dialogue-oriented economic policy' supported by the unions. This encourages direct co-operation of *Mittelstand* firms, spreading of marketing support, encouragement of technical and professional exchange, and the co-ordination of research and innovation activities among SMEs, universities, and research institutes.

In this respect, it seems abundantly clear that it is the *Mittelstand* firms that adhered most to traditional organizational structures, hierarchical management, long product-development cycles, low innovation, and low value-added creation that were the most vulnerable to the effects of recession. Meanwhile, others had embraced a model which broke down internal and external barriers, engaged in more associational modes of business co-ordination, and focused on their strengths. By following iterative processes of monitoring and learning about a customer-focused mode of innovation, they appear to have identified a pathway to future improvement in performance without undue sacrifice of employment opportunities.

THE ROLE OF INTERMEDIARIES

In addition to the more formal governance structures discussed earlier, Baden-Württemberg has a wide range of private or semi-private governance bodies active in the promotion and representation of economic interests in the *Land*. Here, five such governance 'communities' of special relevance to industry and economy are highlighted.

Research   The R&D infrastructure is rich and varied with sixty higher education institutions (nine universities) and some one hundred major independent research institutes (including fourteen Max Planck and fourteen Fraunhofer Institutes). Government and industry research expenditure of some 15 billion DM and a total R&D workforce of 94,518 in 1987 contribute to a gross expenditure on R&D as a percentage of GDP (GERD) statistic for Baden-Württemberg of 3.6 per cent (see Cooke and Morgan, 1991*a*; 1994*a*; Heidenreich, 1996). The *Land*'s pre-eminent position in Germany with, for example, 25 per cent of the country's Max Planck and Fraunhofer Institutes, stems from a classic example of *Politikverflechtung* largely explicable in terms of these two private associations' interest in maximizing their resources from this prosperous regional economy. Moreover, the heads of these institutes play a leading role in strategic thinking for the *Land* economy, as with the 1985 Bülling Commision, headed by the director of Fraunhofer IAO, specializing in work organization. The research resource is also actively exploited in economic promotion by GWZ, the *Land* inward investment agency.

Business Associations   An important mechanism in traditional German government–industry relations are the business associations or *Verbände*: the most important in Baden-Württemberg for which regional offices exist are VDMA (machinery), VDW (machine tools), VDA (automotive), and ZWEI (electronics). Their role in the governance, economic development, and innovation process is exemplified in the following. In 1991–2, Japanese competition reached high-end markets for automotive products with the launch by Toyota of the Lexus car. The VDMA and VDA became instantly aware of the proposal by, in particular, Mercedes-Benz to outsource more innovation to *Mittelstand* firms. The latter, also represented by the *Verbände*, claimed they were unable to bear the extra costs. The VDMA communicated this difficulty to the *Land* Ministry of Economics who commissioned US consultancy Arthur D. Little to study it. Recommendations were made that SMEs should co-operate in model projects on R&D and innovation. These, including an incentives package, were put to them but rejected because of their fear of losing proprietary know-how. A Fraunhofer Institute was invited to act as 'honest broker' protecting confidentiality, the firms accepted this, and a series of model-projects was instituted. The timescale from problem identification to policy implementation was less than one year.

Unions   Trade unions also have a regionalized structure with offices in Stuttgart. IG Metall is the most important one for Baden-Württemberg manufacturing employees, ÖTV for public sector workers. Because of its importance in German industry overall, the Baden-Württemberg branch of IG Metall usually conducts the initial and main negotiation on pay and conditions for the whole of the German metal and machinery industry. Negotations are conducted with *Gesamt Metall*, the German employers' association, which also has a regionalized structure. German unions are often proactive on matters outside the confines of shopfloor politics. In Hessen and North Rhine-Westphalia, they have been active in innovation policy, the latter's SoTech initiative being substantially union inspired (Latniak and Simonis, 1994). The CDU regime in Baden-Württemberg was reluctant to engage in concertation until the Späth government in the late 1980s included IG Metall and others in the expert commission on the social effects of technology which fed into the implementation of the *Land*'s project to establish a Science City at Ulm.

Chambers of Commerce   The *Industrie und Handelskammern* (IHK) play a significant role in the governance of industry and commerce throughout Germany. Their function is no different in Baden-Württemberg. They were founded by Public Law as 'self-governing' organizations and membership for firms is compulsory, payment being made by a levy on company profits. Membership is thus high and, in good times at least, IHKs are well resourced. At 30,000 members, the Stuttgart IHK is large, but not especially so: elsewhere, Aachen in North Rhine-Westphalia has 40,000 and Hamburg 85,000. Nevertheless, a wide range of services to members is offered including training, technology transfer, export services, and so on. The training and technology transfer functions are of key importance. The Chambers (sixty-nine in Germany, thirteen in Baden-Württemberg) supervise all vocational training programmes and the examination process in the country. This involves some one-million training contracts and nearly two-million apprenticeships annually. The IHK also acts as a gateway for technology transfer to consultants who are its members, also operating eight special Innovation Consultancy Bureaus in the *Land*.

Steinbeis Foundation   This technology-transfer agency is the most innovative enterprise support organization in the Baden-Württemberg economy. It dates from 1971, modelled on the first such service established in 1851 by Ferdinand von Steinbeis at Esslingen near Stuttgart. It expanded, as a private company, from 1983 when the post of State Commissioner for Technology Transfer was created by Minister-President Lothar Späth and occupied by the Steinbeis Foundation Chairman Dr Johann Löhn as Späth's nominated special adviser on technology matters. Löhn had been a professor in a *Fachhochschule*. All higher education expenditure is controlled by the *Land* Ministry of Education, Science, and Culture, a high-status department, and the government agreed a policy of using *Fachhochschule* professors as 'Transfer Centres' or consultants to whom SMEs would come for paid (though, in effect, subsidized) technology transfer. The number of centres grew rapidly to 100 by 1990 and 220 in 1996 (Heidenreich, 1996). The Steinbeis Foundation is 90 per cent self-financing based on a 7 per cent 'finder's fee' paid by users of its services. Some such fees come from government departments contracting with Steinbeis to evaluate applications for grants or loans from, for example, *Landeskreditbank*. Steinbeis is interesting for the light it sheds on the way in which *Politikverflechtung* within the *Land* can produce very rapid and successful results under the influence of a strong-minded policy chief such as Lothar Späth. It is criticized, however, as a source of unfair (subsidized) competition by IHKs and their members who are private technology consultants. The problem with Späth's approach, and one that ultimately rebounded on him, is that industry has to be a close ally if such schemes are to be pushed through. The kick-backs that this happened to entail cost Späth his position, while the institution he built goes from strength to strength.

CONCLUSIONS: EMBEDDING FOR THE FUTURE

Baden-Württemberg is a good example of a regional industrial system that has supported innovation in a context suited to the demands of the 'embedded firm' (Grabher, 1993*a*). This has operated in three distinctive ways. First, the federal system in Germany functions on a consensual basis in which 'co-operative federalism' results in 'policy inter-weaving', 'policy interlocking', or 'policy entanglement', depending on whether the observer's perception of the system is sanguine or sceptical. So policies which are ultimately implemented by the *Länder* will nearly always have had a strong *Land* input even though they originate legislatively at federal level. This means that the *Länder* agree to policies which, although based on a compromise of all the interests of differentially advantaged or disadvantaged *Länder*, are furthering their interests too. However, they also retain some room for manœuvre to develop *Land* policy initiatives at the margin, in their own right.

Secondly, corporate interests are also involved in the lobbying and consultation process at both federal and *Land* level, thus adding to the complexity of the compromises necessary in 'co-operative federalism' but adding to the robustness of the agreed policy lines once these have been resolved. Thirdly, between government and corporate interests, lie the regionalized institutions and organizations that perform the valuable intermediary role in assisting government to understand policy demands, and business to take full advantage of policy programmes. In an era of incremental economic growth under conditions of social and political stability, such a *governance* system is capable of guiding change while maintaining the given economic and industrial trajectory.

However, as Grabher (1993*a*) notes, such arrangements can lead to 'lock-in' in relation to a particular trajectory and so-called 'path-dependence' upon it

(Arthur, 1994). Baden-Württemberg's governance system is, at the end of the twentieth century, grappling with the three kinds of lock-in that Grabher identifies. The region's high degree of economic integration in automotive, mechanical, and electronic engineering, in a context when newer sectors display higher growth rates, gives the region *functional* lock-in. Secondly, the belated recognition of the force of Asian competition and the widespread consensus concerning the correctness of the 'high road' strategy of intense non-price competition by regional firms displayed strong features of *cognitive* lock-in. Finally, to the extent that innovation policies have been designed to support the core sectors, the system betrays *political* lock-in.

Among the factors causing a serious policy revaluation are: first, the undoubted 'pulling out' of Baden-Württemberg firms, either for purposes of location of production in established overseas markets or, more frequently, for the sourcing of systems, components, and parts, testifies to a sea change in the mentality of employers in the *Land* as elsewhere in Germany. That both Germany's leading luxury car producers should not only have established production facilities in the USA, with Mercedes in Alabama and BMW at Spartanburg, South Carolina, but be seeking to develop local supply chains through a mix of indigenous and transplanted suppliers, is witness to a quantum leap in recognition of the need for full offshore production facilities.

Secondly, there are interesting signs that as German parent companies such as Daimler-Benz are pulled out into the outside world, by, for example, seeking quotation on the New York Stock Exchange, so their system of corporate governance is having to change. Thus, the banks are criticized for their inability to monitor the very companies in which they are stakeholders. Greater transparency in reporting of corporate financial positions is, for example, one consequence of Daimler's listing. Moreover, such arrangements are necessary if German foreign investors are to borrow capital abroad (Waller, 1993). This may still not overcome what has been called an 'insider culture' which benefits domestic institutions and firms but it signals a significant change nevertheless.

Thirdly, exposure to global competition and the pressures of relatively new market entrants upon both Germany's foreign and domestic markets has caused a re-think about the generous welfare, working, and wage conditions that German employees have enjoyed during the past decades by comparison with those elsewhere. Large-scale job losses in companies such as SEL in Baden-Württemberg where the workforce declined from 23,800 in 1991 to 14,300 in 1996 have had a chastening effect and weakened union bargaining power. Thus, as Norman and Münchau (1996) noted, Hans-Olaf Henkel, president of the German Federation of Industry, stated that the German trade union movement was in terminal decline and that a more Anglo-Saxon style of individual self-reliance would become the model to imitate. Clearly, there is some element of hyperbole not to say gloating in such a view, but it signifies a weakening of the consensus that has served German industry well in the past.

So, in which direction strategically and in policy terms is Baden-Württemberg and the wider German industrial economy headed for the future? Three indicators are worth re-asserting here. First, we saw earlier that there is every likelihood for the foreseeable future that German industry will remain on a 'high road' trajectory. That is, there will be more R&D, innovation, managerial, marketing, consultancy, and advanced business services activity with high skill, qualification, and income requirements, but price-sensitive production work will continue to disappear, migrate, or be bought-in from abroad. German firms will become systems integrators far more than they were in the past. Policies to support the development of that kind of labour market can be perceived in initiatives such as Science City Ulm and even the *Solarinitiative* and *Multimedia Region* projects.

By contrast, Baden-Württemberg firms must and will remain wedded to innovative adaptations, incremental but perhaps also radical, within the established core sectors of automotive or mechanical engineering. Already firms such as Trumpf of Ditzingen near Stuttgart, one of the world's leading manufacturers of laser-cutting machine tools, has begun producing low-tech machines for the US and UK markets, only to find they are also in demand from the German market that hitherto expected technological advances but has more recently become accustomed to simpler but also cheaper Japanese, Korean, and Taiwanese models.

Finally, there is evidence that new efforts are being made to recast and develop aspects of the associative model of interactive innovation in Baden-Württemberg industry. The example of the Steinbeis Foundation's technology-transfer work based on public-private concertation and technology–education partnership is merely the best known of these. The *An-institutes*, with their collaborative mode of stimulating more efficient university–industry research and consultancy linkages, is another. Finally, the model projects which seek to assist SMEs to become innovators, as large enterprises 'hollow out', are perhaps the most indicative illustrations of how highly valued a co-operative ethic is within the *Land's* industrial governance system.

5

Emilia-Romagna: From Civic Culture
to Global Networks

INTRODUCTION

Today, Emilia-Romagna is one of the world's wealthiest regions; the province of Modena, home to the knitwear networks of Carpi, the ceramics of Sassuolo, which account for 2 per cent of total Italian GDP, and the advanced automotive engineering of Ferrari, Maserati, Lamborghini, and Bugatti, has sometimes registered as high as *second* wealthiest European locality and is seldom out of the top ten. But, as in the case of Baden-Württemberg, this was not always so. As Putnam (1992) in his excellent study of Italian regions notes:

In 1901 Emilia-Romagna ranked just at the national median in terms of industrialization, with 65% of its workforce on the land and only 20% in factories. By way of comparison Calabria was slightly more industrial . . . Emila-Romagna's infant mortality rate in the first decade of this century was worse than the national average, whereas Calabria's figure was slightly better. (Putnam, 1992: 153–4)

Calabria is nowadays one of Europe's poorest regions with a GDP that has actually registered a decline in recent years (Leonardi, 1993) despite having experienced, in principle, the same national institutional and administrative system as well as substantial transfers from both the Italian state and the European Union because of its disadvantaged condition.

For students of economic development policy, energized by the idea that poverty can be moderated by active state intervention, this comparison must have a sobering effect. For, through the national system, Calabria has been a regular recipient of financial assistance, while Emilia-Romagna has not. And herein lies the enigma of Italy for, despite the Napoleonic model of the centralized system to which it nominally adheres, the Italian state is, in reality, weak, its governments change as though assisted by a revolving door, and the system as a whole is racked by incompetence and corruption in roughly equal measure.

Since 1992, in particular, the most remarkable scandals concerning bribery and even alleged complicity in murder at the highest levels of the state have caused tectonic turbulence to the party system in particular and the state apparatus in general. The demise of the Christian Democrats, who had ruled since 1945, as a consequence of corruption scandals which affected former heads of govenment as well as a quarter of members of parliament, ushered in Silvio Berlusconi's *Forza Italia* in coalition with the regionalist *Lega Nord* and the neo-Fascist MSI. Their failure to reform a fiscal and budgetary regime which had resulted in the public deficit reaching 104 per cent of GDP (against the Euro-pean Union nominal convergence requirements of 60% for European Monetary Union) then led to replacement by Lamberto Dini's 'government of technocrats' which did little better. And in April 1996, a new left-of-centre government led by former economics professor and head of IRI (the state industrial holding) Romano Prodi was elected with a mandate to resolve the public debt problem while keeping the partnership with the PDS (the former Italian Communist Party) in his 'Olive Tree' coalition intact.

During all this, and before, the government and politicians of Emilia-Romagna (themselves mainly PDS) have remained apparently uncontaminated. This, in turn, gives a hint as to how to interpret and perhaps resolve the Italian enigma. The enigma, of course, is how, in a chaotic national system of governance, has the Italian economy, in general, and that of its northern regions, of which Emilia-Romagna is a paradigmatic case, performed as successfully as it has? A perceptive answer to that question has recently been offered in a path-breaking study by Locke (1995). His argument, to which we shall return, is that tradi-tional analyses and perceptions have sought to understand Italy in terms of its proximity to or distance from 'national models' of political economy. That is, it is assumed that successful countries develop national modes of political regulation and economic co-ordination that are more or less well adjusted to serving the needs of their citizens and companies. Moreover, in this way, they find their place in the competitive system of national political economies to the extent that they display maturity and efficiency in uniting their national interests *vis-à-vis* those of their competitior nations. They may be *dirigiste* like France, corporatist like Sweden, or liberal like the USA, but their evolved systems are both attuned to the institutional structure of their countries and coherent in pursuing developmental programmes in the international arena.

Locke (1995) argues that this approach helps understanding of Italy's failure of governance but not its relative and admittedly incomplete (given the prob-lems of the south) economic success. His case, which is also germane to the argument of this book, is that instances of both economic advantage and severe disadvantage are found in Italy, situated in different geographical locations. What is of interest is that the different locations tend consistently to display differ-ential levels and types of *associationalism* and, in consequence, local or regional governance. These, in turn, are expressed in regional and local economic dis-parities. It is this mosaic of advantage and disadvantage, proactivity and reaction, co-operation and distrust that comprises 'Italy'. These traditional social struc-tures and their persistence to the present day explain the failure of the Italian nation state to become integrated in the way those starting their analysis of 'national models' from above fail to see.

This governance relationship between nation and region as it operates in Emilia-Romagna is the subject of the first main section of this chapter. More-over, in that section, attention will be devoted particularly to the regional level of governance which, by comparison to the German case, is both relatively new and comparatively weak. Nevertheless, within the space available between a nominally centralist system which accounts for the vast majority of regional expenditure and the limited powers of regional government, interesting policies, different from those of neighbouring regions, can be shown to have been pursued with positive effect, especially concerning regional economic and SME development. The role of the Italian national system of innovation, as described by Malerba (1993), and its relationship with innovation within Emilia-Romagna will also be explored (Bianchi and Gualtieri, 1993).

This will act as a prelude to an account of the postwar history and development of what came to be called the 'Emilian model' of small-firm development (Brusco, 1982). The role of craft firms in first absorbing demand from larger customers outside the region, then evolving into networks of co-operating and competing sub-contractors, often found in 'industrial districts', will be examined. Thereafter, the ways in which such restructuring as has been necessitated in the districts by competitive pressures from within and outside Italy, Europe, and elsewhere will be identified. The question of whether, 'this alternative model of production will diffuse throughout the Italian economy and even to other national systems' (Locke, 1995: 16) will be addressed, as will the questions of whether the model is already in decay and whether it is migrating towards service industries from manufacturing.

The role of intermediary associations, organizations, and institutions in sustaining the Emilian model is pronounced and, as with much institutional life in Italy, politically structured; artisans' associations affiliated to both left and right provide a wide range of aids to small businesses, including payroll and accountancy services as, in different ways, do the *servizi reali* of the regional government business service centres and the consultancies affiliated to the chambers of commerce. Bestriding these often localized services are the wider economic development functions of the *Ente per la Valorizzazione del Territorio* (ERVET). This agency is itself funded 75 per cent by the regional government, the rest by thirty non-governmental shareholders such as chambers, entrepreneurial associations, credit banks from Turin, Siena, and Naples, as well as local and nonlocal private and mutual loan banks. Nicola Bellini (private communication) advises that the involvement of banks was 'a sort of goodwill behaviour with a view to establishing themselves in the local market. In fact banks have been very unconcerned shareholders in ERVET's history'.

In the 1990s, the ERVET system came under sustained criticism from the political right, represented by *Confindustria*, the Italian employers' association, the chambers of commerce, and the Berlusconi government, as Italy entered, briefly, a neo-liberal experimental phase (Prodi, 1993). This coincided with a reappraisal *within* the left concerning the future of the SME networks and the industrial districts in which they were often concentrated, especially at the time of the first serious recession (1992–4) the economy had experienced in the postwar era. One argument, of the right, was that they should be cut free from the cosseting they had received from the ERVET enterprise support system and allowed to develop more 'naturally'. Comparisons with the globally successful Benetton company, located in nearby Veneto, which also happened to be a Christian Democrat fiefdom, were made. Another right-wing argument was that the *servizi reali* themselves were both a misuse of taxpayers' money and unfair competition for private consultancies in consequence. To which the left responded that if the consultants were so entrepreneurial, why had they not established such services, for which there was an obvious demand, sooner? Such nuances and anxieties concerning the role and function of the intermediaries and the enterprises with which they interact will be further explored in subsequent sections of this chapter, but first we shall return to the intriguing question raised and apparently settled in Putnam's (1993) observation, based on remarkable longitudinal statistical analysis, that: 'The civic regions did not begin wealthier, and they have not always been wealthier, but so far as we can tell, they have remained steadfastly more civic *since the eleventh century*. These facts are hard to reconcile with the notion that civic engagement is simply a consequence of prosperity' (Putnam, 1992: 153; emphasis added).

Emilia-Romagna is the most civic of the regions Putnam analysed. He has been criticized for allowing the interpretation that prosperity depends on a thousand years of associationalism, a time-frame somewhat beyond that of the average contemporary politician. We will suggest that the good govenance of Emilia-Romagna coincides, from the regional economic development viewpoint, with the much more recent regional reform of 1970 in which the social economy was transformed into a cohesive politico-cultural identity for the newly amalgamated provinces of Emilia and Romagna.

THE REGIONAL GOVERNANCE SYSTEM

The Italian state was formed in the *Risorgimento* of 1860–70 through the alliance of the Moderate Party, led by Cavour, standing for a confederation of the Italian states, and the Action Party, founded by Mazzini as a republican party. The latter was revitalized by Garibaldi who led the Sicilian Expedition of the Thousand in the symbolic march to the north, which brought the unification of southern land-based interests with those of the liberal industrial north and hence the formation of the state (Gramsci, 1971). Because of the myriad city-states and imperial provinces of which the state had previously consisted, a federal constitution was contemplated, but fear by the élite of the centrifugal forces of regionalism and the emergence of radical liberal movements in both northern and southern localities led to the creation of a Napoleonic, centralized state structure in 1865. This newly unified state 'was far from being a solid reality and threats came from the reactionary forces, wishing to restore the old states (especially in the South) rather than from the radical liberals. The Napoleonic structure was a defensive act of liberalism rather than the opposite' (Bellini, private communication).

Fascist interregnum from 1922–43 obviously took advantage of the constitution's centralist tone in tightening the state's grip on the central organs of power and massively widening the incorporation of hitherto private institutions, notably banks and industry. The residue of these actions echoes down to the present-day problems of Italy's bloated public sector and associated public debt. However, despite the disaffection of postwar Italians and their Christian Democrat-led coalition governments for such centralization, little was done to promote moves towards a widespread regional devolution although regional powers were specified in article 117 of the new Constitution of 1948 (Putnam, 1992: 19; Leonardi, 1993: 221). Rather, attention was focused on the needs of the five 'special' regions, with distinctive ethnic and autonomist capacities, of Friuli-Venezia-Giulia, Trentino-Alto Adige, Val d'Aosta, and the islands of Sardinia and Sicily. All, apart from Friuli, received their designated powers over government, police, agriculture, planning, and commerce in 1949, Friuli in 1964. Serious political resistance delayed the establishment of regional governments in the other fifteen regions until 1970 as the Christian Democrats (CDU) feared the rise of the Communists (PCI) in the 'Red Belt' regions of Emilia-Romagna and Tuscany. Even then, the adminstrative, financial, and parliamentary processes of implementing the enabling Laws 281 and 775 took until 1972 for nominal and 1977 for actual reform of the government machinery enabling regional government in the fifteen to be implemented. As Leonardi (1993) puts it:

In financial terms the decrees gave the regions control of approximately 25% of the entire national budget with some estimates running as high as one-third; 20,000 offices were abolished or transferred to the regions, and 15 general directorates and a large number of divisions within the ministries were abolished. (Leonardi, 1993: 231)

But despite the apparent devolution of national powers and the opportunity for creativity in interpretation of responsibilities at regional level, successive national governments refused to incorporate regional influence into central decision-making as the legislation required. It was not until 1983 that the first meeting of the Conference of Regional Presidents occurred, despite its enactment in Law 775 in 1977.

However, by 1989 it was possible to discern the bare outlines of the spending patterns of the regions and thus their areas of responsibility, as Putnam (1992) demonstrates for Table 5.1. Patently, health expenditure accounted for the majority, reflecting its political importance in affecting the daily lives of ordinary citizens. But, in essence, regions were here acting as mere distributors of nationally allocated funds. In the spheres where relative autonomy was given, such as urban planning, environment, and in managing the organization of health, considerable improvements were still made in some regions. But the overall capacity to make radical changes was severely circumscribed, something further exacerbated by the actual decline in revenue raised by the regions themselves from 4.3 per cent in 1980 to 1.8 per cent in 1989.

TABLE 5.1. Regional expenditure in Italy, 1989

Function	Total ($US m.)	Percentage
Health	37,208	56.3
Agriculture	5,029	7.6
Transport	4,525	6.8
Administration	4,325	6.5
Housing	3,842	5.8
Debt and other	3,351	5.1
Industry and commerce	2,289	3.5
Education	1,908	2.9
Environment	1,607	2.4
Social	1,387	2.1
Culture	594	0.9
Total	66,054	100.0

Source: Putnam (1992: Tables 2.1, 25).

Governance of Innovation

The previously noted constraints on regional governance apply to Emilia-Romagna, as to other Italian regions, but there is scope for creativity in the manner of regional enterprise support and Emilia-Romagna has been one of the most creative in designing support for innovation in SMEs. The Italian national innovation architecture is scarcely 'systemic'. Rather, as Malerba (1993) notes, in line with Locke's (1995) analysis, it is dualistic. There is a small-firm network and a different arrangement for the core R&D functions. In Malerba's words:

Firms in the network are engaged in rapid adoption of technology generated externally and in the adoption and continuous improvement of this technology. The success of the system is based on the atomistic interaction of a large number of firms bound to each other by economic, local, cultural and social factors. Firms incrementally innovate through learning by doing, by using and by interacting with suppliers and users. (Malerba, 1993: 230)

In effect, innovation occurs among firms and within industrial districts in ways that are largely insulated from Italian science and technology policy but supported crucially by regional agencies, local governments and other intermediaries, including vocational training schools.

What Malerba terms 'the core R&D system' does not promote advanced technological capacities and does relatively little to induce innovations or enable Italian industry to improve its international competiveness. While the quantity of R&D expenditure increased from 0.8 per cent of GDP in the 1970s to 1.3 per cent in 1993, the qualitative dimension designating a functioning innovation system remains underdeveloped. The reasons for this are that: several industries lack advanced innovative capability; public support for R&D remains weak; co-ordination of policies is lacking; basic research in universities and research institutes is piecemeal; there are shortages of scientists and engineers; and no tradition exists of co-operation between universities and industry with respect to research because, until 1992, it was forbidden by law. The small-firm networks are involved in a virtuous cycle of learning and incremental innovation while the core of R&D is in a vicious cycle of blocked development regarding innovation. Small firms spend only 8.5 per cent of their innovation investment on R&D compared to 21.4 per cent by large firms but they spend 70.7 per cent on productive investments compared to 43.5 per cent by large firms (ISTAT, 1988).

Because of the innovative success of SMEs two national policies have, over time, developed to support them.

Adoption of New Capital Equipment   Beginning in 1965, the 'Sabatini Law' (no. 1329) allowed deferred payment of five years in expenditure on machinery through credit from Mediocredito Centrale. Further laws of 1976 and 1983 provided grants or loans for new construction and modernization, on the one hand, and purchase of advanced equipment, on the other.

Information and Technology Diffusion   National policies have been blended with regional and local ones to develop research centres for training and technical consultancy. One such is ASTER in Emilia-Romagna, a technology-transfer centre with generic responsibilities. In addition, some fifty formal agreements exist among national research institutes, industrial associations, public agencies, and enterprises to diffuse information and technology. ENEA, the former Italian nuclear energy research establishment, has interacted on technology transfer with Emilian 'real services' centres, for example.

Although these initiatives were not set up with SMEs especially in mind, it is they which have taken fullest advantage of the opportunities offered. Large firms, argues Malerba (1993), have seldom provided an innovation demand or stimulus to domestic producers because they themselves have not been particularly innovative. The few that are, such as FIAT, Italtel, Montedison, Olivetti, and Pirelli source their innovation internally from R&D expenditures of as high as 7.8 per cent of sales in the case of Italtel to as low as 2.4 per cent by FIAT.

Public science and technology policy operates at three upstream–downstream levels:

- *National Research Council* (CNR)—there are basic research programmes in food processing, health, environment, advanced technologies, energy, and so on. Funding is shared between CNR institutes (12%), universities (36%), and companies (44%);
- *Ministry for Scientific and Technological Research* (MRST)—promotes National Research Programmes in electronics, steelmaking, construction, biotechnology, and pharmaceuticals. Only 15 per cent of funding goes to universities and public research institutes.

- *Applied Research Fund*—this grants low-interest loans and subsidies for applied research, mostly in larger companies. In 1982 a Technological Innovation Fund was established by the Ministry of Industry based on similar funding arrangements to those followed by MRST.

Innovation in Emilia-Romagna

It is clear that, in the Italian case, the regional and local levels play more than simply a distributive or allocative role in technical change, the more active of them are key players in assisting in the modernization of the Italian economy more generally, a point made by Bianchi and Giordani (1993). They also update Malerba's (1993) account by noting that, in 1989, Law 168 established the Ministry for *Universities*, Scientific and Technological Research (MURST), a recognition of the failure in the past to include universities in the mainstream of innovation policy and an intent to secure this by the appointment, for the first time, of a minister with direct responsibility for research. In 1991, a further law (317) on 'Interventions for Innovation and Development of SMEs' signified, for the first time, recognition of the innovative role of Italian SMEs.

The approach to supporting innovation as a keystone in the broader economic development strategy in Emilia-Romagna was to give access to new technologies and specialized services to firms, where appropriate, inside the industrial districts. Where services could not be locally focused, they were to take a horizontally rather than vertically accessible form via outreach from a central point. The reasoning behind this approach included:

- the perceived need to get away from enterprise support based purely on the allocation of *grants* which tended to end up with consultants supplying generic not specific advice;
- focusing support directly on production-related issues and influencing firms' relationships with their basic operating environment, encouraging co-operation, and the like;
- helping overcome small firms' difficulties in assimilating technological advances in contexts where there might be inadequate stimuli for this from other local firms.

In consequence, the idea of *servizi reali* was adopted as a means to provide direct assistance from public expert bodies into the firm in, as far as possible, its own local environment.

The kinds of services supplied include: IT services, databases, technology transfer, research and development, standard certification, professional training, management consultancy, as well as helping get better infrastructural services in relation to logistics, communications, and postal delivery. The strategic aim was to bring structural change to regional industry: reshaping business processes, differentiating products, and changing market focus. As Bianchi and Giordani put it: 'If by industrial policy we mean the set of interventions aimed at inducing structural changes in the productive system, then "structural services" may well be considered as an instrument of industrial policy' (Bianchi and Giordani, 1993: 33). The kinds of interventions implemented involved: diffusion of technological innovation to SMEs; stimulation of co-operation among groups of firms by providing collective services; promoting modernization of SMEs by improving their internal functioning; and intervention in external ecomomies, that is, building business innovation centres and technology parks.

Once ERVET was established in 1973, the regional policy was to emphasize all of these, but particularly the second, the provision of collective services. In consequence, centres for ceramics (Centro Ceramico, 1976, Bologna), knitwear (CITER, 1980, Carpi) and earth-moving machinery (CEMOTER, 1982, Ferrara) were set up. Later, centres for the footwear industry (CERCAL, 1983, Forli), metals (CERMET, 1986, Bologna), and agricultural mechanical engineering (CESMA, 1987, Reggio Emilia) were established. Horizontal service centres such as ASTER (1986, Bologna) for generic technology transfer, RESFOR (1987, Parma) for mechanical engineering sub-contracting advice, and SVEX (1989, Bologna) for export services were also founded. In this way, and through some fourteen such centres, the innovation requirements of a wide range of business sectors and localities are met, with varying degrees of success, by the regional governance structure.

CHANGING INDUSTRIAL ORGANIZATION

If we wish to understand the evolution of the network-firm system in the typical Emilian industrial district, there are two ways to proceed: first, structurally; and secondly, paradigmatically. Since we have evidence from both perspectives, we will begin with the story of a paradigmatic case, that of Carpi in the province of Modena. Carpi is blessed with a beautiful, oblong, Renaissance *piazza* with two churches occupying a short and most of one longer axis and the outlets of the main shopping street occupying the other long axis. The fourth side is open, blending with the main road out of town as it narrows. One block behind the shopping street lies *Centro Informazzione Tessile Emilia-Romagna* (CITER), the most successful and famous of the Emilian real services centres, servicing the knitwear firms which, in Carpi and its neighbouring communes, number 2,500, employing 18,000 people.

In CITER, which occupies two floors of a terraced building in a largely residential street, there is a library of fashion and design catalogues and magazines, a lecture theatre and a workshop in which the *Citera* CAD-CAM system is demonstrated. This consists of a workstation, electronic graphics tablet, and pencil, linked to an automatic loom. A design from a fashion magazine is scanned into the computer and, by use of the electronic pencil, myriad colours and designs can be called up for experimentation from the electronic library that is stored inside. When a creative and appealing design is selected, it is saved and ready to be transferred for weaving and make-up by the computer-aided-manufacturing part of the system. Owners or workers of the district's firms come to CITER to browse the library, experiment with the CAD, and, occasionally, purchase the system which costs some £30,000. If they are lucky they may catch a showing of the video that, scripted by Sebastiano Brusco and Mario Pezzini—two scholars of the Emilian model—describes the postwar history of the industrial district of Carpi.

The town is on the flatlands leading to the delta of the River Po, set in a rich agricultural landscape now largely owned by agribusiness. This was once the source of employment of thousands of *braccianti*, the agricultural labourers who were some of the earliest Italian proletarian rebels, who, in turn, gave birth to the PSI, the Italian Socialist Party, in response to the emergence of capitalist agriculture in the region (Gramsci, 1971; Sabel, 1982; Murray, 1983; Cooke, 1984). Despite the region's agricultural wealth, workers and their families were poor. One of the ways families supplemented their incomes was by using the willows and reeds that flourished in the marshes to make baskets and 'straw' goods, notably straw hats. In the first half of the twentieth century the straw hat was *de rigueur* in both women's and men's fashion. The market for men's straw hats rose as the career of the French singer and film star Maurice Chevalier waxed.

However, by the 1950s the bottom had been knocked out of the straw hat business and the hundreds of home-working and small artisan businesses that had followed the local leaders into the business and flourished, were decimated. The key actors in the straw hat business had been some five or six artisans in touch with the final market, not only in Italy but other European countries and the USA. In dealing with the buyers in Macy's and Bloomingdales in New York they rapidly realized the straw hat business was in terminal decline, but one entrepreneur also noticed the postwar popularity of the T-shirt in the USA. He brought back the idea that Carpi hatters should diversify into T-shirts just in time to catch the Italian economic miracle of the 1950s to 1960s and the impact on men's and women's casual war of anti-hero fashion of the kind sported by Marlon Brando and Marilyn Monroe.

Hundreds of firms, one and two-person artisan shops supported by home-workers in the main, sprang up to meet the burgeoning and apparently insatiable demand. Eventually these firms diversified into sportswear, children's wear, men's dress shirts, and women's up-market knitwear and the number of firms evolved to the 2,500 registered in 1991 (Cooke and Morgan, 1991*b*). Of the 2,500 only some 700 were then in direct touch with the market, supplying department and chainstores in Europe and the USA. Of that 700, only fifteen employed more than fifty workers. The rest were engaged in some part of the sub-contracted tasks of looming, embroidering, finishing, and packing. The fifteen final producers had, in 1991, 30 per cent of total value of sales in knitwear with 42 per cent of production exported.

The arrival of CITER in 1980 was recognition that Carpi represented many of the best features of the social economy. It was *associative* with artisans' associations of both the right (CGA) and left (CNA—the predominant organization) making up thousands of pay packets a week, dealing with taxation matters, and acting as a medium for communicating learning opportunities for firms too small and too busy systematically to keep up with developments in organizational or product innovation (Rubbini, 1986). It was *co-operative* in the manner in which chains of hundreds of sub-contractors, each tending to focus on a particular position in the division of labour, functioned effectively to sell internationally and provide work for 18,000 people. And it was politically *progressive*, voting consistently and strongly for decentralist socialism and policies that supported small firms in small communities. So an economic project to help keep Carpi competitive through co-operation became a political project to maintain the political hegemony of the PCI; in the process an identity was formed of an honest, well-managed region that attracted the attention of the world and reflected favourably on its citizens who continued to support the region's political leaders.

But the arrival of CITER also reflected the fact that competition was intensifying. T-shirts were easy to copy and Indian producers were undercutting the Carpi prices by as much as two-thirds. They, in turn, were forced to innovate and move slightly up-market by printing motifs on hitherto plain garments. The 'Tiger T-shirt' was very popular for a while, but Indian producers once again copied and undercut, having seen the design at the fashion trade fairs. It was at this point, with the by now elaborate network system once more in peril, that the firms, artisans, and their associations communicated the problem of imitation to ERVET and regional government personnel through CITER. Given the advanced technology inclination of the ERVET system, contact was made with ENEA, with laboratories in Bologna, charged with a new technology-transfer brief following the Italian government's policy to turn away from nuclear energy research. ENEA and CITER together devised *Citera* which revolutionized the time economies of the design process by a factor of ten, allowing Carpi producers to introduce four or even six new designs per year ('*pronto moda*' or quick fashion) and enabling them to escape the imitation trap.

And this has been the recent trajectory in this particular district. In a study of the practices of *Citera* adopters (Cooke and Morgan, 1992), we found network leaders reluctant to share know-how of the new technology with subcontractors or even their own staff, fearing depreciation of their investment. But such is the openness, curiosity, and competitiveness of this way of doing business that both codified and tacit knowledge diffuse quickly around the system like gossip in a common-room. There is even evidence that such external economies allowed Carpi and other Emilian industrial districts to perform better in the 1992–4 recession than firms in the same sector but which were not in districts (Franchi, 1994).

If we take the more structural route to explaining the evolution of the Emilian districts (Brusco, 1990; Bianchi and Gualtieri, 1993; Brusco and Pezzini, 1990), the eventual picture is not radically dissimilar from that just presented. It can be summarized as proceeding through a three-phase process.

Phase I This occurs in the 1960s and 1970s and finds small artisanal firms, many in districts, some more diffused, being discovered by large firms from Lombardy and Piemonte (and abroad) as potential suppliers, through sub-contracting, of inputs hitherto produced in house but, after Italy's *autunno caldo* or 'hot autumn' of strikes in 1969, subject to interruption, low reliability, and difficulties in delivery. Emilia-Romagna's artisans, many of whom had learned skills in manufacturing when dragooned into Mussolini's war-goods factories, only to be thrown out of work when the CDU dismantled these latent hotbeds of Communism after the war, were ready and able to meet large-firm demand whether from FIAT's or Bloomingdales' purchasing divisions.

Phase II This was the period of the 1970s and early 1980s when the new, flexible, network form of externalized production had begun to coalesce into a competitive, often district-based, system which could out-compete large firms still wedded to a mass production model.

Phase III The period of conscious intervention after 1980 but accelerating into the 1990s when the ERVET system of enterprise support was put into place to assist the network firms to deal with competition based on advanced technologies, on the one hand, and cheap overseas labour, on the other.

The debate for the future revolves around the extent to which the industrial districts can survive inevitable economic downturns and the equally inevitable corporate raids from larger predators seeking to acquire the most innovative performers to boost their own competitiveness (not uncommonly by killing off a competitor). The latter argument is particularly associated with Harrison (1994) who argued that acquisition was killing the districts. This was rejected by Dei Ottati (1994) and Bellandi (1992) who showed that, despite acquisition, firms retained strong links within their district and also that firms were continuing to display creativity in dealing with increasing competitive pressure.

However, there is one area where there is agreement that some change has already occurred and another where it is considered to be necessary. The first area concerns the need to reduce production costs in order to remain competitive. Already by the 1980s, Emilian firms were outsourcing some labour-intensive parts of production to cheaper, neighbouring regions and to the *Mezzogiorno*. Thereafter, outsourcing even as far as Hong Kong and other Asian locations became almost the norm and thousands of production jobs have been lost to the districts. Conversely, rather as in Baden-Württemberg, there is acceptance of the idea that the districts may have to reconfigure to interact more fruitfully with *universities* as sources of innovation in addition to the real services centres (Cooke, 1996b). Interestingly, ERVET is now conducting research to identify and design enterprise support, if needed, for advanced business services, themselves conceivably district based, in advertising, multimedia, and financial engineering.

THE ROLE OF THE INTERMEDIARIES

Much of what has been written about Emilia-Romagna's economic success creates the not wholly incorrect impression that there is an umbilical connection between the moderate, decentralist 'communism' of the PCI (now PDS—Democratic Party of the Left) and the region's economic development. The voting patterns of the electorate (predominantly PCI/PDS; with PSI, the Italian Socialist Party, being the minor left recipient and occasional coalition partner) strongly suggest this. It may easily be assumed that the linkage between regional government, the ERVET system, the industrial districts, and PCI/PDS voting is the main or only connection of importance mediating public and business activities.

However, it is important to remember that firms in Emilia-Romagna are proprietorial in the main, though some co-operatives exist, especially in the larger agricultural concerns. There is an extremely powerful and well-organized Regional Chamber of Commerce headquartered in Bologna at the heart of a massive trade-fair and exhibition hall complex, for which it has managerial and major financial responsibility. The Chamber, through its local branches as well as its central organization, represents firm interests to government, provides services for export markets, business information, contact lists for sub-contracting and tendering, and a multitude of other services including transportation, insurance, technology, and training facilitation to its membership.

Then there are the business associations, also private but nevertheless important intermediaries, mainly, as with the Regional Chamber, representing the medium to larger rather than artisan firms employing less than twenty-two workers, in defence of their interests on taxation, wage levels, conditions of work, and so on in relation to governmental regulation at regional and national level. With respect to the latter, *Confindustria*, the employers' organization is the key umbrella organization but it also has regional representation and was seen to be flexing its muscles considerably more publicly than hitherto in regional debates during the Berlusconi government's interlude in power.

Two other private organizations that perform a crucial role in selling services to the very sizeable artisan sector of the Emilian economy are the politically affiliated CNA (Confederazione Nazionale dell'Artigianato—the PCI/PDS and PSI-affiliated Artisans' Federation) and CGA (former CDU affiliated as the Confederazione Generale dell'Artigianato), relatively less prominent than the CNA in Emilia-Romagna for obvious reasons. Some 44 per cent of all businesses in Emilia-Romagna are artisan firms and over half belong to one of the artisans' associations. The services offered mimic many of those offered by the Chamber of Commerce and the trade and industry associations for firms with more than twenty-two employees:

- income tax, payroll, and accountancy services of the kind normally conducted in house in larger enterprises;

- organization of vocational training and professional courses for both employers and employees;
- promotion of artisan bulk purchasing for raw materials, research, product development, and marketing;
- assistance in acquiring credit from local banks and the creation of partnerships or consortia as means of securing such access;
- supply of technical services such as discounted hardware and software for business machinery;
- support to new business firms, including start-up loans, technical advice, property, and training programmes.

In describing the way the CNA has held meetings which led to the establishment of artisans' clubs in which know-how exchange and mutual trust-building among entrepreneurs are facilitated, Rubbini (1986) referred to the associations as: 'a living workshop which has allowed the spreading of experiences, knowledge and innovation, and this is the distinctive feature and the main strength of a network system of enterprises' (Rubbini, 1986). The association is a shareholder in ERVET, the regional development agency, and actively involved in the design of 'real services' offered through the ERVET system of service centres.

In discussing the manner in which the policy of establishing centres selling real services to small firms developed, Bellini (1993) comments first on the way they began as a form of public support for SME *associationalism* to demonstrate the PCI's political leaning in favour of small and against large business. But the success of the system, attracting some larger, medium-scale firms in addition to the anticipated artisans, led to a stress on *sectoral* rather than scale aspects and *co-operation* with a wide range of economic interests rather than defence against big firms. He continues:

In due course, administration boards were defined by virtue of the official presence of various associations ranging from the Confindustria to artisan associations, and these associations were empowered . . . to represent exclusively the interests of entrepreneurs, with the latter able to apply to the [service] centre and public bodies which support it exclusively through them (Bellini, 1993: 120)

Thus, the evolution of the 'centre' concept moved towards an associational perspective. But this accommodation to the prevailing *private* industrial governance structure held dangers, since, on the one hand, it made it harder to change the locus of power while, on the other, leaving the regional government open to the accusation that the service centres were merely recycling the tax receipts of the associations' members. This move would subsequently lead to a paralysis and subsequent watering down of the alternative enterprise-support system the centres once represented.

The 'real service' centres themselves, though, had proved, by the early 1990s, to have performed variably and by no means all could be considered a success. CITER, the Carpi textile centre, received a good deal of publicity precisely because it was seen as a success, not least by its users. Research conducted in

1992 (Cooke and Morgan, 1992) into user perceptions of CITER and particularly its Citera workstation elicited the following judgements:

- 'CITER's role in informing the company's decision to adopt CAD was
  considered helpful, but not a determining factor. Independent consultants
  were also used to assess the benefits to the company . . . follow-up support
  on Citera was considered to be excellent . . . Training of staff in Citera was
  also of a high quality';
- 'The company sought advice from a wide array of sources before adopting
  Citera . . . But its membership of CITER was clearly an important influence
  in the decision to adopt the system; the company was "joining the club"
  of local innovators';
- 'CITER was appreciated for its continuous flow of information on innovation and on new equipment on the market . . . In addition, CITER was able
  to offer rapid assistance in solving day-to-day technical problems';
- 'Although this company had decided against using the Citera system it
  was still an active member of CITER, using a wide range of the centre's
  technical and fashion forecasting services';
- 'Finally, as to whether the company would diffuse the Citera technology
  to its subcontractors the answer was emphatically no' (Cooke and Morgan,
  1992: 70–6).

Even a centre as successful as CITER faced two problems from the firm viewpoint: first, distrust as a public sector agency, which suggests entrepreneurs in
Carpi strongly distinguish business from electoral practices; secondly, it was
seen to be helping 'leader firms' who are not themselves too keen on sharing
their know-how (even though it gets diffused informally anyway).

Other service centres performed less well than CITER, some disastrously
so. The shoe-industry centre, CERCAL, fell into the underperforming category,
as did the earth-moving machinery centre, CEMOTER, at Ferrara. At various
meetings during the 1992–4 recession and onset of the Italian political crisis,
the whole ERVET system was brought under the microscope, within the left and
by representatives of the Regional Chamber of Commerce and *Confindustria*.
Citing the poor performance of some of the centres and making a belated case
for their closure or privatization, the right caused the PDS leadership of the
region to make concessions. The key compromise reached in 1994 was that the
ERVET system should survive in principle, but that the centres would have to
bid for projects and not have their public funding ring-fenced as had been the
case previously. Inevitably, it was seen that the better-performing centres would
survive, because of market demand for their services (even in 1990, CITER
was 70% self-funding) while the weak ones would go to the wall.

Already, by the mid-1990s, the recognition was beginning to become widespread among policy-makers and their advisers in Emilia-Romagna that the
service-centre idea may have served a valuable interim function in enabling
microfirms to survive in the hostile, international environment of the 1980s and

early 1990s. But, thereafter, groups of lead firms that had been forming to seek internal economies of scale to match external economies of scope were clearly in need of access to a more full-blooded regional or even national system of innovation (Cooke, 1996*b*). The kind of technological advice on product or process development that will be necessary for Emilian small firms to develop and maintain a competitive edge rather than play 'catch up' are likely to require closer interaction with universities and research institutes such as ENEA rather than the centres themselves, despite the latter's success as a gateway to ENEA assistance with the Citera system.

RE-MAKING THE SME NETWORKS

There remains a residual, possibly subconscious, belief among many who have observed the Emilian model and the ERVET system or comparable ones elsewhere, that the industrial districts and small-firm networks are ultimately doomed. This is because, at the common-sense level, it defies logic to think that small firms can compete with larger ones *ceteris paribus* given the experiences of town-centre greengrocers' shops in the face of the insurmountable market power of the large out-of-town shopping centres and supermarkets. Sober economic textbooks generally confirm such common sense by their privileging of scale economies as unbeatable competitive weapons and accordingly correct business aspirations. Among those for whom the 'big firms must win' belief is pronounced are Harrison (1994) and Amin (1994). Their arguments regarding the re-making of SME networks and the development of industrial districts deserve attention because their analyses are frequently based on sound empirical observations. However, the counter-arguments from such as Dei Ottati (1994; 1996), Bellandi (1992; 1996), and Belussi (1996) also deserve attention for, from similar empirical observations, they draw different conclusions.

Harrison's (1994) lines of questioning rest on a scepticism about the robustness of the co-operative form as a basis for economic co-ordination. How likely are these districts to survive as systems of quite symmetrical economic power distribution between small firms in networks? To what extent does their success invite acquisition by larger outsider firms and to what extent, in any case, does hierarchy develop as leader firms emerge from the pack? And are the benefits equally shared when such districts demonstrate competitive strength in international markets? In tackling the first question, about survival, Harrison explores the *localized learning* and trust-formation that are said to characterize small-firm networks in Emilia-Romagna and elsewhere. In this, he begins by demonizing the activities of the SASIB company in the Bologna machinery district. This firm acquired smaller firms, organized the networks into a hierarchy, keeping the high-value-added design work in house but putting lower-value-added production out to sub-contractors. There are two responses to this observation: the first is that this is an isolated case and the analysis is prone to the fallacy of composition, that is, taking a single high-profile case of a hypothesized future trend actually to be the trend itself. A second response, made by Dei Ottati (1996) regarding large-firm acquisition of a software firm in the Tuscan textile district of Prato, is that despite Olivetti having acquired one of the district's leading machine-automation software companies, it has not significantly interfered with the organization of the company, nor has it helped destroy relationships between it and the network firms with which it maintains business contact. It could, further, be added that networks may still function as such even if they evolve from a more to a less horizontal organizational structure (Robertson and Langlois, 1995). Harrison's essential point is an egalitarian one and, as we have seen from the Carpi case, industrial districts are not necessarily strongly *egalitarian* but rather inclusive and perhaps, to some degree, *communitarian*, from the outset.

A different argument is made by Amin (1994) who sees districts inevitably evolving to become mere shells of their initial, productive selves as their firms are forced to put out production work to more and more remote, cheaper, locations in order to remain competitive at all. His work on the Santa Croce leather-working district is offered in support of this forecast, since firms have become more design and marketing-intensive and less production-oriented over time. However, two features of this analysis invite scepticism regarding the generic nature of the process being described. First, Santa Croce seems, from Amin's account, to be an artificial district. Twenty years previously, he states, it was not a 'district' in the sense being used in this discussion. Rather, it consisted of a small number of vertically integrated tanning firms, albeit located in the same town. Because of the associated pollution, the local authority, somewhat curiously, refused planning applications for more modern factories. With market demand for Italian leather goods soaring in the 1980s, this led to a sudden proliferation of artisanal firms. Some 300 artisan firms employing 4,500 workers and 200 sub-contractors employing a further 1,700 workers evolved. But, secondly, the tanners were also designers and gradually they placed more emphasis on this higher-value activity, even opening foreign retailing outlets. Production went elsewhere in what is plainly a poorly embedded, inadequately serviced, highly entrepreneurial 'quick buck' environment. In other words, it looks, once again more like an exceptional than a universal case.

Bellandi (1996) makes precisely this latter point more technically in dealing with Amin's prediction of 'hollowing out'. In arguing that such processes do not necessarily lead to 'the subjugation of the local to the global' he refers to a view that was first articulated by Alfred Marshall (1927) in *Industry and Trade*:

although the opening out of new sources of supply or new markets for sale may quickly overbear the strength which old districts have inherited from past conditions: yet history shows that a *strong centre* of specialized industry often attracts much new shrewd energy to supplement that of native origin, and is thus able to expand and maintain its lead. (Marshall, 1927: 287; emphasis added)

Bellandi equates this 'strong centre' with the conscious, innovative, enterprise support system found in districts capable of evolving without fragmenting, as described by Brusco and Pezzini (1990) in terms of the advance from a mark I to a mark II model of the industrial district.

Perhaps more to the point, in terms of more general reflection and theorized speculation on the future of small-firm networks of the kind found in Italian and, typically, Emilian industrial districts, are the sober yet not pessimistic analyses of writers like Belussi (1996) and Varaldo and Ferrucci (1996). Belussi, in particular, makes the departure point of her analysis clear from the outset:

It is, therefore, necessary to clarify that it is not the intention of this piece of work to tag on to the array of defenders of the virtues of an almost disappeared world of small firms in antithesis to an economic world dominated by giant oligopolies . . . and it will by-pass the dry well of discussion in favour of or against industrial districts. (Belussi, 1996: 6)

Her thesis, informed by evolutionary economics, is that firms are social entities capable of learning, judging, emulating, and distancing their practices *vis-à-vis* other firms. They are not merely atomistic units of rational economic calculation. Local development is thus conditioned by the governance of inter-firm co-ordination, the thickness of interconnections among agents, the existence of Marshallian 'attractors' capable of evolving new strategies, and the diffusion of relationships beyond the local or even national market. Successful industrial districts share a common 'productive culture' involving high levels of trust and loyalty and low levels of opportunism owing to the existence of social integration or a 'community market'. Support from 'real services' is also significant to the competitiveness of local systems.

In consequence, and here Belussi's (1996) argument merges to some extent with that of Varaldo and Ferrucci (1996), local systems are in a process of constant change, they may be pulled forward by leaders or by specialized networks. Given the present stress in processes of economic co-ordination on matters of free trade and globalization (see e.g. Ruigrok and Van Tulder, 1995), local systems that succeed will tend to evolve globally because markets and technological linkages are presently tending in that direction. Belussi deduces that co-existence between a variety of small-firm network types and multinationals will occur to the extent that each recognizes the importance of linkage between global and local networks. Varaldo and Ferrucci (1996) see this as conceivably entailing a dissociation over time between the practices of lead firms and those of the rest in the industrial district. They envisage a 'pulling out' of key firms towards global networks and the evolution of tightly integrated districts into looser clusters which are still capable of the kind of system flexibility they will have inherited from the past.

To the extent that firms and districts have had to be capable of responding to new challenges including external market competition from cheap production countries; the need to move up-market in order to secure sales through exacting distribution chains elsewhere in Europe and the USA; the imperative to diffuse the use of advanced technologies developed overseas to enhance the competitiveness of district firms; the need to begin to develop more innovative, learning relationships with advanced knowledge-centres such as universities or research institutes; and the need to recognize the centrality of advanced business services to the capacity of district firms to remain competitive in future, then it may be said they are conforming with the logic of the evolutionary economics perspective. They are doing this by a judicious combination of learning from past mistakes, learning from changing political environments, and learning from others.

CONCLUSIONS

At the outset of this chapter, the point was made that, although Emilia-Romagna is a rich region, it was not always so. It became so because of the willingness of its people to learn and change, to take advantage of an initial, long-established, social endowment of an active civic culture and, in formal and informal ways, transform it into an engine for economic growth. Such *associationalism* and its successful, perhaps not entirely self-conscious, deployment gave force to the insight offered by Locke (1995) that to understand the economic success of Italy we must move beyond the national level of governance to the local and regional levels where the secrets of that success lie. The analysis offered here would not have been different had Locke's advice not been available but in the context that it is, it receives substantial support. This is not least because the account we have offered shows how, excepting some national legislation giving incentives which, inadvertently, advantaged SMEs, and the important laws responsible for creating the regions, most of Emilia-Romagna's prosperity has been acquired by the collective efforts of its people operating outside or beneath the national system.

It was made very clear in the analysis of the Italian national system of innovation proffered by Malerba (1993) that there were two innovation circuits, one national and feeding large-firm requirements and the other, local and regional, significantly less well funded and operating formally and informally through small-firm networks and industrial districts. Innovation in the secondary circuit was largely divorced from R&D expenditure, a normal but inadequate index of the innovativeness of economies, while R&D in the core circuit appeared substantially divorced from innovation.

At the regional level of Emilia-Romagna, it was evident that economic development, innovation, and enterprise support were conceived as part of a political project by the PCI. Eventually distancing itself from a more hard-line stance, the Emilian party embarked upon a successful experiment in decentralist socialism based on gaining and keeping the support of the large number of artisans and other small entrepreneurs by fostering a system of collective business-services provision. Complementing the already established institutions representative of business interests, the regional government, although poorly funded and with little discretion, created a policy which in turn reflected back to the citizenry and outwards to those looking for both progressive and successful policies to help give the new region an identity that its diverse cultural and historic origins had denied it. Even President Clinton has visited, and stressed what he had learned, in advocating the Emilian model of collective entrepreneurship to the G7 heads of state at their Detroit meeting in 1994.

But politics are a two-way street and we have seen how, as political environments change, even apparently successful models can be scrutinized, not always for the best of motives, and found wanting. The ERVET system of enterprise support was a specific initiative for a particular time. It served some of the needs of Emilia's firms well but it did little for others served by centres that lacked the spark and imagination provided by the leadership of CITER. Now, as elsewhere, market and technological imperatives are pulling the Emilian system out into the wider world of globalized markets and production. We have suggested that co-operative yet still competitive systems such as that of Emilia-Romagna will learn, adjust, and evolve. Time alone will be the judge of whether or not we are correct in that expectation.

6

Wales: Innovating through Global–Local Interaction

INTRODUCTION

Can peripheral regions innovate? More precisely, to what extent can less favoured regions enhance their innovative capacity when their economies are dominated by mature industrial sectors or externally controlled branch plants? If innovation is understood narrowly, to mean the generation of new technologies or the ability to introduce radical product innovations for example, then peripheral regions are clearly not innovative because they lack the competence to engage in such activities. But if innovation is understood more liberally, to mean new methods of working in the factory, more effective networking relationships between firms in the supply chain, more dynamic synergies between public and private sectors, and so forth, then it is not at all fanciful to speak of innovation in the context of a less favoured region.

All too often our notion of what constitutes 'innovation' is derived from the technological frontier—from activities like R&D, from places like Silicon Valley —even though most regions depend on far more prosaic economic activities. Here we would do well to remember the prejudices which litter the study of innovation, with the result that scientific knowledge is privileged over 'lower' forms of knowledge like engineering, and the early stages of the innovation process are held in higher esteem than the equally important production-related stages (Rosenberg, 1976).

In this chapter we try to compensate for such prejudices by taking these 'lower' forms of knowledge seriously. Among other things, we explore the possibilities for innovation in the context of a region—Wales—which is dominated by the branch plants of large multinational firms. Just as the innovation literature has downplayed the significance of production-related activities, so economic geography has downplayed the role of branch plants. Indeed, not so long ago, it would have been totally unthinkable for the branch plant to be treated as a potential source of innovation because it was perceived to be part of the problem in peripheral regions (Firn, 1975).

That branch plants might be a more innovative force than we have hitherto acknowledged clearly owes something to the fact that, from the corporate standpoint, these plants are now expected to contribute much more to their parent companies. But it also owes something to the fact that, in some regions at least, regional policy is finally beginning to address itself to a *developmental* agenda in which branch plants have a large role to play.

Although regional policy has a long history in the UK, stretching back to the Special Areas legislation of the 1930s, it has never been much more than a spatial variant of social policy in which the overriding aim was to reduce unemployment rates in peripheral regions by offering subsidies to induce mobile capital to set up in those regions. Regional policy was thus largely concerned to redistribute resources *to* these regions, which is hardly the same as trying to raise the developmental capacity *of* these regions. In other words, it was addressing the symptoms rather than the underlying causes of peripherality.

Compared to many of their European counterparts, the UK regions lack the institutional capacity to construct a developmental agenda (i.e. policies which aim to upgrade the innovative capacity of the region). The absence of a regional tier of government, and the dearth of region-wide institutions in the public and private sectors, means that the UK is not well equipped to pursue a decentralized approach to economic development. Indeed, with the exception of Wales and Scotland—where a modest degree of economic devolution exists—the design and delivery of economic policy are extremely centralized and this, as we shall see, is part of the developmental problem in the UK.

Modest though it is by European standards, the evolution of institutional capacity in Wales is still significant when compared to the English regions. Whatever its limitations, this embryonic state apparatus has enabled Wales to pursue a more robust economic strategy than its regional counterparts in England. In fact, Wales can be considered something of a regional laboratory in economic development terms in the sense that it has developed a number of institutions and a policy repertoire which simply have no equivalent in the English regions. What we have here is a 'regional innovation system' in the making and our main aim in this chapter is to examine the developmental potential of this system. But we have to remember that this 'regional system' has evolved, often against the odds, within a British framework which is at once both centralized and fragile.

LOW TRUST AND SHORT-TERMISM: THE ANTI-INDUSTRIAL SYNDROME IN BRITAIN

Once hailed as the 'first industrial nation', Britain could now more accurately be described as the country which has led the world down the road of deindustrialization. On almost every economic measure—employment, output, productivity, trade performance—Britain finds itself at or near the bottom of the international economic league of major OECD countries. Of all these measures, Britain's manufacturing output performance best illustrates the scale of the problem. In the two decades to 1992, for example, manufacturing output remained virtually static in Britain, compared to increases of 27 per cent in France, 25 per cent in Germany, 85 per cent in Italy, and 119 per cent in Japan (House of Commons, 1994). Output has stagnated largely because of Britain's dismal record of manufacturing investment since the 1960s and chronic under-investment has constrained technological innovation, induced unemployment, and retarded skills formation. The much vaunted 'economic miracle' of the 1980s did little to alter this trajectory because productivity growth was largely achieved by cutting pay-rolls, while the benefits of higher productivity went into higher dividends rather than developing new products and expanding output (Kitson and Michie, 1996).

Debating the causes of Britain's relative economic decline has been a national pastime which has its origins in the 1880s, when Britain's status as the 'work-shop of the world' first began to be threatened by foreign competition. There is no single cause of Britain's poor industrial performance; rather, what we have is a very complex interplay of mutually reinforcing problems which constitute a *systemic* weakness, an anti-industrial syndrome. This syndrome consists of a number of problems, the most important of which are the lack of 'patient money', a low commitment to R&D, a woefully inadequate system of skills provision, weak inter-firm networks, ineffective professional associations, and a central-ized state system that has manifestly failed to provide a stable and stimulating regulatory framework. Each of these problems merits some attention because, collectively, they define the structural context for economic development in Britain.

The lack of 'patient money' for industrial investment has been a constant refrain in the debates over relative decline in Britain. In most conventional accounts, the source of this problem is located in the 'short-termism' of the City of London. The influence of the stock market is so much greater in Britain than in most other countries because public companies represent over 80 per cent of GDP in the UK, compared to 59 per cent in the USA, and just 23 per cent in Germany. Whereas private investors are dominant in the USA and banks in Germany, the UK stock market is dominated by financial institutions such as pension funds and insurance companies, who own some 60 per cent of the shares in UK quoted companies (Charkham, 1995). A survey of finance dir-ectors of major British companies found that 90 per cent of them believed that 'City institutions are excessively preoccupied with short-term earnings' (House of Commons, 1994).

The high priority which the City attaches to short-term profits and growing dividends makes it that much more difficult for public companies to justify long-term investment, but it has also fostered a deal-driven culture in which acquisitions are exalted over organic growth. The ultimate sanction against firms which fail to play by these rules is the threat of takeover. Given this peculiar corporate governance culture, it is perhaps not a coincidence that the UK is the most merger-active country in Europe, that hostile takeovers, which are virtu-ally unknown outside the USA, are a constant threat, and that dividend pay-outs in the UK are far higher than in any other OECD country. This deal-driven culture also helps to explain why, even in the recession of the early 1990s, dividends increased as a proportion of post-tax profits while companies reduced their layouts on R&D (Office of Science and Technology, 1995). When the City is inclined to view shares as trading counters, when trust and loyalty are low, it is not surprising that companies have shown 'a clear preference for dividend payments over R&D' (IAB, 1990).

But what conventional accounts of short-termism often ignore is that British industry is itself culpable: while the City is cast as the villain of the piece, the truth is that companies also help to sustain this culture by insisting on good short-term results from their own pension funds, hence creating a rod for their own backs.

Although R&D expenditure is not synonymous with innovation, not least because this figure says nothing about the *quality* of R&D activity, it is nevertheless a good proxy indicator of innovative behaviour. Britain's R&D record has been causing concern for many years on account of the level and the composition of expenditure. In terms of gross expenditure on R&D, Britain has been lagging other major countries for many years: it was one of the very few countries where the rate of growth of R&D was lower in the 1980s than the 1970s, and in the first half of the 1980s it was actually the *only* OECD country where growth of R&D expenditure was lower than growth in GDP (OECD, 1989).

The composition of R&D spending is also problematical for a number of reasons. First, government R&D expenditure has historically been heavily biased towards military spending: in 1990, for example, the UK government spent a total of £4.8 billion on R&D, of which nearly 50 per cent was absorbed by defence, which does little to sustain innovation in the civilian economy. Secondly, in the decade to 1991, the growth of industry-financed R&D has lagged behind Britain's major competitors and barely kept pace with GDP growth. Thirdly, some 95 per cent of R&D in manufacturing is carried out in just a hundred firms, a very much higher level of concentration than in most other OECD countries (Trade and Industry Committee, 1994). The scale of the problem is best captured by the fact that the combined R&D expenditure of just five Japanese companies—Hitachi, Toyota, Matsushita, NEC, and Fujitsu—equals the entire R&D spending of the UK private sector. This comparison led a pro-industrial alliance to warn: 'Without change, we shall at best become a manufacturing arm of Japanese, American and German companies, whose governments have for years taken a more positive attitude to science and technology and to manufacturing industry than UK governments' (Parliamentary and Scientific Committee, 1992).

But the exploitation of science and technology is only as good as the stock of skills, management, and workforce skills. By general consent, Britain's woefully inadequate level of skills lies at the heart of its poor manufacturing record. The general level of formal qualification among UK management is very low and, of those managers with qualifications, these tend to be biased towards finance and marketing rather than manufacturing and technology. Even so, the most acute skill problems are not at managerial and graduate levels but at craft and technician levels. In 1989, for example, the proportion of the workforce *without* vocational qualifications was 64 per cent in Britain, compared to 26 per cent in Germany (Prais, 1993).

While the vocational education and training (VET) system is often seen as the source of the skills problem, not least because the main delivery vehicle of vocational skills, the Further Education colleges, carries a cultural stigma of 'failure' in Britain's highly élitist education system, this supply-side conception is only one part of the problem. Equally if not more important is the *demand side*: the demand for skills is inextricably bound up with a whole series of other issues, like firms' product-market strategies, work organization, job design, employee involvement, and so on, none of which are addressed by public training policies. Recent labour market research suggests that the absence of a highly skilled workforce can partly be explained by the fact that many British firms are pursuing low-cost, low-quality product market strategies, using Taylorist methods of work organization, and a low-skilled, tractable workforce is perfectly compatible with these corporate strategies (Keep and Mayhew, 1994). If this is a logical match between supply and demand in the short term, it is not sustainable in the long run for either the companies concerned or the country as a whole. Above all, this analysis demonstrates the shortcomings of the training policy philosophy in Britain, which supposes that a supply-side boost to VET provision can lead to a higher skilled economy without tackling the internal workings of the firm, particularly the product and technology strategies which condition the quality of labour within the firm.

While public training policies have failed to make the connection between firms' skill levels and their wider business strategies, this connection is pivotal in the 'vendor-building' programmes which Japanese companies have introduced into Britain. As we saw in Chapter 2, integrated supply chains offer enormous benefits for firms that have the patience and the skills to craft them. Since Nissan opened its British plant at Sunderland in 1986, for example, it has tutored its suppliers in the art of continuous improvement (*kaizen*), to help them to reduce stock, prevent defects, and improve productivity. Suppliers have found that dealing with Nissan impacts on virtually every aspect of their internal operations, especially design, development, production, *and* training (NEDO, 1991).

Being exposed to the advanced manufacturing practices of Japanese customers came as something of a cultural shock to most British supplier firms, a point which illustrates not just how far they had fallen behind in technical terms, but also how weak inter-firm networks were and are in Britain. With some notable exceptions, like Marks and Spencer, British firms display the same kind of low-trust, short-term ethos in dealing with their suppliers within manufacturing as the City does to industry in general, so much so that weak inter-firm networks are an integral part of the anti-industrial syndrome.

To illustrate the problem, let us take a sector which is rarely discussed as a 'strategic' sector, but which is of enormous importance to the British economy: food and drink. In the early 1990s, Britain was running a trade deficit of nearly £6 billion, of which more than £5 billion was attributable to the deficit in food and drink. The most perplexing feature here was that 63 per cent of this sectoral deficit was accounted for not by exotic foodstuffs, but by products from northern European countries which had no climatic advantage over Britain. An inquiry into the trade gap found that one of the key factors was the lack of collaboration between producers, processors, and retailers, a problem which the Minister of Agriculture explained away in a colourful mixed metaphor by saying that 'we are better at rowing our own boat than getting into bed with other people' (House of Commons, 1992).

The recourse to the 'national character' is less persuasive as an explanation than the weak inter-firm networks which pervade the food chain in Britain. More generally, a tradition of weak inter-firm networking is perfectly compatible with an industrial economy which seeks to compete on the basis of price rather than quality, an economy in which firms value 'exit' above 'voice' in their dealings with other firms.

Weak inter-firm networks are perhaps not unrelated to the weakness of professional associations in Britain. In contrast to Germany and Japan, professional engineers in Britain have found it virtually impossible to forge a strong, common identity, not least because they have jealously guarded their narrow technical specialisms, a point illustrated by the fact that thirty-nine different professional engineering institutions exist to represent the profession. Although a new Engineering Council was formed in 1996 to try to unify the profession, this fragmented history helps to explain why the engineering fraternity has had such a muted voice in industry and government, and such a low status in British society.

Similar problems afflict trade associations. In 1993, there were some 2,000 registered trade associations in Britain, compared with 1,200 in Germany and 1,000 in France. While some of these associations, like the Chemical Industries Association, are well resourced and play an important role in keeping their members abreast of new trends in regulation, markets, and technology, the vast majority have a less than illustrious record. In 1972, the Devlin Report offered a damning indictment of the duplication and confusion among trade associations in Britain, warning that 'you can have competition of services but not competition of voices' (Devlin, 1972). Over twenty years later, little has changed, so much so that in 1993 a government minister launched a new drive to rationalize the number of associations, saying 'a good deal of the input from trade associations is both negative and of a low quality' (Heseltine, 1993). Much the same could be said of the Chambers of Commerce: poorly resourced, because of low business membership, the British Chambers are a pale imitation of their counterparts in northern Europe.

Key management functions like purchasing and supply also remain poorly organized in terms of professional associations. The most important association for these managers in Britain is the Chartered Institute of Purchasing and Supply (CIPS), which had a British membership of just 17,500 in 1996, less than 20 per cent of the total. The fact that Britain's 120,000 odd purchasing and supply managers annually spend some £750 billion means that these managers have enormous potential for raising the innovative capacity of British industry, much more so in fact than any government department. But this potential has never been tapped, partly because the purchasing manager is a poor relation to finance and marketing managers and partly because most firms have not recognized the strategic significance of this corporate function. For example, in a survey of 400 major British companies in 1993, CIPS found that nearly 25 per cent did not believe any benefits could come from better supply-chain management, while another 17 per cent could not even identify the percentage of their total costs spent on purchasing goods and services, all of which led CIPS to conclude that 'most companies are still in the stone age as far as managing the purchase and supply chain is concerned' (Cassell, 1994). Another reason, clearly, why inter-firm networks are so weak in Britain.

No account of the anti-industrial syndrome would be complete without some reference to the manifest failure of the British state to offer a stable and stimulating regulatory regime for industrial innovation. The roots of this failure lie in the inability of successive governments since 1945 to forge a constituency for the modernization of British industry, a strategy which would inevitably have posed a challenge to the City, the main locus of the ascendant culture of short-termism. Indeed, far from trying to reverse the anti-industrial syndrome, the Conservative governments of the 1980s actually exacerbated the problem by peddling the notion that the way ahead for Britain lay in the direction of a post-industrial, service-based economy. Paradoxically, the most trenchant critique of this anti-industrial stance came from the most antiquated part of the state system, the House of Lords, which argued that the 'national attitude' to manufacturing needed to be radically changed 'if we are to avoid a major social and economic crisis in our nation's affairs' (House of Lords, 1985).

Echoing the House of Lords report, an influential inquiry into 'Tomorrow's Company' concluded that the key problems in Britain were threefold: short-termism, adversarial inter-firm relations, and a corporate governance system in which the shareholder was king (RSA, 1995). The RSA argued that these attributes are the antithesis of what the innovative company requires today: such a company caters for stakeholder interests rather than just shareholder values, it sets a premium on managing a network of relations with employees, customers, suppliers, investors, and the community and it recognizes the significance of qualities such as trust, loyalty, and respect for the individual.

Although large swathes of British industry have been forced to retreat from the competitive frontier, there are of course notable exceptions. Britain continues to have its islands of innovation, particularly in pharmaceuticals and military electronics, sectors which rely less on production skills than élite science. While the British science base has been one of the most fecund in the world, leading firms like Glaxo and ICI now consider this science base to be in both absolute and relative decline (House of Commons, 1994; Kay, 1994).

Given the fragile nature of the British industrial base, it is perhaps surprising that Britain has done so well as a location for foreign direct investment (FDI). But certain weaknesses, like low labour costs and the lack of strong indigenous sectors in cars and electronics, two of the key FDI sectors, become strengths in the race to attract inward investment. In addition to these locational advantages, the political commitment to FDI has been stronger in Britain than in any other European country, where governments have been partly concerned to protect their indigenous sectors. While the outflow of FDI from Britain far exceeds the inflow, the latter plays an enormous role in the British economy: in 1994, for example, foreign-owned companies accounted for nearly 20 per cent of all manufacturing jobs, 24 per cent of net output, 32 per cent of manufacturing investment, and 40 per cent of all British exports. Significantly, the value added per head was 40 per cent above the British-owned manufacturing sector and investment per head was 112 per cent higher (Invest in Britain Bureau, 1995; Eltis, 1995).

Successive Conservative governments since 1979 have sought to use foreign firms, especially Japanese firms, to tutor British firms in the art of innovative management; indeed, FDI is seen as the chief means of reviving an industrial base which has been eroded by the attrition of domestic industry (Morgan and Sayer, 1988).

In recent years, the government has conceded that Britain needs a far more robust institutional framework for innovation because the existing system, based on a bewildering multiplicity of public and private enterprise-support agencies, had proved both ineffective and wasteful. Three key developments deserve to be mentioned here:

- in 1994, the government published a White Paper on Competitiveness, which contained over 300 measures to boost Britain's economic performance, including a new commitment to manufacturing, which was said to be 'essential' for long-term prosperity (DTI, 1994);
- in the same year, it launched the Technology Foresight exercise, designed to promote better technology-transfer networks between government, industry, and academia, a process which identified fifteen key sectors for priority treatment (OST, 1995);
- in 1993, the government unveiled a new initiative to overhaul the delivery of enterprise-support services since the existing system had resulted in 'unproductive rivalry and variable quality standards' (DTI, 1992). The Business Link network of one-stop shops is designed to offer firms a single point of access to a wide array of business services.

One of the novel features of this new policy of enterprise support was the growing emphasis attached to *localizing* the design and delivery of business services, a trend pioneered with the creation of Training and Enterprise Councils in 1990 and extended with the formation of Business Links, which are supposed to be locally driven business-support agencies. While this signals an advance over the centralized system of enterprise support, the government continues to be overly prescriptive as to how these local services should be delivered, which effectively undermines the claim that Britain has a locally driven system of enterprise support (Bennett *et al.*, 1994; Morgan, 1996).

As part of its drive to rationalize and localize the system of enterprise-support services, the government also created new Integrated Regional Offices (IROs), which unified the functions of four Whitehall departments in each of the English regions. While the IROs are relatively powerless, the fact that they were created at all was a belated admission that economic renewal was being hamstrung by the lack of a coherent institutional framework at the regional level in England.

Like the USA, the most innovative economic development thinking in Britain over the past decade has come, not from central government, but, rather, from a host of networking experiments at the local and regional levels. These may seem modest when set against the systemic nature of Britain's anti-industrial syndrome, but they suggest that the days are passed when Britain's regions meekly accepted that Whitehall knows best. The belief that stronger regional governance capacity is necessary to encourage more robust forms of regional development owes much to the experience of Scotland and Wales, where a concerted effort has been made to address some of the weaknesses of Britain's industrial syndrome. In other words, the creation of regional governance capacity is a vital step in the process of building a more stimulating institutional framework for innovation and economic development at the regional level in Britain.

GOVERNANCE CAPACITY: THE RISE OF THE REGIONAL STATE IN WALES

The capacity to design and deliver policies which are attuned to the needs of a regional economy—which is what we mean here by sub-central governance capacity—is an important part of a country's regional policy repertoire, and this in turn depends on the degree to which political power is devolved to the level of the region. In Britain, which has one of the most centralized political systems in Europe, sub-central governance capacity is extremely limited. Such centralism has had two debilitating effects: it has over-burdened central government with too many responsibilities and it has denuded the regions of the capacity to use their own local knowledge to design and deliver policies for regional regeneration. To this extent, we can speak of a crisis of sub-central governance capacity in the British political system.

Because of their status as *nations* within Britain's multinational state system, Wales and Scotland have enjoyed a degree of relative autonomy which has been denied to the English regions. Modest though it is by some European standards, such relative autonomy has given these Celtic nations a limited capacity for self-government and this has been used to develop more locally attuned economic-development policies.

The rise of the regional state in Wales began in earnest when the Welsh Office was created in 1964 in the face of opposition from both Whitehall civil servants and a number of centralist-minded Labour Party ministers (Osmond, 1978). From this inauspicious start, the Welsh Office grew from just 225 civil servants at the outset to over 2,000 in 1996, when it had an annual budget of some £7 billion which was financed through a block grant from central government. Today the Welsh Office has absorbed the functions of seven Whitehall departments, which means that it is responsible for policy development in agriculture, industry, employment, education and training, health, transport, and the environment. Unlike the functional departments in Whitehall, the territorial departments in Wales and Scotland thus have a dual character (Rhodes, 1988). While they are first and foremost part of the apparatus of central government, they are also part of their territory, a dual status which means that they have to satisfy two very different constituencies.

Although the Welsh Office does not have the power to resist policy initiatives from central government, it can tailor these initiatives to local requirements. The informational resources of the Welsh Office are developed through direct interaction with firms and cognate public bodies, whereas central government tends to rely on indirect contact through its network of regional offices in England. So, in principle, the Welsh Office ought to be closer to its partners and clients than its London-based counterparts in Whitehall. In practice, however, its capacity to forge robust partnerships was vitiated by the fact that, between 1979–97, it was controlled by the Conservatives, a minority political party in Wales which was completely at odds with the rest of the regional state system.

Unable to win power through the ballot box in Wales, the Conservatives extended their influence by appointing the boards of dozens of quangos, the non-governmental organizations which deliver a wide array of services on behalf of the Welsh Office. In other words, the dominant political party in Wales, the Labour Party, had no role in setting the priorities of the Welsh Office, nor did it have any direct influence over the quango appointments process. In other words, there was an enormous democratic deficit at the heart of the governance system in Wales (Morgan and Roberts, 1993).

This democratic deficit was more than just an affront to political democracy. Because quangos are not publicly accountable to the communities in which they operate, they lack the political legitimacy which is necessary for forging high-trust partnerships with other public and private sector bodies in Wales. This lack of political legitimacy has marred their effectiveness because, in the case of the Welsh Development Agency for example, we have a classic case of a quango which has been forced to defend itself politically when it should have been wholly focused on its economic development brief. Far from being luxuries, public accountability and political legitimacy are vitally important ingredients of an effective economic development strategy (Morgan, 1997*b*).

Being at the apex of the governance system, the Welsh Office is ideally placed to promote a networking ethos in the public and private sectors in Wales. Although it is formally committed to working in 'partnership', its local partners are critical of the way in which the Welsh Office seems more concerned to retain control for itself than to empower the wider network. This criticism was endorsed by a European Commission evaluation of the partnership framework in South Wales. Whereas the local partners saw partnership in a *horizontal* sense, in which equal partners worked towards common goals, the Commission found that the Welsh Office saw partnership in *vertical* terms, in which the Welsh Office saw itself playing the decisive role. The EC concluded by saying that 'working relationships in industrial South Wales, although reasonably good, are limited in scope' (European Commission, 1991).

These two problems—the lack of public accountability and the need for more effective partnerships—have fuelled demands for a more democratic governance system in Wales in the shape of a directly elected Welsh Assembly (Osmond, 1994). What this means is that the traditional form of devolution is no longer perceived as acceptable, hence the demand for *democratic* devolution.

Aside from the Welsh Office, the other main component of the political governance system in Wales is local government, which consists of twenty-two unitary authorities. Local government in Wales, as in Britain generally, has been emasculated by a series of centralist measures under successive Conservative governments. Its powers and functions have been greatly reduced, so much so that it is now dependent on central government for around 80 per cent of its spending, it can no longer set its own budget, and many of its functions have been hived off to unelected quangos.

Given the systemic weaknesses of local government as an institution in Britain, it is fortunate that Wales has managed to develop a significant regional state apparatus in the Welsh Office and its associated network of non-governmental organizations (NGOs), because it is this apparatus which has taken the lead in promoting economic development initiatives, as we shall see below. In the economic development field the most important NGO is the Welsh Development Agency (WDA), which was established in 1976 and which is now one of the largest and most experienced development agencies in the European Union.

Between them, the Welsh Office and the WDA provide Wales with a regional governance capacity that has no parallel in the English regions, where one of the key problems is 'the bewildering profusion of economic development bodies' (House of Commons, 1995).

The need for coherent governance structures is a key issue in contemporary Britain because the 'hollowing out' of the state (through the privatization of public sector functions for example) has led to a fragmentation of control of economic development, education, training and transport, and so on. The very fact that 'governance' has replaced 'government' in British political discourse reflects the extent to which functions formerly controlled by central or local government have been transferred to private or non-governmental organizations, a process which poses new problems of co-ordination and accountability (Rhodes, 1994).

These problems are particularly acute in the field of vocational education and training (VET), which has a key role to play in economic development policy.

Responsibility for VET provision in England and Wales is now split between eighty-two TECs (which are privately run, employer-led bodies), Further Education colleges (which were transferred from local authority control in 1993), and Upper Secondary schools (which are encouraged to offer VET courses in competition with FE colleges). The newly created VET 'market', in which colleges and schools compete for the same students under a funding system driven by student numbers, makes it virtually impossible to co-ordinate VET provision.

Although Wales is subject to the same pressures as the English regions, it has regulatory mechanisms which help to temper the problem of unproductive rivalry in the new VET system, mechanisms which simply do not exist in the English regions. The most obvious mechanism is the Welsh Office, which has been less than enthusiastic about the new competitive ethos despite Conservative control. As we shall see below, the WDA has sought to involve FE colleges in training schemes which entail collaborating rather than competing. Then there are informal regulatory mechanisms, like Fforwm, the association of FE colleges, which provides a Wales-wide forum for promoting joint solutions to common problems (Morgan and Rees, 1994).

Even though these mechanisms are not able to resolve the systemic problem of unproductive rivalry, they do allow for more concerted action in VET provision than has been possible in the English regions. These experiences have persuaded the VET community that a much more robust VET system could be created in Wales if it had more autonomy to design its own policies, via a Welsh Assembly for example. This potential for innovating in the periphery was recently acknowledged by the *Times Higher Education Supplement*, when it said:

Wales has the supreme good fortune to be far away from Whitehall. It has been possible for the universities, colleges and funding councils there to work away quietly at devising a system for post-compulsory education without too much attention or interference from the centre . . . It is smaller and its institutions more homogenous than those in England. (*The Times Higher Education Supplement*, 1996)

Tapping the capacity of the regional state is all the more important in a context, like Wales, where the private sector has historically played a rather muted role in promoting economic development initiatives, reflecting a more general picture of low civic engagement on the part of the regional business community. During the 1930s, for example, when business interests played an active role in helping Britain's depressed regions to alleviate the inter-war slump, South Wales was unique in the fact that the business community (and the coal-owners in particular) was conspicuously absent from the work of the Development Council, so much so that the Council's income was entirely drawn from local authority sources. Contemporary experts had no doubt that the low civic role of the business community in South Wales was due to the preponderance of an 'immigrant business class' in the region (Marquand, 1936). Indeed, such was the limited effect which the coal-owners had on society, politics, and culture in Wales that one economic historian commented that when they disappeared, with nationalization in 1947, it was as if 'they had never been' (Williams, 1980).

Although some branch-plant managers are beginning to play a more active role in both economic and civic life, the fact remains that Wales does not have the robust business associations which play such an important role in regulating and animating corporate development in regions like Baden-Württemberg and Emilia-Romagna. For example, Chambers of Commerce in Wales are a pale imitation of continental chambers and regional trade associations are similarly weak. Although the Welsh division of the Confederation of British Industry (CBI) is one of the most proactive of the CBI's regional divisions, this does not compensate for the systemic weakness of business associations, a weakness which Wales shares with the rest of Britain.

Regions which lack strong private sector business institutions are that much more dependent on their public institutions taking the lead in forging a developmental strategy, a point we develop further below. Here it is worth noting that the public authorities in Wales have tried to fashion a developmental coalition (loosely composed of the regional state, organized labour, and the regional business community) which champions a strategy which is less socially divisive and more associative than the mainstream Conservative agenda. For example, while conservative governments sought to attract inward investment to Britain by stressing the availability of 'union-free' facilities, the WDA studiously avoids this anti-union line preferring, instead, to stress the benefits of single union as opposed to non-union agreements (Morgan and Sayer, 1988).

The fact that the WDA eschews an anti-union line in its marketing campaigns, a position tacitly endorsed by the Welsh Office and the Wales CBI, is mainly because it wants to retain the goodwill of the Wales TUC, on whom it depends for 'the maintenance of orderly industrial relations' (Morgan and Sayer, 1988). More generally, we can say that the relationship between state, business, and labour is less ideological and more pragmatic in Wales than it is in Britain, and this makes for more productive interactions between these key institutions.

But the main weakness of this developmental coalition under the Conservatives was that it lacked political legitimacy because core elements, like the Welsh Office and the WDA, were controlled by political appointees who had no democratic mandate within Wales. This made the coalition less stable than it might otherwise have been, not least because it was exposed to the ideological whims of the Secretary of State. This is precisely what happened between 1993–5 when John Redwood, a leading Thatcherite, tried to overturn existing priorities by setting a new, right-wing agenda for the Welsh Office. To overcome these problems, the association of local authorities in Wales called for the Welsh Office to be made more publicly accountable, through the creation of an elected Assembly for Wales, and this is tied to its demand for more powers to be devolved to the Welsh Office from Whitehall and Westminster (Welsh Local Government Association, 1996). The motivation for these demands is not just to create a more democratic governance system but, also, to fashion a more robust strategy for economic development. Without a more autonomous regional state, empowered to design locally attuned policies, Wales will be in a weaker position to address the problems and possibilities of economic renewal.

CORPORATE RESTRUCTURING: THE SCOPE AND LIMITS OF FDI

Like many areas which 'took off' during the nineteenth century, Wales is still grappling with the social and economic legacies of its once-dominant coal and steel industries. Although these sectors no longer dominate the regional economy, the effects of narrow sectoral specialization are still evident today. That Wales is still heavily reliant on external capital, for example, reflects the fact that industrialization was largely sponsored by an immigrant business class with few ties to the localities in which it invested. An indigenous business class failed to develop largely because these industries were geared towards semi-skilled manual occupations with little or no scope for career advancement, a social structure which was thus ill equipped to spawn new firms. Given the absence of a strong internal dynamic, the postwar modernization of the Welsh economy was propelled by a combination of public sector investment in the state-owned coal and steel industries on the one hand and by foreign direct investment (FDI) on the other.

With the subsequent decline of the coal and steel industries, the Welsh industrial economy became ever more dependent on foreign-owned plants. In the early 1990s, Wales, with just 5 per cent of the UK population, was said to be 'the number one performing region, attracting around 20% of total new foreign projects entering the UK annually' (Hill and Munday, 1994). By 1996, the foreign-owned sector accounted for some 74,000 employees, equivalent to 33 per cent of all manufacturing jobs in Wales, nearly twice the foreign share of UK manufacturing. We shall focus here on this foreign-owned segment of the Welsh economy, not simply because FDI has been prioritized in Wales but because it raises the question as to whether FDI offers host regions a genuine *developmental* opportunity, a route through which they can upgrade their regional economies. With some notable exceptions, this question is rarely taken seriously in the British context, where branch plants are often seen as having little if anything to do with development in any meaningful sense: indeed, many of these plants, especially Japanese plants, are dismissed as mere 'warehouses' (Williams *et al.*, 1992).

The cruder versions of the 'branch-plant syndrome' portray these plants as low-pay, low-skill, assembly-based operations which have little or no multiplier effect because they have limited linkages with firms and training institutions in the regional economy. While there is a good deal of truth in these claims, this stereotype nevertheless needs to be revised to take account of the changes that are under way in this FDI sector. While branch-plant wages are lower than those in the traditional coal and steel sectors, they tend to be higher than the wage levels of the domestic manufacturing sector. While Wales is a land of low pay within the UK (with average weekly full-time wages in 1995 at 95% of the GB level in manufacturing and 89% overall), the fact remains that manual wages for both men and women in manufacturing are slightly *higher* in Wales than in Great Britain as a whole (ONS, 1996). In other words, the most important sources of low pay in Wales are not branch plants—as the stereotype would have it—so much as the public and private service sectors.

While Welsh manufacturing is certainly biased towards manual occupations, the growth of non-manual occupations in engineering, like managers and professional engineers, scientists and technologists has been increasing significantly higher, albeit from a low base, than in the UK as a whole (Lawson and Morgan, 1991). This suggests a process of occupational upgrading which is inconsistent with the image of assembly-only activities. Indeed, it reflects the growing complexity of production, on the one hand, and the addition of development functions on the other. While we are not suggesting that full-blown R&D laboratories are blossoming out of these foreign branches, we should no longer equate the branch plant with low-level assembly functions.

Along with wages and skills, local purchasing is another index of the 'embedded' branch plant. Traditionally, the level of local purchasing has been very low in Wales and, generally speaking, remains so. But this situation is not set in aspic because foreign plants are no longer so impervious to local supply, providing it can meet exacting standards with respect to quality, cost, and delivery. Although this new stance is still in its infancy, it is creating opportunities for local suppliers that were simply not available even five years ago.

One of the most prominent examples of this new sourcing stance is Sony, which first located in Wales in 1974 and which now employs some 4,000 workers in what is the company's largest complex in Europe. As part of its shift to a just-in-time strategy in the late 1980s, Sony set a premium on working with locally based suppliers wherever possible. To this end, it persuaded its specialist plastic-mouldings suppliers to relocate to the region because it preferred face-to-face contact to meet the challenge of ever shorter product-lead times. This is more than just a simple purchasing relationship because Sony has tutored these suppliers in a wide range of skills, including quality control, factory layout, tooling, and integrated materials management (Munday, 1991). Furthermore, Welsh-based companies are beginning to figure more prominently in Sony's Quality Awards, which have been held annually since 1989 to pay tribute to the best European suppliers.

As we saw in Chapter 2, branch plants are coming under pressure from their headquarters to deliver much more than was hitherto expected of them, especially as regards new ideas for improving product, process, and organizational innovation. Within Wales, a number of branch plants are beginning to act as 'learning laboratories' in which new information is being generated for their parent companies. These include:

- the multi-skilling programme at Ford's Bridgend plant, which has gone further than any other plant in Europe in implementing integrated manufacturing teams, through which radical productivity improvements have been secured;
- through its interaction with Nissan, the local branch of Valeo pioneered a new model of collaborative manufacturing with its own suppliers and this model has subsequently been adopted by Valeo plants worldwide;
- the Welsh branch of Northern Telecom took it upon itself to develop a more interactive relationship with its key suppliers and formed a suppliers' association to give this institutional expression, the first such association anywhere in the NT group;
- by interacting with the UK-based Japanese automotive firms, the local plant of Bosch has learned far more about the realities of lean production than its HQ in Stuttgart, one of the reasons why its productivity is much higher than comparable German plants;
- General Electric's aircraft-maintenance plant has gone further than any other plant in the GE empire in realizing the concept of the 'supervisorless' factory through the use of autonomous work teams, with the result that this Welsh plant is something of a 'Mecca' for managers throughout the company;
- TRW's plant at Resolven has developed a Suppliers Park to create a 'family supplier organization' to enable the plant to iterate more effectively with its key suppliers and this concept, developed by local managers, is a first for TRW worldwide.

These organizational innovations represent genuine achievements for both the plants and the parent companies, even though the latter still find it difficult to accept that they have anything to learn from their outposts in the periphery. Because these innovations do not directly involve *product* innovations, which is what tends to generate new jobs, critics of FDI might legitimately ask how organizational innovations of this sort benefit either the plant or the host region? As for the plant the main benefits are felt in terms of plant security and potential *re*-investment: the most important form of FDI is now repeat investment, which accounts for over 60 per cent of new FDI in Wales today, and this tends to be focused on the most innovative branch plants in the company. As for the host region, the main benefits are the tutoring effects which branch plants are having on local suppliers and local training institutions.

Although Wales has earned itself a reputation as a key FDI location for manufacturing activities, there are real limits as to how far branch plants can be the platform on which to build a more innovative, R&D-based regional economy. The most that can be expected is that these branch plants are encouraged to secure broader product mandates, more development responsibilities, and greater managerial autonomy, so that they are empowered to tap their local knowledge—this is the meaning of 'innovation' in the context of a branch-plant economy. In other words, there is more scope for innovative activity at the level of the branch plant than is commonly thought, both within the plant itself (in the form of management–labour practices, multi-skilled and autonomous work teams, incremental product innovation, etc.) and between the plant and its local milieu (through interactions with training colleges, suppliers, and regional development agencies, etc.). The more successful these interactions, the more the plant becomes embedded. However, the process of embedding branch plants depends on a whole series of factors, including a high grade infrastructure, a proactive development agency, and, perhaps most important of all, a robust operational record within the plant itself (Amin *et al.*, 1994).

Whatever its shortcomings, FDI has played a key role in helping Wales to weather the decline of its traditional industries on the one hand and the wider process of UK deindustrialization on the other. This helps to explain why, in the decade to 1995, manufacturing output in Wales grew by over 40 per cent, more than double the UK rate, and why manufacturing employment in Wales grew by over 5 per cent, when it declined by over 15 per cent in the UK. The combination of higher productivity and lower wages also means that Wales now has significantly lower unit labour costs than the UK as a whole. While this constitutes a major locational advantage from the *corporate* standpoint—illustrated by the very high level of FDI which is repeat investment—the *regional* challenge is to enhance wage levels without compromising above-average productivity levels. Upgrading the quality of branch plants is only part of the answer here. What is equally, if not more important, is for Wales to address two other interrelated weaknesses, namely, a weak R&D base and a population of SMEs with a low capacity for innovation.

These weaknesses have not been addressed until recently, largely because of the inordinate attention devoted to FDI, which has dominated the thinking of regional state agencies to a degree which is hard to justify. While the FDI sector accounts for a third of all manufacturing jobs, this is just 6 per cent of total employment in Wales, a figure which puts FDI into proper perspective and highlights the significance of the indigenous sector.

Wales is at or near the bottom of the UK regional league table for R&D expenditure, owing to the fact that industry and government-financed R&D are both relatively low in Wales, though the picture in higher education is somewhat more favourable. No amount of organizational innovation in branch plants and supply chains can ever compensate for the lack of product innovation, which in turn depends on R&D activity (Edquist *et al.*, 1996). Bad as it is, this problem may be overstated because R&D is recorded not in branch plants but in registered offices, while many SMEs undertake development work but rarely account for it separately.

On the SME front, most firms in Wales do not perceive 'innovation' as a strategic priority and, when they do engage in product or process innovation, it is often due to customer pressure. For most SMEs, the main source of innovative ideas is the supply chain, while the biggest barriers to innovation are lack of available finance and inadequate technical expertise (Henderson, 1995). These indigenous firms cry out for the same kind of support which has been lavished on the foreign-owned sector, not least because over 90 per cent of all net new job creation in Wales in the 1990s has been in indigenous firms. However, since some of these indigenous firms will be supplying the region's foreign-owned firms, we should not push this distinction too far.

For all its success in attracting FDI, Wales continues to lag below the UK average on a number of key developmental indicators. While the Welsh unemployment rate is no longer well above the UK average (6.8% in March 1997, compared to 6.1% in the UK), Wales continues to suffer from lower GDP per head, lower earnings, and lower activity rates, and these problems are not resolved overnight. But one of the most encouraging features of Wales today is that the regional authorities have finally begun to acknowledge the need for a radically different kind of developmental strategy, a strategy which harnesses the skills and resources of a much wider constituency than was considered necessary in the past. Belatedly, the WDA and other agencies are now crafting a strategy to build innovative capacity in both public and private sectors, a strategy predicated on the principle of associational action.

BEYOND CLASSICAL REGIONAL POLICY

Classical regional policy in Britain was essentially a glorified subsidy regime for attracting mobile capital. Looking back on over sixty years of regional policy, the most damning thing one can say is that it did little or nothing to enhance the developmental capacity of the regions it purported to help: it did little to raise the learning and innovative capacities of firms in receipt of regional aid, it never countenanced the creation of inter-firm networks or business service centres through which firms might have been persuaded to collectively upgrade their capabilities, and it made no attempt to raise the calibre of public agencies so as to render them more dynamic interlocutors in the corporate economy. In other words, while regional policy helped to redistribute economic activity and contain the spread of unemployment differentials—a laudable social goal—it was not designed to engage with the organizational structures, managerial cultures, and absorptive capacities of firms in the assisted regions, issues which lie at the very heart of the economic development process.

As we argued earlier, the most innovative strains of regional development thinking in Britain have come, not from central government, but from a wide array of *bottom-up* local and regional initiatives, the full significance of which has been lost because they remain too scattered and too localized to have a transformative impact. Here we want to examine some of these bottom-up initiatives in Wales because they signal a radically different kind of approach to regional development, an approach which genuinely tries to engage with the issues of learning, innovation, and capacity-building (in both firms and public agencies), with associational action being the common thread.

The Development Agency as Animateur

Most of these initiatives have been sponsored by the WDA in conjunction with other public and private sector actors. For most of its career since 1976, the WDA strategy was based on the triad of land reclamation, factory building, and inward investment, what we might call the 'hard' infrastructure. Since 1990, however, the Agency has been setting a higher premium on business support services, technology transfer, and skills development for both indigenous SMEs and foreign-owned branch plants, what we might call the 'soft' *info*-structure. What induced this new shift? A number of factors conspired to the same end, in particular the novel demands of existing branch plants, complaints that the Agency had been neglecting indigenous SMEs by chasing FDI, and the simple fact that regional aid, the mechanism through which FDI had been secured, had been progressively reduced since 1979.

The early generations of branch plants made few demands on the regional economy, which was not surprising when all they required was a pool of low-cost, tractable labour, cheap premises, and an adequate physical infrastructure —prosaic requirements which could be easily met by the WDA's 'hard' competencies. Over the past decade, however, the more innovative branch plants have begun to make novel, and more exacting, demands on the regional economy. Among other things, they have shown themselves to be interested in the quality of technical skills, the calibre of local suppliers, the availability of digital telecommunications links, and better after-care services. Taken together, these demands required a new set of competencies within the WDA and a more innovative approach to the way it designed and delivered its services.

Satisfying the demands of existing inward investors has become an ever-more important issue because, as we have seen, the major form of FDI is repeat investment: indeed over 60 per cent of FDI in Wales today takes this form. The changing form of FDI requires new skills and new institutional arrangements because the factors which are important for greenfield FDI, like the upfront grant package for example, may not loom so large when it comes to repeat investment. To secure these new rounds of investment, local branch-plant managers need to convince themselves, along with their HQs, that the region offers *sustainable* attractions in terms of skills, suppliers, and after-care services. The WDA has woken up to the fact that after-care covers such a wide spectrum of services that no single agency could possibly satisfy these requirements. For this reason, the WDA is obliged to work in and through a host of other agencies to ensure that firms get the right package of service.

In other words, the Agency is evolving from a position where it was engaged in the direct provision of a wide portfolio of services to a point where it plays the role of animateur, in which it seeks to weave its own specialized services with the complementary offerings of other agencies (Morgan, 1997*b*). This is easier said than done because the Agency has no formal control over the cognate bodies (like TECs for example) with which it is obliged to collaborate. Hence this constellation of agencies is not so much an empire as a commonwealth, where trust and reciprocity are the keys to successful collaboration. In assuming the role of animateur, which calls for a delicate balance between leadership and forbearance, the WDA's most useful apprenticeship has been its work in managing the Regional Technology Plan for Wales.

Learning to Innovate: The RTP Exercise in Wales

Sponsored by the European Commission, the Regional Technology Plan (RTP) was part of a new generation of EU programmes to promote innovation in less favoured regions. Wales was invited to be one of the four pilot regions for the RTP because, in the eyes of the Commission, the regional authorities had demonstrated their resolve to upgrade the economic fabric through a collaborative effort between public and private sectors. In the Commission's view, the RTP exercise would be most fruitful 'in areas where well-founded cooperation between the public and private sectors is—or can be—established' (European Commission, 1994*b*).

The merit of the RTP programme is that it signals a decisive break with past EU regional policies; for the most part, these equated innovation with R&D activity and the latter was too often perceived as a supply-side problem, where the 'solution' was more investment in technical infrastructure, a diagnosis which neglected the social, institutional, and commercial dimensions of innovation. More recently, a new diagnosis has begun to emerge because the Commission now argues that 'regional planners have to address not only a supply problem (the lack of RTD capacity and mechanisms for diffusing technology) but also —and probably most importantly in the first place—a problem of demand' (European Commission, 1994*a*). It is in this context that we have to understand the RTP exercise, the key aim of which is to promote an iterative regional innovation *process* in which the region's stakeholders are enjoined to define a commonly agreed, bottom-up strategy for their regions. In contrast to classical British regional policy, the RTP is designed to stimulate a collective learning process among the key regional players—the regional state, private firms, public agencies, social partners, and a wide array of intermediary organizations spanning education, training, and technology transfer. Equally important, the RTP exercise is predicated on the notion that the initial impetus for regional renewal must come from *within* the region and that this turns on the region's networking capacity, that is, the disposition to collaborate to achieve mutually beneficial ends (Morgan, 1997*a*).

Because the process (collaboration) was widely perceived to be integral to the success of the product (raising innovative capacity), the RTP consultation exercise lasted eighteen months and over 600 organizations were actively involved in what turned out to be the most comprehensive iteration process ever undertaken in Wales in the field of economic development. Whatever its limits, the RTP Action Plan, which was officially launched in June 1996, was very much a bottom-up collective endeavour. The Action Plan identifies a total of sixty-six projects to be implemented under six priorities for action, with project champions ranging from private firms in projects related to technology transfer, supply chains, and finance for innovation, and so on, to trade union bodies in projects dealing with skills formation and new qualifications. Of course, everything hinges on how well the RTP projects are implemented and whether public and private partners make good their commitments with actual investments.

Orchestrating the RTP exercise was an invaluable experience for the WDA because it forced the Agency to engage with a much wider spectrum of organizations than had been customary in the past. Many of these organizations—in the business, labour, education, and training spheres—had never been formally involved in the design of a regional strategy before, which meant that a wider intelligence was being tapped for the first time. To this extent, the RTP clearly met one of its principal aims of providing an opportunity 'to break old habits and to create new openings' (Shotton and Miege, 1994). Through this iterative process, the WDA has been able to gain a better understanding of how firms acquire their information, how they learn, and how their receptivity to innovation is conditional on the agency with which they are dealing. This confirmed the WDA in its belief that firms learn best from other firms—whether they be suppliers, customers, or competitors—because they see their corporate peers as being more credible interlocutors than public agencies. These findings resonated with the Agency because it was already coming to the conclusion that the most effective business-support initiatives were those which were designed *with* rather than *for* firms, and this represents a major departure from the traditional supply-driven approach to enterprise-support thinking in Britain (Morgan, 1996).

While it is too early to judge the success or otherwise of the RTP exercise, since the implementation phase is only now getting under way, it is worth looking at some related initiatives which, in the spirit of the RTP, are predicated on the principles of collective learning and associational action.

Building Supply Chains

One of the most creative business-support programmes which the WDA has ever designed is based on the idea of using the supply chain as a mechanism for promoting learning and innovation among both customers and suppliers throughout the regional economy. A high quality local supply base was seen as a key factor in attracting more sophisticated FDI projects on the one hand and raising the local multiplier effect of foreign investment on the other. Building more localized supply-chain linkages was also an obvious way to support both indigenous firms and branch plants at one and the same time. To this end, the WDA launched its Source Wales programme in 1991, a collective brand-name for a range of services which aim to identify supply opportunities (sourcing) and enhance supplier performance (development). To achieve these aims, the WDA acts as an intermediary in the supply chain, seeking to build and develop long-term, high-trust partnerships between major corporate buyers and Welsh-based suppliers (Hines, 1992). One of the most distinctive features of the development side of this programme is the emphasis on self-help through self-organized networks, that is, groups of firms which are committed to improving their performance by sharing their expertise for mutual benefit.

On the sourcing side, the WDA has targeted original equipment manufacturers (OEMs) in the electronics, automotive, information technology sectors and major institutional purchasers like the National Health Service and the Ministry of Defence. To assist in the identification of suitable suppliers, the Source Wales database now holds details of over 2,000 Welsh companies and, when a sourcing opportunity has been identified, the database can be interrogated for the most appropriate candidates. Since 1991, the number of sourcing projects has been running at around 120 per annum, with some 50 per cent of these yielding 'deals' for Welsh companies.

On the development side, the WDA offers different services to different firms, depending where they stand on a pyramid of scale and ability, as we show in Figure 6.1. The programme has concentrated on the top two tiers of the pyramid, where companies have reached a stage where they can benefit from the services on offer. For companies in the top tier, the WDA has developed a series of 'best practice' programmes designed to help them to become 'world class manufacturers'. These programmes include:

- *the Time to Market Programme* which aims to improve the product development process so that firms can bring products to market more quickly and more efficiently. This programme, delivered in a shared learning environment, lasts for two years;
- *the Supplier Association Programme*, known by its Japanese name of Kyoryoku Kai, aims to build long-term, high-trust relationships between client companies and their key suppliers with the objective of raising performance through the supply chain;
- *the Materials Management Network Programme* aims to disseminate 'best practice' in materials management through the formation of regional network groups.

For the smaller companies in the second tier of the pyramid, the WDA has designed a series of supplier development programmes, like the Manufacturing Improvement Networks programme, which aims to raise awareness of world-class tools and techniques. A new programme to improve awareness of the Japanese tool *Gemba Kanri* was launched in 1995 and this is designed to improve quality, operations, and maintenance at the shopfloor level. Common to both the best practice and supplier development programmes is a growing commitment to *benchmarking*, an activity which helps to make firms more receptive to new ideas because, for smaller firms especially, 'seeing is believing'.

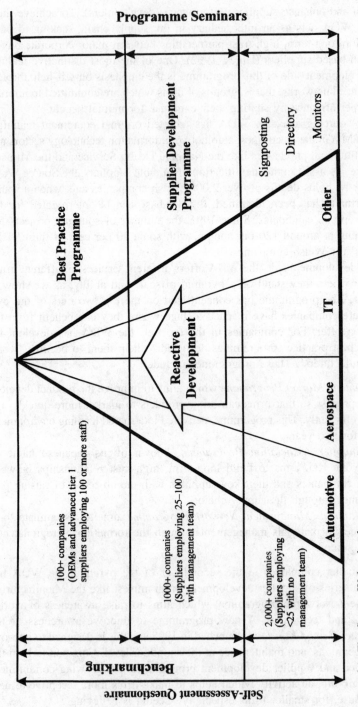

FIG. 6.1. The Source Wales development strategy

Source: Welsh Development Agency

Of all these services, one of the most innovative to date has been the Supplier Associations. To our knowledge, the WDA was the first development agency in Europe to adapt the concept of the *Kyoryoku Kai* to local conditions and, thus far, well over twenty supplier associations have been crafted in Wales. The first of these was launched in 1991 by Calsonic, a Japanese automotive-components firm, which had recently acquired Llanelli Radiators, a well-regarded firm which was voted 'supplier of the year' by GM in 1994. With an initial membership of just ten firms, limited in number so as to ease the delicate trust-building process, the Calsonic association has delivered major benefits to its members across a wide range of problem-solving skills through the use of interactive workshop techniques in which each firm tutors its peers in its own specialized field (Hines, 1994). In principle, the jointly defined curriculum—covering issues like product development, logistics, target costing, and total quality management—could have been delivered by external service providers, but in practice the members of the association attached more importance to the tutoring skills of their peers, which reinforces our earlier point about how firms prefer to learn (Morgan, 1996).

The Source Wales initiative was independently evaluated for the first time in 1996. While more effort was said to be necessary as regards the monitoring and evaluation of the output of the programme, the general verdict was very encouraging. The delivery process for sourcing was said to be effective and the Agency's approach was seen to be 'professional and impartial' and generally welcomed by the participating firms. On the development side, the evaluation said the success of the best practice programmes was down to three factors: (1) the credibility that WDA backing gave the programmes; (2) the extent to which the programmes were subsidized in the early years; and (3) the capability, enthusiasm, and drive of the WDA's consultants. The evaluation concluded by saying that:

most of the companies had a clear desire for some form of continuing forum which would allow them to keep up to date on the latest issues, as well as being a mechanism which would keep the existing network in place. There may be a role for WDA to monitor the situation and ensure such a network is retained, but there is evidence to suggest that the participants would bear the full cost of such an initiative. (Segal Quince Wicksteed Ltd., 1996)

By inserting itself as an intermediary in the supply chain, the WDA came to be seen as part of the learning process, bringing skills, like that of the honest broker for example, which the firms did not, indeed could not, possess. What this shows is that public agencies can be innovative interlocutors when they have earned the trust and the respect of the firms which they are trying to help.

The Self-Organized Technology Forum

Apart from building vertical networks of firms in the supply chain, the WDA is also active in promoting horizontal networks of firms in key sectors of the

Welsh economy. Based on the same philosophy which informs the Source Wales programme—that firms learn best from other firms and that inter-firm networks help to facilitate this process—the concept of the Technology Forum has been developed in an effort to help firms to help themselves. The ultimate aim here is to create a capacity for self-organization in key sectors so that firms and cognate institutions can begin to interact more fruitfully so as to find joint solutions to common problems. Although the WDA has no technical competence in the sectors it has targeted under this initiative—healthcare, new materials, opto-electronics, food and information technology—it is once again trying to play the role of honest broker by orchestrating the disparate sources of expertise in sectorally based technology fora.

This concept was launched in 1992 with the formation of the Welsh Medical Technology Forum, which consists principally of firms supplying healthcare products and services, the National Health Service, the Welsh Office, the Design Council, and university-based medical research teams. In short, this industry-led Forum brings together producers, users, and regulators, with the WDA acting as the secretariat, and its self-declared aims are to encourage the sharing of ideas and experiences in the medical sector so as to improve innovation, research, and commercial advantage. Members themselves define the agenda of their meetings and this helps to explain the impressive attendance rates achieved so far. Indeed, the most recent evaluation of the Forum concluded by saying that 'this grouping of firms and industry actors has clearly promoted a greater feeling of shared destiny amongst members' (Henderson, 1995). Such has been the progress that Forum members are now planning to create a jointly owned medical-products development company to exploit local research results.

In 1996, the Welsh Opto-Electronics Forum was created out of a joint initiative on the part of the WDA, the firms and related education institutions to fortify the growing opto-electronics cluster in North Wales. While its aims are essentially the same as its medical predecessor, the Opto-Electronics Forum is also interested in forging strategic business alliances with firms in and beyond Britain and forging technical links with overseas professional institutes like the Fraunhofer Institute in Germany, the Institute d'Optique in France, and Oitda in Japan. In other words, there is no set 'menu' of activities in the concept of the Technology Forum as each Forum's agenda is shaped by the common interests of its membership. Far from trying to impose a sectoral strategy on these groups, the WDA encourages them to use their collective knowledge to identify the weaknesses of their sector and to address these through concerted action.

Collaborative Training Provision

The weak training culture in Britain seems to be impervious to the successive waves of government reforms to promote a better system of skills provision. Now that (publicly funded) training provision has been localized in the TECs, there is currently more scope to experiment with new forms of skills provision and the WDA has been actively exploring these possibilities. Here we want to focus on two of these experiments in the Welsh automotive-components sector, one for SMEs, the other centred around the Ford engine plant at Bridgend. One of the key pillars of the Welsh economy, the automotive-components sector in Wales, has acquired a reputation for being one of the most cost-effective clusters in Britain, a position it needed to bolster if it was to remain viable in a sector demanding ever higher levels of quality and performance (Delbridge *et al.*, 1990).

In conjunction with the TECs, the WDA brought the most promising SMEs together to discuss their common skills-related problems, the aim being to get the firms to define their own training needs. By acting in concert, the firms saw two benefits: first, they would be able to reduce the costs of training since the WDA and the TECs would share the costs and, secondly, they would get training tailored to their real needs rather than having to choose from a pre-given menu of training programmes. Working in partnership with Further Education colleges, where the trainers began to see the limits of traditional supply-side provision, these firms were able to gain local access to courses that were defined *not* by colleges but by themselves. Although this collaborative training programme is not without problems—like getting firms to release scarce staff on agreed dates—it helps to overcome the standard criticism which British firms level at much college-based training, namely that it is not specialized enough, that it is dated and of variable quality (Morgan and Rees, 1994).

Building on this collaborative approach, the WDA has now developed a far more ambitious strategy in the form of the Automotive Training Centre (ATC), which is located alongside Ford's engine plant at Bridgend in South Wales and which opened in 1997. The aim of the ATC is to be a 'centre of excellence' for a wide array of auto-related training courses and it already enjoys preferred supplier status for all Ford courses, some fifty-six in all, throughout the region. Far from being a dedicated training centre for Ford, the ATC is designed to overcome the fragmented nature of existing training provision, it therefore aims to become a focal point for state-of-the-art courses for the 150 odd auto suppliers throughout South Wales. With Ford's imprimatur the ATC hopes to engender a new training culture in the auto cluster and, with it being industry led and locally rooted, this would seem to be an improvement on the top-down initiatives from central government.

While this initiative has yet to prove itself, the very creation of the ATC is a good example of associational action: although the WDA and Ford were the principal architects, this initiative also involves the TECs, the universities, and Further Education colleges, all of which stand to benefit from closer interaction with a training-conscious company like Ford. For its part, the Ford management at Bridgend was keen to defend its status as a high productivity plant within the company and one way of doing this was by forging stronger links with local support agencies, without which the ATC would not have been possible. In other words, the ATC was designed to meet the needs of the company and its suppliers for higher quality skills provision, while also meeting the developmental agenda of the WDA, which wanted to create an industry-led training centre capable of keeping the region's auto cluster abreast of new labour skills.

All the initiatives we have examined here are very much at the embryonic stage and only time will tell whether they will succeed in raising the innovative capacity of the region's key sectors. The common thread running through these initiatives is the new *associational* strategy of the WDA, which has sought to create the conditions under which firms can more easily engage in a mutually beneficial process of collective learning. Its role in animating these networks was valued by the participating firms because it was contributing an asset—the role of honest broker—which none of the firms possessed. Indeed, the networks would not have emerged had it not been for the WDA's involvement. Being involved in the networking process, the WDA assumed a role which government more generally needs to assume if it wants to be a more credible, more innovative interlocutor, namely, 'an unobtrusive participant rather than an intrusive spectator' (Sabel, 1992).

CONCLUSIONS

Although less favoured regions often seem powerless to act for themselves in a world dominated by international capital flows, one of the key lessons from Wales in recent years is that the branch plants of multinational firms are not delocalized units of a corporate hierarchy; on the contrary, they have a regional context and the latter is becoming more, rather than less, important to their performance. Even so, the challenge for regions which are heavily dependent on FDI is how to exploit this global–local interaction, so that the benefits accrue to the region as well as to the firm, the familiar problem of development *of* the region versus development *in* the region (Morgan and Sayer, 1988). Whereas classical British regional policy was ill equipped to meet this challenge, the WDA, for so long obsessed with merely attracting FDI, is at least beginning to address the right targets, such as how to embed foreign investment, how to strike a more judicious balance between FDI and the indigenous sector, and how to stimulate self-organizing networks in which firms, foreign and local, can develop an interactive learning capacity.

While FDI has played an important part in the modernization of the Welsh economy, it is now perceived to be an ingredient of regeneration rather than the recipe itself. However, the most that can be expected from the FDI sector is that these plants are encouraged to secure broader product mandates, more R&D functions, and greater managerial autonomy, all of which would create better opportunities for locally based suppliers, universities, and training colleges. This is what we mean by innovating through global–local interaction. While this is more an aspiration than a reality in Wales today, the initiatives being pursued by the WDA and its partners suggest that this is a feasible aspiration.

If the embedding of FDI is a key priority for the future, even more important is the task of raising the innovative capacity of the indigenous SME sector. This is particularly important with respect to product innovation capacity, which tends to be the most job-intensive form of innovation (Edquist *et al.*, 1996). The mechanisms for raising the innovative capacity of SMEs include better supply-chain networks, in which the customer is encouraged to act as tutor, and a better, more locally attuned enterprise-support infrastructure.

A more locally attuned infrastructure raises the issue of how far regional institutions are empowered to design and deliver policies which resonate with the needs of the regional economy. Despite recent trends towards localization of enterprise support, the British policy-making system remains highly centralized, so much so that there is little scope for significant policy innovation below the level of central government. With the advent of a Labour government committed to constitutional reform, including elected regional governments for Wales and Scotland, there promises to be more scope for genuine regional experimentation than at any time this century.

Of itself, of course, regional government will do little or nothing to enhance economic performance (Garmise, 1997; Evans and Harding, 1997). But it could make a difference if, using its local knowledge and its enabling powers, it helped to foster more robust networks of collaboration between public and private sectors on the one hand and a more customized support infrastructure on the other. By removing the democratic deficit in Wales, an elected regional government might be better able to achieve these things because, being of the region, it would command greater legitimacy than a Welsh Office run by a minority political party, which was what the Conservative Party was in Wales until 1997. But time alone will tell whether the practice of democratic devolution matches its promise.

7

The Basque Conundrum: Regional Autonomy and Economic Decline

INTRODUCTION

Perhaps to a greater extent than any other region in the European Union, the Basque Country has been forced to pursue an extreme version of the endogenous model of economic development. For a variety of reasons—economic and political—the Basque Country has been unable to secure anything like the amount of foreign investment that has gone to Madrid and Catalonia for example, thus forcing the Basque Country to rely almost entirely on its own efforts and its own resources. Acutely conscious of having to go their own way, and equally conscious of their separate political identity in Spain, the Basques are struggling to define a model of development which is both consistent with and supportive of this distinctive political identity.

But this strong political identity is both a strength and a weakness. On the positive side, it has fuelled demands for a degree of regional autonomy that has few, if any, precedents in Europe. On the negative side, however, the Basque Country is plagued by endless internecine ideological conflicts, the most extreme version of which involves the political terrorism of ETA, the nationalist separatist movement, which makes it that much more difficult for the Basques to attract foreign investment.

A strong regional identity can often be an important factor in helping regions to harness their resources for collective ends but, in the Basque case, it also leads the political authorities to externalize the source of their problems from within the region to Madrid, the seat of the Spanish central government. So long as there remains unfinished political business between central and regional government over the degree of devolution, which is the case in Spain today, regional leaders can always criticize the 'centre' as a surrogate for self-criticism in the 'periphery', and this too can be a weakness.

Notwithstanding these problems, the Basque Country has gone further than most of Europe's old industrial regions in building a regional innovation infrastructure to support the modernization of its traditional industries on the one hand and nurture new industrial and service activities on the other. In pursuing this endogenous model of development, the regional government sets great store on the devolved powers which it acquired under its Statute of Autonomy of 1979, powers which it hopes will give it the political capacity to regenerate the regional economy.

To some extent, the Basque Country offers a unique opportunity to explore a question which lies at the heart of contemporary regional development thinking: to what extent, if at all, can a regional government, which enjoys considerable political autonomy, alter the trajectory of its regional economy? While the political power of the Basque government is quite considerable by European standards, this government also faces some of the most intractable economic problems in Europe, problems which stem in large part from the fact that, being the cradle of the industrial revolution in Spain, the Basque economy specialized in and became inordinately dependent upon the heavy industries associated with nineteenth-century industrialization, for example, iron, steel, and metal manufacture. Although new industrial and service activities are struggling to emerge, the belated restructuring of the heavy industries is the main reason why the Basque Country today suffers from one of the highest rates of regional unemployment in the European Union.

We can also use the Basque Country to explore another question which resonates in contemporary regional development thinking, and that is whether a region with a strong and cohesive cultural identity is more able to develop the associative forms of action that are nowadays deemed to be so important to innovation and economic development. Drawing on the example of the Mondragon co-operative movement, a unique experience by any standards, some writers have gone so far as to claim that a corollary of Basque cultural identity is a strong ethos of 'mutual co-operation' in business life. While this claim is hopelessly exaggerated as it stands, there are indeed signs that associative action is beginning to emerge on a much wider scale than the particular Mondragon experience, but this owes less to some primordial cultural identity and more to the active construction of sectoral alliances of firms, public agencies, and training institutes.

These two questions—the scope and limits of the regional state and the construction of associational strategies—are the two key themes of this chapter. Before exploring these questions, we need to understand the wider national context of the Basque Country because many of its problems are associated with a Spanish system which has been something of a hothouse of economic and political change since it joined the European Community in 1986.

FROM FRANCOISM TO FEDERALISM: LATE MODERNIZATION IN SPAIN

It is quite impossible to understand the radical changes being wrought in the 'national system' in Spain without some reference to Francoism and its institutional legacy. Driven by growing economic stagnation, Spain had begun to accommodate itself to the international capitalist economy long before Franco's death in 1975; in fact, the 'modernization' of the Spanish economy which began in the late 1950s, under the influence of technocrats associated with the

secretive Opus Dei sect, inadvertently contributed to the dissolution of the
Francoist system because it created an unsustainable tension between economic
liberalization and political authoritarianism. Even so, the formidable apparatus
of the Francoist system, in which *self-sufficiency* was the highest priority, was
not going to be uprooted overnight.

As an authoritarian form of corporatism heavily biased towards strict economic autarchy until 1959, the Francoist system had spun an enormous web of
state control over virtually every aspect of the Spanish economy. Among the
most palpable signs of state control were the state companies: Endesa in energy,
Seat in transport equipment, and, above all, Instituto Nacional de Industria (INI),
the huge state holding company which exists to this day. Progressive controls
over the banking system culminated in 1962 with the nationalization of the
Bank of Spain. On the labour market front, where the legacy of Francoism was
strongest of all, the visible hand of the state was most clearly enshrined in the
Ordenanzas Laborales, a wide array of paternalistic measures which regulated
working conditions, job categories, promotions, demarcations, and redundancy
terms. Repressive and stultifying as they were in limiting labour mobility, these
measures nevertheless contained important social benefits: they offered workers
an extensive system of job protection to compensate for the fact that wages were
low and unemployment coverage was limited. Unions and employers' organizations had little influence over this *de facto* pact because free associations
of labour and capital were officially banned, with *sindicatos*—bodies which in
principle represented both employers and employees in given sectors but which
were in practice organs of the state—acting as a poor surrogate (Salmon, 1991).

Most of these systemic features remained in place through the Francoist 'economic miracle' between 1959–73, a period of growth which was spatially concentrated in the three core industrial regions of Madrid, Catalonia, and the
Basque Country. But this period of rapid growth masked deep structural problems: large swathes of industry consisted of firms which were small scale and
technologically backward, the service sector was under-developed, social and
economic infrastructure was woefully inadequate by EC standards, and the
labour market was virtually cast in aspic. These and other problems surfaced
with a vengeance in the decade to 1985, when Spain was shaken by a traumatic and semi-permanent economic recession, the most telling sign of which
was the surge in unemployment from less than 4 per cent in 1975 to what was
then a postwar peak of nearly 22 per cent in 1985. The structural weaknesses
rendered Spain ill equipped to survive the more intensive competition which
followed the two oil shocks of the 1970s and this, together with the rapid wage
increases unleashed by the restoration of democracy, induced a savage bout of
labour shedding throughout the economy, especially in older industrial regions
like the Basque Country (OECD, 1994b).

To a large extent, this decade-long recession was stemmed and spectacularly
reversed by Spain's entry to the EC in 1986, a move which signalled a new
era for Spain as a political democracy and a 'normal' capitalist economy. Being

a member of the EC brought both benefits and costs, though the former were more apparent in the short term. For the first five years of EC membership, Spain enjoyed the highest growth of output and employment in the entire OECD area and this boom was largely driven by an unprecedented influx of foreign investment, which increased fivefold between 1986 and 1993, making Spain one of the most important recipients of foreign direct investment in the EC. With its significantly lower labour costs Spain offered inward investors 'high rates of return on newly-installed capital and technically-advanced equipment' (OECD, 1991).

But in keeping with Spain's feast-to-famine economic cycle, this rate of growth was unsustainable. Rapid expansion induced the usual symptoms of uncontrolled growth—severe inflationary pressures and growing trade deficits—which provoked a deflationary response from the Socialist government.

The end of the EC-induced boom in 1991 once again exposed the underlying problems of the Spanish economy, where the key problem is again unemployment. Having fallen during the boom, Spain's unemployment rate surged to 24 per cent in 1994, a new postwar peak and the highest rate in Western Europe. The high level of unemployment for a country with one of the fastest output growth rates in the OECD highlights 'the predominantly structural nature of the problem' (OECD, 1994b). Even though this problem may be less severe than the official figures suggest, on account of the 'invisible factories' in the informal sector of the Spanish economy (Benton, 1990), it still constitutes the main problem in Spain today.

Following Spain's accession to the EC in 1986, the most important structural changes have been associated with the *liberalization* of the economy and the *regionalization* of the state system, each of which merits some attention.

Before it joined the EC, the Spanish economy was the most protected in Western Europe, with a 'protection rate' three times higher than the average in other EC countries (OECD, 1991). Liberalizing this vast protectionist apparatus was the price Spain was obliged to pay to become a bone fide member of the EC and this external obligation helps to explain why the Socialist governments which held office from 1982 to 1996 were forced to prosecute what left-wing critics saw as a 'neo-liberal' programme, a strategy which has been pursued with greater alacrity by the Conservative government which assumed office in 1996. In varying degrees, this liberalization programme has touched virtually every aspect of the Spanish economy, including the lowering of tariffs on trade, privatization of state firms, deregulation of banking and utilities, welfare cuts, and the progressive removal of labour market controls.

Draconian as these measures may seem by Spanish standards, their effect in eradicating the state as an economic actor should not be exaggerated. Most of the privatizations were designed to ensure that the state retained a stake and, in the case of INI, which owns over 50 companies and has a stake in 450 others, the government refused to countenance privatization so that INI could continue to exert some state influence in key industrial sectors. Overall, it was estimated that the state still accounted for at least 50 per cent of total Spanish GDP in 1991 (Bruce, 1991).

Liberalizing the highly regulated labour market has proved to be the most difficult and most contentious issue for successive Spanish governments. Motivated by mounting unemployment, escalating labour costs, and growing business opposition to rigid regulations, the government made a determined effort to deregulate the labour market after 1992. The key labour reform of the 1980s was the introduction of temporary, fixed-term contracts, a move designed to create a more flexible workforce to compensate for the rigid rules governing permanent contracts. These new contracts proved immensely popular with employers, so much so that 'temps' accounted for a third of the total Spanish workforce in 1993, the highest level in the OECD. While temporary contracts offered short-term benefits to employers, they also involved less visible costs: continuous labour 'churn' meant that firms lost skills which had a detrimental effect on human capital and overall productivity (OECD, 1994*b*).

But the labour reforms of the 1980s left untouched the biggest problem for employers, namely the rigid rules governing workers with permanent contracts: two-thirds of the workforce. Rooted in the *Ordenanzas Laborales* of the Francoist era, and further reinforced in the Workers Statute of 1980, these rules were the *bête noire* of the business community, especially the foreign-owned stratum. Of all these rules, employers were most vociferously opposed to the redundancy rule for permanent employees which meant that Spanish dismissal costs were among the highest in the world, a factor which helps to explain employers' reluctance to hire permanent staff (OECD, 1994*b*).

In the face of fierce trade union opposition, the Socialist government introduced its most radical labour market reforms in 1994, the main aim of which was to undo the employment protection regulations which had been passed during the Franco and post-Franco periods. Alongside the liberalization of trade, industry, and services, the deregulation of the labour market had finally brought Spain more into line—or perhaps less out of line—with its fellow member states in the EC. Even so, a number of things still distinguished the Spanish economy in the EC context, not least abnormally high unemployment, relatively poor social and economic infrastructure, a weak national system of innovation, and low-productivity industry. Time alone would show whether the Spanish economy was fit enough to withstand the 'convergence' pressures unleashed by the Maastricht Treaty on future European integration.

The other key structural change in Spain in recent years was the regionalization of the state system, which was one of the main provisions of the 1978 Constitution. By far the most sensitive issue in the post-Franco period, the regionalization process had to steer a middle ground between the left, which favoured a more federalist settlement, and the right, which feared for the national integrity of the Spanish state. Given the radically different traditions across Spain's seventeen regions, the Constitution identified three types of region (or autonomous community), the most privileged of which were the 'historic' regions of the Basque Country, Catalonia, and Galicia, which had been granted autonomous status in the 1930s, before this was brutally suppressed by Franco's centralist government. These 'historic regions' were given the right to assume their functions sooner than the other regions.

More a process than an event, regionalization only seriously began with the passing of the Law for the Financing of the Autonomous Communities in 1980 and these arrangements, along with the devolution of powers, continue to be refined and contested even now. However, the regionalization process was supposed to conform to four key principles: first, it should not undermine the unity of Spain; secondly, it should not impede the central government's ability to ensure internal and external stability; thirdly, solidarity between regions had to be ensured through transfer mechanisms to protect the poorer regions; and fourthly, the regional governments should have sufficient resources to finance the activities devolved to them.

The competencies devolved to the regions to date fall into two broad categories: social and economic. In the former, the regions have acquired competencies in health, welfare, education, housing, environment, and culture, while in the economic category the most important functions are infrastructure, agriculture, industrial regulation, and economic development in general. While central government has relinquished most of the spending powers transferred to the regions, it has retained, for macroeconomic reasons, most of the taxing powers. The only taxes transferred to the regional governments are the so-called *ceded* taxes on inheritance, wealth, property transactions, legal acts and gambling. In all, the regions' tax-raising competence accounts for just over 25 per cent of total regional government funding. Clearly, the bulk of regional governments' financial resources comes from the central state, where the most important single source is their share of central state tax revenues. Even so, the regional governments are free to dispose of more than 80 per cent of their total revenues as they see fit (OECD, 1994*b*).

Inevitably perhaps, creating a new regional tier of government has been more costly than originally envisaged: considerable overspending on prestige projects, salaries which are often higher than in central government departments, overstaffing, growing levels of debt, and weak financial management. In theory, central government staffing levels were scheduled to contract as the new functions were transferred to the regions. In practice, however, this barely happened: between 1982–91, for example, the number of civil servants in the seventeen regional governments increased twelvefold to 565,460, while central government numbers fell by just 23 per cent (Chislett, 1994). Indeed, the burgeoning budgets of the regional governments have been a major cause of Spain's growing government deficit in the 1990s.

Aside from costs, central and regional governments will have to address another issue in the 1990s—the calibre of staff in the public administration. One of the hallmarks of the Francoist system was endemic corruption among public officials and, while much of this has since been eradicated, public officials in Spain are still perceived to be low calibre, self-serving, and inefficient bureaucrats (Nieto, 1984). Although the first Socialist government was alive to the fact that a modern and efficient public administration was essential on both democratic and developmental grounds, serious proposals to modernize the public administration only began to emerge in the early 1990s.

At the moment, the political system in Spain is precarious and highly fluid: while it is no longer a centralized state, it still falls short of being a federalized state like Germany. Even so, with the fate of the Conservative government in the hands of the Basque and Catalan nationalist parties, both of which aim to achieve greater regional autonomy in the future, federalism may be the only way to guarantee the national integrity of the Spanish state system.

For Catalonia, with its robust economy and its successful record in attracting domestic and foreign investment, greater autonomy would seem to pose few problems. In contrast, the Basque Country has progressively slipped down the regional economic league in Spain over the past twenty years, as Madrid and the Mediterranean Arc regions have emerged as the key centres of economic activity in post-Franco Spain. In other words, nationalist parties are pressing for ever more political autonomy at a time when, economically, the Basque Country has never been weaker. This is the Basque conundrum.

THE GOVERNANCE SYSTEM IN THE BASQUE COUNTRY

Governance should be understood in the broad sense to mean all the institutions which govern political and economic life, as well as the rules and regulations, the norms, networks, and associations through which these institutions interact with one another. These remarks are especially germane in the Basque context because, as we shall see, the networking capacity of its key political and economic institutions leaves something to be desired. To look at this issue in more detail, we look first at the institutions of *political* governance.

Following the Statute of Autonomy in 1979, the Basques lost no time in establishing a new system of regional government. The Basque Country possess *four* autonomous governments: in addition to the regional government itself, there are also the provincial governments (*Diputaciones Forales*) of the three provinces of Alava, Bizkaia, and Gipuzkoa. In contrast to Catalonia, where the provincial tier has been sidelined by the regional government, the provincial governments of the Basque Country, historical territories with a pronounced sense of their own identity, remain very important institutional actors. As well as having extensive powers to promote industry, training, and economic development, these three provincial governments also have a unique status in the European Union: they are empowered to raise income tax revenue, a portion of which is shared with regional and central governments.

In addition to these regional and provincial governments, there is also the municipal tier, the basic unit of local government. With a population of just

2.1 million the Basque Country seems to be somewhat 'over-endowed' with governmental institutions because, whatever the merits of this governance system, the potential for inter-governmental conflict is that much greater. Because the provincialist ethos is so much stronger in the Basque Country than in other Spanish regions, the Basque government finds it that much more difficult to develop a truly regional perspective on economic development, a problem exacerbated by the fact that some 40 per cent of the Basque population is concentrated in Greater Bilbao, the region's largest city.

Deep political divisions within the Basque Country serve to compound the problem of institutional co-ordination. In all, there are seven main political parties, ranging from the moderate regionalism of the Basque Socialist Party to the radical separatism of Herri Batasuna, the political wing of ETA. Since the first democratic elections, the two consistently largest parties have been the PNV (the moderate nationalist party) and the PSE (the Basque Socialist Party), and since the 1986 elections these two very different parties have formed PNV-led coalition governments. Where the PNV is nationalist, conservative, and Catholic in orientation, the PSE eschews ethnic politics, prides itself on its trade union links and its urbanized political base, and professes a secular outlook. In short these coalition partners have little in common other than a pragmatic desire to govern.

While it is the largest single political party, the PNV is not as dominant in the Basque Country as its nationalist counterpart is in Catalonia. Not only is it condemned to share power with the socialists, but it also competes with smaller, more radical parties for the nationalist vote. Although the collective nationalist vote hovers between 50–60 per cent of the total, which signals a clear majority in favour of greater autonomy for the Basque Country, the nationalist movement is fractured by deep divisions over ideology, language, violence, and indeed over what constitutes the 'real' Basque identity.

Whatever its weaknesses, the PNV is committed to winning further powers from Madrid. The demand for a Basque central bank to regulate the regional financial sector, a move which could undermine the regulatory authority of the Bank of Spain, is unlikely to be met. Indeed, it is even opposed by the PNV's own coalition partner, thus fuelling the animosity between the two governing parties. Much more realistic is the demand for more control over vocational training because this has been woefully inadequate when run as a nationally organized system by INEM, the central public employment office. Decentralization of vocational training promises to be the most effective way to overcome the problems inherent in the 'Latin' system, which involves a strict separation between the school and the firm. The positive experience with the 'workshop' schools in Spain, which are run by regions and municipalities, illustrates the importance of decentralizing training provision so as to take account of local and regional nuances.

As well as tackling the problems of vocational skills, the Basque government has been active in trying to create a more effective university system.

Until the creation of the public university (Universidad del Pais Vasco) in the
early 1980s, there was just Deusto University, a private, Jesuit-run university
which was created by a group of Bilbao business notables in 1886. Few social
networks in the Basque Country can compete with the Deusto alumini, a
network which embraces industry, banking, and politics. Much more than a
simple university, Deusto was 'the reproduction centre of the ruling elite that
emerged in the heat of Bizkaia's industrialisation' (Burns, 1989). Like its counterparts in Spain, however, the public university system in the Basque Country
is highly bureaucratic and it has yet to forge the partnerships with industry that
are necessary for endogenous regional development.

Partly because of the limitations of the university system, the regional government has sought to create a new enterprise-focused technology-transfer system.
The key elements of this system are SPRI (a regional development agency),
the EITE network (a group of seven technology centres), and technology parks
(special sites for advanced technology sectors, the largest of which is in the
municipality of Zamudio outside Bilbao). These institutions are designed to
attract the specialized skills which are necessary to engage with the private
sector, skills which the regional government does not possess in house. It is
primarily through these economic development institutions that the government
has tried to promote its regional innovation policies and we shall examine the
scope and limits of these institutions below.

In terms of political governance, the Basque Country would seem to be somewhat unique by European standards. With a population of just 2.1 million, it
has *four* autonomous governments as well as a local government tier. Whatever
the merits of this 'over-endowed' system, there is no doubt that it creates its
own set of problems, and the problems of institutional mismatch on the one
hand and high duplication costs on the other are the two most serious problems facing this governance system (Serrano *et al.*, 1993). There is no easy
answer to this dilemma because the nationalist community is deeply divided as
to whether the 'true' seat of political power should be the regional government
or the provincial governments (*Diputaciones Forales*), based as they are on the
historical communities of the region. Nowhere, it seems, does the past weigh
so heavily on the present as in the Basque Country.

Having looked at the institutions of political governance, let us briefly consider some of the key institutions of *economic* governance. As in most other
European regions, the majority of firms in the Basque Country belong to Chambers of Commerce, of which there are eighty-six in Spain as a whole, roughly
one per province. Under the 'continental system' which operated in Spain until
recently, all firms above a certain threshold were obliged to belong (and pay
fees) to a local chamber of commerce. These chambers offered an array of
services—export information, training provision, and the like—but, because the
quality of these services was variable, firms objected to compulsory membership
in a campaign which recently won support from the *Tribunal Constitucional*,
Spain's constitutional court. If the chambers are no longer able to count on

compulsory membership fees, they will have to compete with other business-service vendors to secure their income. Never particularly effective as a business association, the chambers' status has now been thrown into question in the Basque Country as elsewhere in Spain.

More important than the chambers are the employers' associations in the Basque Country, which are organized along provincial lines. As we shall see later, one of the most innovative experiments in associative action—the Machine Tool Institute at Elgoibar—has been partly organized through ADEGI, the employers' association in the province of Gipuzkoa. Given what we have said about the limitations of the national vocational training system in Spain, this initiative at Elgoibar demonstrates the value of having a locally based and locally attuned system of skills provision. Generally speaking, though, employers' associations are weak in the Basque Country, as they are in Spain as a whole, partly because they were banned under the Francoist system.

A key component of any private economic governance system is the banking network. Unlike most older industrial regions, the Basque Country is home to some of the leading banks in Spain, notably Banco de Bilbao and Banco de Vizcaya. After the merger of these two banks in 1988, the new bank, Banco Bilbao Vizcaya (BBV), is now the second largest bank in Spain. With stakes in dozens of Basque companies, and some 33 per cent of its equity still in Basque hands, BBV can claim to have a good knowledge of the regional economy. While it may be large by Spanish standards, it is not particularly big in the international banking league, where its aspirations lie, and this helps to explain why its energies are no longer directed to its home region. Together with the local *cajas*, the savings bank network which is deeply embedded in the locales of the region, this banking system still constitutes a potentially important resource if it can be tapped for economic renewal purposes.

The potential of what associative action might achieve in the regional financial arena is perhaps best exemplified by Elkargi, the mutual guarantee society of the Basque Country. Created in 1980 as a joint venture between the four governments on the one hand and a consortium of banks and employers' organizations on the other, Elkargi is a non-profit association of over 6,000 Basque companies, making it the largest mutual guarantee society in Spain in terms of both the number of associated firms and the level of guarantees. Its *raison d'être* is to socialize the management of risk by acting as a guarantor of loans made by the banks to SMEs. From guaranteed loans of just 633 million pta. in 1981, Elkargi provided guarantees for 9.8 billion pta. in 1992, with a bad debt rate of a mere 1.45 per cent of all guarantees made (Ikei, 1995).

Chambers, employers' associations, banks, and the mutual guarantee society are the key components of the private economic governance system in the Basque Country. What matters most of course is not the number but the calibre of these institutions and their networking capacity. With notable exceptions—like the Elkargi society and the Elgoibar training system—these institutions have found it difficult to promote associative action among their members or clients. The former head of SPRI, the regional development agency, attributes this state of affairs to 'the deep individualist ethos of Basque entrepreneurs' (Velasco, 1994a), an ethos which contradicts the traditional image of a region which is said to be highly disposed to 'mutual co-operation' in business (Mead, 1993).

In an effort to promote mutual co-operation between the four governments, business, and trade unions, the Basque government created a tripartite governance forum for industrial policy in 1991. Designed as a consensus-building exercise to overcome the divisions among the three key stakeholders of the region, the results of this exercise have been disappointing to date, not least because the nationalist trade union, ELA, prefers company agreements to a broader regional agreement. However, if the Basque Country is to develop a more robust regional renewal strategy, these key stakeholders will have to find more common ground.

CORPORATE RESTRUCTURING: THE SHADOW OF THE PAST

At the time of Franco's death, in 1975, the Basque Country was still enjoying its status as the wealthiest region in Spain. Under the Francoist system of national autarchy, the regional division of labour was such that the Basques specialized in steelmaking, metal manufacturing, and shipbuilding, all of which prospered in the heavily protected Spanish market. The fact that the regional economy was based on a 'mono-culture of metal' is the key to understanding the rapid deindustrialization of the region over the past twenty years (Ikei, 1995).

Whereas most European steel producers were able to restructure in a fairly measured way under EC guidelines, Spain's late entry to the EC meant that the restructuring of its heavy industries was far more sudden and this was nowhere more traumatic than in the Basque Country, the traditional centre of Spanish capital-goods production. What perhaps best symbolized this process of hot-house restructuring in the 1980s was the closure of the huge Euskalduna ship-yard near the centre of Bilbao, the massive rationalization of Altos Hornos de Vizcaya (AHV) outside Bilbao, the biggest private-sector steel producer in Spain, and the heavy cutbacks at Babcock and Wilcox, the heavy engineering company, all of which caused a haemorrhage of employment in the Greater Bilbao area in particular. Less visible, but no less important, were the indirect job losses among the hundreds of smaller supplier firms in the surrounding districts of the region. In short, what we had here was a tightly integrated 'metal-processing district' in the throes of a crisis which had no parallel elsewhere in Spain.

Aided and abetted by the Reconversion Plans which the (central) government launched in 1984, which sought to ease the trauma of restructuring by creating Zones of Urgent Reindustrialization (ZUR) throughout Spain, the Basque Country was awarded ZUR status along the banks of the Nervion river, the worst affected area in the region. Too little, too late, the Nervion ZUR failed to produce the number of new jobs which was originally projected for the area (Velasco, 1989).

But these measures did little to alter the key problems of the Basque economy. Cosseted by protectionism, large swathes of Basque industry faced nothing short of a cultural revolution in having to introduce new technologies, higher quality standards, better management methods, new organizational practices, and a more international outlook to markets all at the same time. And even though R&D expenditure in the Basque Country was and is high in Spanish terms, it still remains extremely low by international standards (SPRI, 1994*a*). Another problem associated with narrow industrial specialization is the fact that the Basque economy is under-represented in services; even though some advanced services have been internalized in the larger firms, the regional economy remains heavily dependent on producer services from other Spanish regions (Ikei, 1995). In fact, the main source of new service employment has come from the rapid growth of public sector functions which have grown in association with the regional government apparatus.

Modernization and specialization have gone hand in hand across most sectors of the Basque economy. In the steel industry, for example, the most successful companies are those which have specialized intelligently and focused on new export markets, a strategy pioneered by the likes of Aristrain in long products and Tubos Reunidos in seamless pipes.

Outside the traditional heavy industries, the most promising sectors have been automotive components and machine tools. In 1991, the automotive-components sector consisted of 156 firms which together employed a total of nearly 28,000 workers. This sector has also evolved into one of the most export-oriented sectors in the Basque economy, with some 85 per cent of firms engaged in export markets (SPRI, 1994*b*). Furthermore, many of these firms are becoming heavily involved in supply-chain linkages with car assemblers around the world and, through this mechanism, they are being exposed to advanced manufacturing practices (Alaez *et al.*, 1996).

But perhaps the most successful industrial sector of the Basque economy is machine tools. With eighty-one companies employing over 5,000 workers in 1991, the Basque machine-tool sector accounts for some 75 per cent of the Spanish machine-tool sector in terms of both number of companies and employment. Basque machine-tool firms are also more technologically advanced than their Spanish counterparts: for example, 47.5 per cent of Basque output was equipped with numerical control in 1989 (up from just 9% in 1980), whereas the Spanish average stood at 40.4 per cent in 1989. One of the most export-oriented sectors in the Basque economy, these machine-tool firms have established a strong presence in sophisticated markets like Germany, their largest export market, where they compete on price. With an average workforce of fifty-five employees, the Basque machine-tool sector is largely composed of SMEs (SPRI, 1994*c*).

What is most distinctive about the Basque machine-tool sector is that, like a classical 'industrial district', it has a spatially concentrated character, with some 75 per cent of the firms based in Elgoibar, Urola, and other districts of the province of Gipuzkoa. As we shall see, a number of these firms are small co-operative enterprises which are linked under the corporate umbrella of the Mondragon Co-operative Corporation. The origins of the 'industrial district' in Elgoibar are to be found in the local needs of Estarta y Ecanarro (EyE), a factory which made sewing-machines under licence from the Singer Company before the Civil War. Having no local supply of parts, EyE took this activity upon itself and, through a gradual process of vertical disintegration, a number of new firms were spun off to produce machine tools which were previously made in house. Under a SPRI-sponsored restructuring plan for the sector in the 1980s, many of these small firms were encouraged to work in groups to collectively enhance their capacity to the point where they could produce flexible manufacturing systems. Here we have a very successful example of associative action between public and private sectors to upgrade the innovative capacity of a key part of the Basque economy (Cooke *et al.*, 1989).

The potential of associative action is nowhere more apparent than in the Mondragon Co-operative Corporation (MCC), as it became known in 1991, probably the most impressive example of collective entrepreneurship in Europe. From its inauspicious origins, in the poor and remote mountain-bound town of Mondragon where the first co-operative was formed in 1956, the group has grown to the point where, in 1995, it had a turnover of nearly $5 billion and a workforce of 26,000, the bulk of which is in the Basque Country. Now the most important business group in the region, and the twelfth largest in Spain, MCC has fired the imagination of people the world over for having combined co-operative status with commercial success. For this reason, most attention has been focused on MCC as an innovative *social* phenomenon, a model which seems to offer a 'third way' between the vagaries of private capitalism and the stifling centralism of state socialism.

Our main interest here, however, is in MCC as a system of innovation which is, by virtue of its social constitution, so territorially embedded that it has few parallels in Western countries. Indeed, some writers claim that this peculiar territorial character, in which capital is to a large degree 'locked' in the region, helps to explain why MCC has been a self-propelling 'territorial innovation complex' (Stohr, 1989). What is it about MCC that has enabled it to perform so much better than the Basque economy in general?

MCC is nowadays a holding company for some a hundred co-operatives which straddle industry, financial services, distribution, as well as a host of other activities, including education, training, social welfare, and housing. At the heart of the MCC system lie three key groups:

- the *Industrial Group*, which accounted for nearly 60 per cent of total MCC employment in 1993, covers a wide array of products, the most important of which are machine tools, domestic appliances, automotive components, and electronic devices. Although employment in this group has fallen gently in recent years, this contrasts with the fact that the regional economy as a whole lost some 50 per cent of its industrial jobs in the two decades to 1994;

- the *Financial Group* revolves around Caja Laboral, which was formed in 1959, and is now one of the largest savings banks in Spain. Charged with the task of securing the financial stability of MCC in general and with funding new business development in particular, Caja Laboral constitutes the financial nerve-centre of the MCC system;
- the *Distribution Group* largely consists of the Eroski group, a supermarket chain which has expanded throughout Spain and into France.

Over and above these three groups is the Corporate Activities group, the strategic centre of the MCC system. Among other things this group includes:

- *Ikerlan*, the Technological Research Centre which was created in 1974 to generate and disseminate advanced technologies throughout the organization. In 1993 Ikerlan had a high grade technical staff of 133 and a total income of 1,026 million pta., a third of which was funded by the regional government to support generic research projects of relevance to the regional economy as a whole;
- *Ideko*, a specialist R&D centre for the machine-tool sector, was created in 1986 in response to the demands of the Debako group of machine-tool co-operatives based at Elgoibar, which felt that the costs of R&D could no longer be met at the level of the individual co-operative;
- *Eskola Politeknikoa*, which was originally created in 1943, includes a number of education and training centres which specialize in engineering, business, and management studies, with over 2,000 students today, half of whom are engaged in engineering studies. The most recent addition to the Eskola is Otalora, a centre which was created in 1985 with two specific aims: to organize advanced management courses and to diffuse co-operative values among MCC members, especially among its managers.

MCC's success cannot be explained simply by reference to its social constitution. A fuller explanation would have to include many other factors, three of which are of decisive importance in our view. First, the progressive creation of key organizational assets—especially the Eskola Politeknikoa, Caja Laboral, and Ikerlan—testifies to the high premium which MCC attached to technical skills, financial autonomy, and R&D, the hallmarks of the innovative firm. These microeconomic factors were reinforced by a supportive macroeconomic environment which afforded total protection to domestic producers under the Francoist system.

Secondly, MCC seems to have struck a judicious balance between central control and local initiative. All the co-operatives are obliged to transfer 10 per cent of their profits to the MCC holding company, 20 per cent in the case of the Caja Laboral banking co-operative. This central fund aims to balance the difference between strong and weak co-operatives (e.g. by transferring workers from the latter to the former when conditions dictate) and to finance new product development. Within this central framework, devolution of responsibility is encouraged in the firm belief that each co-operative is taken to be the best judge of its own product, its own market, and its own rivals. Furthermore, each co-operative is free to decide where it sells its products. There is therefore no obligation to purchase from other co-operatives in the corporation because MCC believes that such in-house rules would spawn a protectionist ethos, with higher costs and lower quality standards.

But this is a regime of relative autonomy *not* total freedom: if a co-operative wanted to produce a product which competed with an existing co-operative, it would be overruled by MCC. In other words, each co-operative is responsible for its own strategic plan but the latter must be approved by MCC. While the criteria for assessing these plans are wider, and more socially conscious, than in conventional business accounting, the relationship between the centre and the parts is not unlike the model to which today's multinationals are aspiring.

The third key factor is organizational learning capacity. The creation of Ikerlan in 1974 and Otalora in 1985 signalled a desire to disseminate technical expertise, management skills, and a *kaizen*-like culture of continuous innovation throughout the organization. Just as the large Japanese firm uses peer-to-peer interaction to promote problem-solving skills throughout the firm, so MCC began to adopt similar methods in the 1980s. The best MCC managers are used to tutor their peers in other co-operatives and, where this internal expertise is lacking, MCC has used external consultants. More recently, Fagor, one of the biggest names within MCC, which buys less than 5 per cent of its components from within the Corporation, is beginning to experiment with internal supply-chain links as a mechanism for inter-organizational learning. Although there is no obligation to buy in house, these larger co-operatives are using a portion of their purchasing budget to tutor suppliers within MCC. Some of the co-operatives in the automotive-components division, for example, are fully abreast of international best practice, evident from the fact that in 1992 MCC was named European Corporation of the Year by General Motors (MCC, 1992).

These factors—finance, skills, R&D, and organizational learning capacity—allied to a social constitution which made the sum so much greater than the parts, help to explain why MCC has proved to be such a durable commercial proposition, certainly more durable than most other firms in the Basque Country. In a severe test of its own adage—that vitality is demonstrated by rebirth and adaptation—the Corporation has witnessed some of the biggest changes in its career since 1990. In organizational terms, by far the biggest change was the transition from local *groups*, like the Elgoibar-based Debako group of machine-tool co-operatives, to product-based *sectors*, a move designed to capture the benefits of organizational integration and economies of scale ahead of the opening of the Single European Market in 1992.

As part of this shift from groups to sectors, a process begun in 1989, a more powerful central administration was formed, in the shape of MCC, to offer a wider array of common services to its associated members. Less visibly, this organizational change also induced a new balance of power in central–local relations, since a measure of authority has been ceded from individual co-operatives to the Group and from the latter to the General Council of MCC. No organization is without its internal tensions, but in MCC's case these tensions take on a particular hue because of its unique socio-spatial character. To conclude this review of MCC, let us examine two particular tensions.

The most widely noted tension is the discrepancy between the democratic structure of the General Assembly (the supreme decision-making body where all members, regardless of status, have just one vote each) and the well-defined hierarchies from shopfloor to central management (Greenwood and Gonzalez Santos, 1991). Unless members feel that they have the opportunity for greater involvement in their day-to-day work, as opposed to the annual General Assembly, this discrepancy could undermine the commitment which is necessary, even from a purely economic perspective, for a *kaizen*-like working culture to take root on the shopfloor. Another dimension of these management hierarchies has an equally long pedigree, namely salary differentials. At the outset, the differential between the highest and lowest-paid members was set at a ratio of 3:1, extended to 6:1 at the 1984 Congress, and which has now reached the stage where the most senior managers are allowed to earn 70 per cent of the comparable salary for a Spanish executive. Although some managers have long complained about being underpaid relative to their capitalist counterparts, very few of them ever leave the Corporation, not least because 'this would entail a loss of civic status in their home town' (Goitia, 1995).

The second tension relates to MCC's deeply embedded territorial character, which again distinguishes it from the more spatially mobile capitalist enterprise. Since it began in Mondragon, where it employs nearly 30 per cent of the town's entire working population, MCC has expanded throughout the Basque Country. In recent years, however, it has established a series of manufacturing and retail operations in and beyond Spain, including components factories in Thailand and Mexico. As a principle, MCC does not extend co-operative status to its activities outside the Basque Country and these external activities are justified within the General Assembly as a necessary evil to strengthen MCC within the region. The growth of activities outside the Basque Country means that MCC is now learning to live with two cultures, co-operative and capitalist, within its organization. This dilemma seems set to become more acute in the future because, in 1995, MCC disclosed plans to tap national and international capital markets on the grounds that it needed more capital than it can generate internally (White, 1995). What some members fear is that, far from protecting the integrity of MCC in its Basque heartland, external expansion will inadvertently unleash pressures which threaten that integrity because capitalist finance houses may be fearful of lending to a 'workers' co-operative'.

TABLE 7.1. Regional distribution of FDI in Spain (%)

Regions	1988	1989	1990	1991	1992	1993	1994
Madrid	46.36	40.61	46.46	39.44	40.15	43.45	34.18
Catalonia	23.69	24.57	29.71	42.96	28.89	29.60	28.78
Andalusia	7.56	12.86	5.43	5.47	5.26	5.92	12.16
Valencia	2.54	2.74	2.13	2.17	1.84	4.60	2.34
The Basque Country	2.32	3.91	2.81	1.04	4.36	2.57	0.75

Source: Ferreiro *et al*. (1995).

External expansion beyond the Basque Country signals a new era for MCC, creating new dilemmas as well as new opportunities, and time alone will tell how well the Corporation handles these dilemmas. However, Father Jose Maria Arizmendiarrieta, the architect of the Mondragon project, always urged a pragmatic approach to the future, saying 'we build the road as we travel' (Whyte and Whyte, 1988). More recently, one of the key figures in MCC reinforced this point, arguing that the Corporation was not cast in aspic, indeed 'practically nothing remotely like what turns out to be necessary now was considered then' (Ormaechea, 1991). Whatever the future holds, MCC will continue to play an enormously important role in the Basque economy. Quite apart from its direct contribution to the regional economy, where it accounts for over 6 per cent of total industrial employment, MCC serves as a reminder of what associative action can achieve for small enterprises working in concert.

If MCC has been a modernizing force for its associated members, the Basque economy generally lacked the modernizing impetus that other Spanish regions have enjoyed from the influx of foreign direct investment. In the years following EC entry, foreign investment accounted for nearly a fifth of total private investment in Spain and this helps to explain the above-average growth of Madrid and Catalonia, the two major beneficiaries of foreign investment. As we can see from Table 7.1, Madrid accounted for 34 per cent of foreign investment in Spain in 1994, Catalonia secured nearly 30 per cent, while the Basque Country received less than 1 per cent of the total.

Furthermore, while foreign investment in Catalonia has helped to diversify the regional economy, geared as it is to sectors with strong and medium growth prospects, foreign investment in the Basque Country is actually concentrated in medium to weak demand sectors, thus compounding the problem of a regional economy which is excessively geared to weak growth sectors (Ferreiro *et al*., 1995). While foreign investment has played an important role in boosting employment and sectoral change in Catalonia and Madrid, this stimulus has been relatively absent in the Basque Country.

Looking back over the post-Franco period, it is evident that no region has fallen further down the regional economic rankings in Spain than the Basque Country. Like most depressed regions, the Basque Country now has an unemployment rate above the national average of 23 per cent, in a country which has the highest unemployment rate in the EU. Unlike other depressed regions, however, average wages in the Basque Country are well above the national average, a sharp contrast to Wales. Above-average wages, coupled with below-average productivity, means that the Basque Country has the highest unit labour costs in Spain (SPRI, 1993). At a time when regions throughout the EU are vigorously competing for international investment, the Basque Country is ill equipped to compete in this race. The combination of political problems (like the perceived threat of terrorism) and unattractive economic features (like high unit labour costs amidst declining industry) helps to explain why foreign investors have recoiled from the region. Because the Basque Country has been unable to tap external capital, the regional authorities have little option other than to harness their own resources: hence the priority accorded to a regional innovation infrastructure.

REGIONAL INNOVATION STRATEGIES: CHINKS OF LIGHT?

Perhaps the most important ingredient of a regional renewal strategy is a collective awareness of the need for one. While this may seem all too obvious, it was not apparent to all sections of political opinion in the Basque Country that the regional economy was actually facing a structural crisis. Wedded to obsolete notions of regional economic supremacy, some members of the Basque government refused to acknowledge the scale of the problem even as late as 1986, when the crisis was still being attributed to exogenous cyclical factors in the international economy or to political factors external to the region, like the Madrid government (del Castillo, 1989). In other words, there was a political refusal to admit that some of the problems were internal to the Basque Country, a stance which did little to promote a better collective awareness of the challenges ahead.

Cyclical or structural, the economic problems were sufficiently acute to demand an urgent response and for its part the first Basque government was keen to utilize the newly devolved powers it had assumed from Madrid. Ever since 1981, therefore, the Basque government has sought to create a regional innovation framework to sustain an endogenous strategy of economic renewal.

With some 20 per cent of regional GDP directly under the control of the public sector, via the budgets of the regional and provincial governments, the Basque Country has far more discretion than most regions to tailor its own innovation strategy. Indeed, as much as 60 per cent of the 7 billion pta. total spent on science and technology in the Basque Country between 1988–93 came from the autonomous administrations, compared to 32 per cent from central government and 4 per cent from the European Union (Lavia et al., 1995). Having the capacity to spend is important, but spending it well is more important. To assess the scope and limits of this innovation strategy, we shall focus on the key elements, namely, SPRI, the technology centres, the technology park, industrial clusters, and the Machine-Tool Institute.

The main thrust of this strategy has been directed at enhancing the position of SMEs, since the problems of the larger firms in the crisis-hit sectors of steel and shipbuilding were directly addressed by central government, which was perhaps just as well because these problems would have overwhelmed the budget of the newly formed regional government. In retrospect, we can say that the regional government's SME-support policy has revolved around three main themes:

- schemes to promote sectoral restructuring and labour adjustment in sectors not covered by central government, consisting of subsidies, soft loans, and public guarantees;
- programmes to foster investment, especially in new product and process technologies;
- provision of a wide array of real services, ranging from traditional services like industrial estates to support for R&D, organizational innovation, and inter-firm collaboration.

The significance of these themes has varied over time: the first was more prominent during the worst of the crisis years in the early 1980s, the second has been a constant priority since 1981, and the third theme has been assuming more importance over time (Ikei, 1995). In all these support schemes the key vehicle for public intervention has been SPRI, the regional development agency of the Basque Country.

SPRI: Rethinking Enterprise-Support Policy

Modelled in part on the Welsh and Scottish Development Agencies, SPRI (*Sociedad Para La Promocion Y Reconversion Industrial*) was created in 1981 to spearhead regional economic renewal in the Basque Country. Formally a semi-public agency governed by private law, some 70 per cent of SPRI's budget is jointly financed by the regional and provincial governments on the one hand and 30 per cent from a consortium of six Basque savings banks on the other. With an annual budget of some £15 million and ninety-one employees, it is a modest-sized development agency by EU standards. SPRI's semi-public status should not obscure the fact that it is a highly politicized organization, with the three top positions being political appointees. Although this might not seem much of a problem in a region which has had a succession of PNV-led governments, political stability is sometimes more apparent than real because control of governmental departments oscillates between the PNV and the Socialists, the PNV's junior coalition partner. This impacts directly on SPRI because the Minister of Industry also happens to be the president of SPRI, hence whenever this portfolio changes party hands there are often new plans, priorities, and personalities for the agency to absorb, which deflects it from the task of regional renewal.

Of course, development agencies the world over have to contend with a conflict between operational autonomy and political expediency, but this tension seems more acute in SPRI's case because of the weak political consensus within the ruling coalition government.

This protean political environment helps to explain why, after 1990, SPRI experienced major changes of function, staff, and priorities, such that it now has five key 'areas' of activity: technology promotion, business infrastructure, financial products, international links, and promotion of new and existing firms. During the 1980s, its key brief was to raise the innovative capacity of SMEs throughout the region but, with the onset of recession in the early 1990s, its political masters imposed a new agenda in which short-term policy objectives, like job creation, became the order of the day. These changes also signalled a shift in the balance of power between SPRI and the Department of Industry, with the result that the latter began to assume more control over the design of regional industrial policy, particularly with respect to industrial clusters, a policy which originated in the Ministry of Industry. Although the Industry Department has the money, and therefore the control, it does not have the skills to design and deliver programmes, nor does it have the credibility that SPRI has accumulated in the corporate community.

It was precisely because of the agency's specialized skills that a new unit— the Technological Strategy Unit—had been created in SPRI in 1989. This had two main objectives: first, to help the Industry Department devise a techno-logical plan to establish new guidelines for public support for innovation and, secondly, to provide information about the technology-transfer needs of key sectors in the Basque economy (Isusi, 1991). As it happens, some of the changes signalled by the industrial clusters policy, like the need to prioritize sectors and technologies, had already been anticipated by SPRI, which had come to the con-clusion that public support was being dissipated because it was not sufficiently focused and, because monitoring and evaluation procedures were weak, the gov-ernment did not know the real effects of its own policies (Zumarraga, 1994).

Another weakness of traditional enterprise-support policy was that it was excessively focused on the individual firm, an approach which 'reinforced the solitude in which most Basque SMEs work and therefore impeded the develop-ment of joint actions amongst firms belonging to the same sector and sharing common interests in different fields, like R&D, Quality etc.' (Ikei, 1995).

After 1990, two radically new directions began to emerge in SPRI's enterprise-support policy. First, SPRI abandoned the previous approach of dispensing aid to individual firms in favour of a regime which supported groups of firms that were prepared to co-operate with one another. Secondly, it introduced much tighter procedures to try to ensure that its financial support had demonstrable effects within the firm, a measure which was long overdue because, in the past, aid was distributed with little or no obligations on the firm concerned (Saez, 1994). This new emphasis on value for money was also applied to other pub-licly sponsored innovation agents, like the technology centres, which were no longer regarded as goals, but as tools. In short, the post-1990 period signalled a shift away from a supply-side innovation policy towards a strategy which stressed the need for better *interaction* between service providers and the users of these services, that is, firms.

Enhancing the absorbtive capacity of SMEs—which is less a function of technology than of management and labour skills on the one hand and organizational capacity on the other—is now one of the main priorities of SPRI's enterprise-support policy. A recent example of this new approach is the RETO programme, which was launched in 1995 as part of SPRI's Plan of Integral Support in Management, which aims to enhance the strategic management capacity of SMEs (SPRI, 1995). Although RETO appears to be well designed, SPRI has had some difficulty getting SMEs to sign up to the programme, which suggests that it may be too exacting for many SMEs. Addressing the demand side of enterprise-support policy is clearly a far more difficult endeavour than building a supply-side infrastructure. Even so, the former is now taking precedence over the latter.

In terms of technological support, SPRI is now targeting four priority technologies—manufacturing technologies, information technologies, new materials, and environmental technology—and this support is being focused on near-market projects in specific industrial clusters. Targeting support and promoting interfirm co-operation are two of the most difficult tasks facing public agencies today and, because SPRI is still on a steep learning curve here, it has begun to benchmark its policies against other development agencies in the EU, a move which is long overdue.

The changes introduced since 1990—like the targeting of support on market-focused technologies in key sectors, the emphasis on monitoring and evaluation, the practice of supporting groups of firms rather than single firms, and so on—signal a new direction in the evolution of SPRI's enterprise-support policy. Given its modest size, SPRI cannot hope to regenerate the regional economy on its own: hence the need to harness the resources of other agents, like the technology centres.

The Basque Network of Technology Centres

Aside from SPRI's innovation-promotion programmes, the bulk of the regional government's science and technology budget is directed towards two ends: to build up R&D capacity within private firms and to nurture the Basque Network of Technology Centres, the key (public) mechanisms for technology transfer in the region. Of the 7 billion pta. spent in public support for science and technology between 1988–93, 59 per cent went directly to firms and 28 per cent went to the technology centres. With Spain's national system of innovation being so weak, and with little to build on in the Basque university system, the regional government had no choice other than to try to enhance the existing stock of technical expertise, much of which lay in the technological centres that had evolved as separate institutions at different times in different places, as we can see from Table 7.2.

TABLE 7.2. A profile of the Basque technology centres

CEIT
Founded: 1982
Staff: 61
Scholarship holders: 70
Turnover: 784 million pta.
Location: San Sebastian
Key activities: Materials engineering, microelectronics, applied mechanics and environmental engineering

GAIKER
Founded: 1985
Staff: 60
Scholarship holders: 23
Turnover: 615 million pta.
Location: Zamudio
Key activities: materials, environmental Recycling, industrial biotechnology

IKERLAN
Founded: 1974
Staff: 132
Scholarship holders: 16
Turnover: 1,250 million pta.
Location: Mondragon
Key activities: control engineering, sensors and machine vision, electronics and communications, CAD/CAM technologies, robotics and automation, renewable energies and production systems

INMASMET
Founded: 1962
Staff: 115
Scholarship holders: 35
Turnover: 1,240 million pta.
Location: San Sebastian
Key activities: aerospace, railway and naval, automation, energy and petrochemistry, paper and packing

LABEIN
Founded: 1955
Staff: 176
Scholarship holders: 31
Turnover: 1,997 million pta.
Location: Bilbao
Key activities: materials and construction, environment, mechanics, information technologies and quality procedures

ROBOTIKER
Founded: 1985
Staff: 90
Scholarship holders: 22
Turnover: 933 million pta.
Location: Zamudio
Key activities: design and engineering applications on CAD/CAM/CAE systems, Shopfloor control systems and ISDN applications

TABLE 7.2. (cont'd)

TEKNIKER
Founded: 1981
Staff: 76
Scholarship holders: 37
Turnover: 956 million pta.
Location: Eibar
Key activities: manufacturing technologies, information and communications,
mechatronics, surface technologies

Source: EITE (1994).

As separate entities with their own agendas, the centres were brought together
in 1987 under the umbrella of EITE, which now functions as an association
which represents the centres for contract-research purposes at local, national,
and international levels. The centres are largely funded through four mechanisms: (1) contract research for private and public sector clients; (2) generic
projects which are mainly funded by the regional and provincial governments
on the one hand and by the European Commission on the other; (3) central
government research projects; and (4) fee income from associated firms. While
the details may vary, the funding sources do not differ significantly from one
centre to another. In 1993, for example, 58 per cent of Labein's budget was
funded from contract-research projects, 26 per cent from generic projects for
the regional and provincial governments, with the remainder coming from a combination of central government, the EU, and associated firms (Arribas, 1994).

Since 1990, the centres have been undergoing something of a cultural revolution: like SPRI, they have come under pressure from the regional government
to become more market-focused, more specialized to reduce duplication, more
commercial in their procedures, and, above all, more sensitive to the needs of
SMEs in the region (Cooke *et al.*, 1991). Research managers in the centres
freely concede that their technical staff prefer to work with organizations which
already have a research culture, which invariably means larger firms or other
research centres. In Robotiker, for example, staff were inclined to work with
the same firms because they had 'built up a common code of joint-working
based on trust and familiarity' (Hormaeche, 1995).

The crux of the problem is that the technology centres have a dual vocation.
On the one hand, they are expected to engage in generic research projects which
enable them to stay abreast of leading-edge technology. On the other hand, they
are expected to act as market-focused technology-transfer agencies for SMEs
in the Basque Country. If they veer too far towards generic projects, they lose
touch with the more prosaic needs of SMEs in the region; if they become too
market focused, they may fall behind the state of the art in their technical fields.
This is the paradox of the Basque technology centres (Prospektiker, 1994).

Because generic and applied projects are equally important, if for different
reasons, the centres are learning to live with the paradox of their dual vocation.

As a key source of funds, the regional government is in a strong position to influence the activities of the centres and it has used this mechanism in two important ways: first, to encourage a better division of labour between the centres, since EITE was too powerless to perform this task and, secondly, to make the centres more conscious of their responsibilites to the regional economy.

In the past, the menu of generic research projects to be funded by the regional government was largely determined by the centres themselves, partly because the imbalance of knowledge was such that civil servants were not able to second-guess the technologists. More recently, however, the regional government has used the firms in its industrial clusters programme to help it decide which projects in the centres it should finance from the public purse. Although this helps to prevent the centres from unilaterally determining the research agenda, it has caused its own problems because the centres feel that the firms are overly disposed towards near-market rather than generic projects.

For their part, the centres are trying to reduce the problems of their dual vocation by forming technology-transfer units to scan for applications and, perhaps more importantly, by trying to ensure that there is no systemic division of labour between staff who work on generic projects and staff who work on more market-focused technology-transfer projects (Hormaeche, 1995).

Another way to ensure that the centres stay in touch with the needs of the regional economy, without losing touch with the state of the art, is for them to extend their network of associated companies. Each centre currently has between thirty to sixty associated companies with which it has a close working relationship, each of which pays a nominal fee to belong to the centre. These networks could be extended to include more SMEs and the latter could benefit from being exposed to the research culture of the existing corporate membership.

For all the problems associated with the technology centres, this network constitutes a major resource for the Basque Country. With a budget of some 7,700 million pta. and over 900 researchers, the EITE network is now the most developed technology-transfer system in Spain. Having built up a strong capacity in a dozen key technologies, the centres have clearly fulfilled the *technical* side of their dual vocation. But the real test will be whether they are equal to the task of meeting the *commercial* side of this vocation, where their success will depend not just on their own activities but, crucially, on the absorptive capacity of SMEs in the region (Lopez Egana, 1995).

The Technology Park of the Basque Country

Regions throughout the world have felt it necessary to build science parks to try to exploit the potential synergies between advanced technology firms and the basic science base in their universities and technical institutes. The Basque Country is no exception to this trend. In 1989, a technology park was formally opened in Zamudio, a small town in the province of Vizcaya some 12 kilometres north-west of Bilbao. Set in 320 acres of beautifully landscaped environment, now *de rigueur* for science park settings the world over, this clean and tranquil rural location could not be further removed from the polluted and bustling atmosphere of metropolitan Bilbao. Over 20,000 million pta. have been invested in the Zamudio site since the Park Management Corporation (*Sociedad Gestora del Parque*) was formed in 1985. Through SPRI, the regional government holds a 75 per cent stake in the Corporation, the provincial government of Vizcaya holds another 24 per cent, and the town council of Zamudio has the third, very miniscule stake.

The very construction of the park was a conscious attempt to try to set new standards in the Basque Country for design, materials, architecture, and land-use planning, all of which have been fully realized at Zamudio. But the key aim of the park is to foster a new innovation culture in the Basque Country based on new forms of collaboration between firms, universities, and the technology centres, three of which—Robotiker, Gaiker, and Labein—have facilities on the park.

The Park Management Corporation gives priority to private and public sector organizations which are engaged in their own R&D or the provision of specialist services to advanced technology industry. Potential occupants are therefore judged on their existing activities and their potential for collaborating with local researchers in the universities and the technology centres. The Corporation offers its tenants a wide array of support services, ranging from IT support to legal, financial, and marketing advice, all of which are important to new and small firms in particular.

Having opened in 1989, the park was home to forty firms in 1995 with a total workforce of 1,400, and 90 per cent of these jobs are held by local people. The Corporation claims that only 20 per cent of the Park's firms were not collaborating with either the universities or the technology centres, but this figure seems to be somewhat low. A more independent study has suggested that the number of non-collaborating firms might be much higher, citing evidence from the firms themselves to the effect that the technology centres were considered too advanced, while the universities and the business community were said to be living in separate worlds (Hanratty, 1995). If this is the case, then the technology park looks like having a much more limited impact than the regional government seems to expect. Besides, with a population of just forty firms, the park cannot hope to be more than an ambassador for the collaborative culture which it seeks to foster throughout the region, a goal which very much depends on the complementary actions of universities, technology centres, and, above all, the firms themselves.

Zamudio is no longer the only site of the Basque Technology Park, even though this was the regional government's original plan, as two other sites have since been opened, at San Sebastian in the province of Gipuzkoa and Vitoria in the province of Alava. The origins of these parks lie *not* in technology policy but in the provincialist politics of the Basque Country, where each province insists on having its own facilities. This provincial culture makes it that much more difficult for the regional government to focus resources on locations where they can make the biggest impact.

As it is, the regional government is obliged to present the Basque Technology Park as a single and coherent entity with a campus in each province! The only common thread running through these three parks is that SPRI is the majority shareholder in each one, and this offers some potential for getting the parks to co-ordinate their activities.

Innovating through Clusters?

As we saw in Chapter 3, the concept of industrial clusters was popularized by the work of Michael Porter to such an extent that a great many regions around the world have now embraced this concept to justify their policies for pro- moting inter-firm collaboration. The Basque Country was one of the first regions to take up the cluster concept in a serious way, so much so that it is now a central feature of the regional government's industrial policy repertoire. The origins of the Basque cluster policy tell us much about how rapidly new con- cepts (or fads) travel across borders today, especially when they are perceived to carry the imprimatur of a celebrated business expert.

The cluster concept was actually introduced into the Basque Country in 1990, largely because the new Minister of Industry, a member of the PNV, was per- sonally attracted to it. In fact, he had invited MPs to commission a study of the cluster concept before he entered the new regional government in 1990, when he was still an official of the Bilbao Stock Exchange. Significantly perhaps, the study was eventually commissioned from Monitor, the private consultancy firm of Michael Porter, which is based in Boston.

Between 1990–1, Monitor's consultants conducted a series of bilateral inter- views with key stakeholders throughout the Basque Country, especially with leading firms, technology centres, SPRI, and regional government departments. Being unfamiliar with the region, these US consultants were starting from a low base, indeed a zero-knowledge base. Steered by the Department of Industry, which begun to assume more direct control of economic promotion after the socialists lost the industry portfolio in 1990, the Monitor team conducted their inquiry in a rather secretive fashion. According to one local expert, 'they made no attempt to generate a regional consensus over the cluster concept, so the most important part of the exercise, the *process*, was forgotten' (del Castillo, 1994).

Aided and abetted by Monitor, the regional government identified a number of clusters which were to receive priority treatment and cluster-building initiat- ives begun in earnest in 1992. The official definition of a cluster in the Basque context is 'a group of companies, interrelated and situated in a limited geo- graphic zone, which develop their activities in common or complementary areas and count on the support of service companies, forming between them an inter- active system' (Bilbao, 1995). In selecting the clusters, the main criteria are the importance of a sector to the Basque economy and its strategic inter-relationship

with other sectors. On the basis of these criteria, nine clusters have been identified. These clusters range from clearly defined sectors like steel, machine tools,
automotive components, and home appliances to more amorphous sectors like
the Port of Bilbao, tourism, and the environment, where the core activities are
far from clear.

The cluster programme tries to orchestrate the activities of the key actors,
especially core companies, service providers (like vocational training schools,
technology centres), and the regional government. The industrial clusters are
obliged to follow a common methodology which involves three main phases:
benchmarking the firms to identify their strengths and weaknesses, developing
an action plan and implementing the plan under the auspices of a cluster group,
which is composed of leading figures from the cluster.

By common consent, the cluster-building process is most advanced in machine
tools and automotive components, the two sectors where, unlike the others,
there is a genuine critical mass of firms (Gobierno Vasco, 1994*a*; 1994*b*). But
critical mass does not spell a cluster, which involves a disposition to collaborate to achieve mutually beneficial ends. While the cluster-building process
has indeed helped to induce new forms of collaboration between public and
private actors in these two sectors, it is still too early to judge the full effects
of these efforts.

Even so, we can already say that the biggest problems to date have emerged
in the field of inter-firm collaboration. For example, the plan for the machine-
tool cluster envisaged the formation of six large groups, which would cover
over 60 per cent of machine tool output in the Basque Country. Yet this action
has failed to materialize, not least because the firms found it difficult to reach
agreement. Critics of the cluster policy have suggested that the firms' interest
in collaboration was born of the recession of the early 1990s, when they were
eager to secure financial grants from the regional government, and that this
interest waned with the first signs of recovery in 1994/5.

The former managing director of SPRI, for example, has argued that there
are major flaws with the cluster policy. Among other things, he claims that the
regional government sees the cluster concept as a multi-sectoral panacea, when
in reality only a limited number of sectors have the capacity to exploit this
strategic concept. This has been compounded by a lack of discretion in the
selection of companies, such that both viable and non-viable companies have
been included, with the result that there are too many companies participating
in the exercise. In other words the cluster policy is criticized for being applied
to too many sectors, for dispensing financial grants to firms with a dubious
future, and, more generally, for extending the tradition of public sector 'van-
ity' in which the regional government feels obliged to take the lead in trying
to resolve industrial problems on behalf of the firms, thereby increasing their
dependence on the public sector (Velasco, 1994*b*).

If this is the case, then the cluster policy could be dismissed as a hugely
expensive mistake: although it is difficult to put an exact cost on it, the cluster

policy is part of a much larger technology plan, to which $135 million was committed between 1993–6. But this might be too harsh a judgement because, whatever its limitations, the exercise has proved to be a valuable learning process for all concerned, a process which has shed new light on the inter-dependencies in the Basque economy. The lesson the regional government should perhaps draw from this exercise is *not* that its policy was wholly wrong, but that clusters cannot be induced through political action alone, that not every sector lends itself to a cluster strategy, and that collaboration is not an end in itself. In other words, there must be a perceived need to collaborate on the part of the firms, otherwise cluster-building becomes a very expensive fig-leaf for a crude subsidy regime.

The Machine-Tool Institute: A Model of Associative Action

If collaboration between firms is proving problematical in the context of clusters, the Machine-Tool Institute has proved to be an exemplar of what associational action can achieve when it is predicated on a perceived need. Created in 1991, the Institute was a collaborative venture between the regional government, the provincial government of Gipuzkoa, and the town council of Elgoibar on the one hand and AFM, the Spanish Machine-Tool Association, and ADEGI, the Employers' Association of Gipuzkoa on the other. With its base in Elgoibar, some 55 kilometres from Bilbao, the Institute is located in the very heart of the machine-tool district.

Given the weakness of the vocational education and training (VET) system in Spain, the AFM was concerned that Spanish machine-tool firms needed a better system of skills provision if they were to remain competitive in the Single European Market. ADEGI, too, was painfully aware of the fact that its mem-bers could not rely on the national VET system. Unlike the province of Bizkaya, where most of the larger Basque firms are based, firms which tend to be less dependent on the provincial employers' association, the structure of industry in Gipuzkoa province is much more oriented to SMEs. Because these SMEs have been more actively engaged in their association, ADEGI is today the most proactive of the three provincial employers' associations in the region.

The fact that they were closely attuned to their member firms meant that the AFM and ADEGI were far better placed than the government to design a train-ing programme which resonated with the needs of these firms. Securing the sup-port of the regional government was necessary not just to enhance the Institute's budget, initially set at 850 million pta. per annum, but more importantly to gain official recognition for the courses. By involving the education and labour departments of the regional government, the Institute won the right to design and deliver professional courses for both initial and further training in the machine-tool sector.

Significantly, the Institute takes students from all over Spain and currently it has 200 full-time and a further 500 part-time students on a wide array of courses, ranging from sophisticated apprenticeships in advanced machine-tool technology to courses which combine technology, languages, and business administration skills. By combining practical hands-on training with theoretical knowledge, the Institute has introduced some of the thinking behind the German 'dual system' into Spain, which has always suffered from too little interaction between vocational training schools and the corporate sector. By ensuring that professional training is not just a matter for the schoolroom, but is rather something which the firms should engage with directly, the Institute has become a reference point for best-practice training provision—not just in the Basque Country but in Spain itself. The integration of practical and theoretical knowledge is personified by the head of the Institute, Alberto Ortueta, who is also the director of the AFM, the Spanish Machine-Tool Association.

But the Institute is far more than a training centre. By offering a wide range of services, it acts as a sophisticated information service centre for the machine-tool industry in and beyond the Basque Country (Instituto de Maquina-Herramienta, 1992).

In the five years since its inception, the Machine-Tool Institute at Elgoibar has become a beacon of best practice in the field of professional training. Its success owes much to the fact that it is a creative partnership between private sector associations and the three tiers of government in the region. Most important of all, perhaps, is that the services are sponsored, not by civil servants who are remote from the industry and therefore lack credibility, but by bodies which are deeply rooted in the fabric of the industry (AFM) and the province (ADEGI), bodies which command the respect of the firms.

In contrast to the cluster policy, which tries to promote direct collaboration between firms in areas such as product strategies, professional training is an area which is far less threatening to the independence of the firms, and here they can collaborate indirectly with a third party, the Institute, acting as a neutral broker. Furthermore, the firms themselves are acutely conscious of the need for better initial and further training provision. Hence the Institute fulfils a commonly perceived need, which again is not so apparent with the cluster policy.

CONCLUSIONS

We began this chapter by posing two questions concerning the scope and limits of the regional state and the potential of the new associational strategies. As to the first question, the Basque Country is a salutory reminder that, of itself, regional government is not a panacea for economic regeneration. Arguably, there is no region in the EU which enjoys more political autonomy than the Basque Country, where the provinces have unique tax-raising powers. However, this political capacity is not matched by an equally robust political consensus hence the potential of the regional state apparatus has been compromised in practice by ideological conflicts between socialists and nationalists on the one hand and between rival nationalist parties on the other. Arresting economic decline would be demanding enough with political consensus; without it the task becomes that much more difficult.

Having said that, it would be wrong to conclude that the regional state, which is not yet 20 years old, has been a failure. Quite apart from its role in restoring democracy and giving voice to a distinctive cultural identity, the regional state has been the most active agent behind the construction of a regional innovation infrastructure in the Basque Country. Indeed, it is difficult to imagine that SPRI, the technology centres, or the technology park would be what they are today were it not for the support and encouragement of the regional government. The point is that, given the problems of a mature economy that was late to modernize, these things are simply not enough.

A regional innovation infrastructure is important, but what is even more important is the capacity to utilize it and the capacity to collaborate to achieve mutually beneficial ends, that is, the associational capacity of the region. Clearly, the Basques are alive to the possibilities of associational action, and this is being explored by both firms and public agencies. The most successful example of associational action is the Mondragon Co-operative Corporation, the largest business group in the Basque Country. One of the paradoxes here is that, as it expands, MCC is outgrowing its regional base, so much so that corporate success may not be so congruent with regional success in the future. Even so, MCC's distinctive social constitution means that it is more embedded in, and therefore more committed to, its region than a conventional capitalist firm.

MCC aside, associational strategies have met with mixed results. In most of the sectors targeted by the regional government's cluster strategy, the results to date have been disappointing to say the least, proof perhaps that clusters cannot be created by political injunctions or through mere physical proximity. On the contrary, effective clusters are the result of a self-selection process on the part of firms which see advantages in exploiting their interdependencies for mutual benefit, a process which can be encouraged but not ordained by public agencies (Rosenfeld, 1995).

The fact that firms have not seen sufficient advantage in the cluster concept is the main reason why the strategy has yielded such poor results. The Machine-Tool Institute, in contrast, has been remarkably successful, not least because it resonated with the perceived needs of the firms and its services were designed and delivered in a more organic fashion, which underlines the significance of self-regulated forms of enterprise support.

These lessons will need to be learned if the regional government wants to become a more effective economic animateur. A more mature political strategy will also be necessary because SPRI, the key public development agency, has become highly politicized, to the point where a new regional government seems to entail new management at SPRI. Constant turnover of staff means that SPRI loses its institutional memory every so often, which makes it that much more difficult for it to build durable, high-trust relations with the region's firms. If the Basque Country is to develop a more effective regional development strategy one of the most important requirements is institutional innovation within the sphere of regional government itself, something that is likely to happen only when the Basques have secured greater political consensus.

8

Evolutionary Processes and Reg

In this book our principal concern has been to offer an analysis economic evolution and the role of co-operation as a governance me and policy mediator in that process. Little research has yet been conducted regional evolution itself so this marks something of a fork in the road of region development thinking and associated empirical study. Of fundamental import-ance to the analysis of economic evolution in general is research on processes of innovation. Indeed, innovation studies form the leading edge of research conducted from an evolutionary economics perspective following on from the path-breaking work of Nelson and Winter (1982). In an information-saturated society, *learning* becomes a pervasive feature of the organizational landscape and the individual lifetime. Interactive learning is the process that best describes the present state of industrial and institutional innovation. We have stressed the centrality of both kinds of innovation at many points in the preceding chapters.

However, thus far the policy implications of our mode of analysis, privileging as it does ideas of indeterminacy, alternative developmental pathways, evolv-ing economies and institutions, interactive learning and innovation, networks and co-operative associationism, have rather been left to be inferred. Clearly, in the accounts we have provided of the factory as laboratory or the region as a nexus of learning processes and, particularly, the accounts of the evolution of regional industrial and institutional change, we have pointed to ways in which successful policies have been prosecuted.

We have also pointed to the increasing need for vigilance in a world where information is communicated instantly and yesterday's new trick becomes tomor-row's old news. Hence, when we attempt to tease out the policy lessons of our analysis in the second part of this chapter these will not be instant policy recipes of the magic-bullet variety. Rather, they will be reflections on the processes and elements of an institutional policy architecture and modes of policy evolu-tion in a more heterarchical, less hierarchical institutional world of policy.

We shall, for example, argue for the continuance and significant enhancement of the state at regional level. Unlike associationists who appear to argue for a 'thin' state (Hirst, 1994) and those who see virtue in the maintenance of a 'thick' state (Amin, 1996), we will argue for a regional state that may evolve towards thinness for some policy areas as it evolves towards thickness for others. This is predicated on our emphasis on divergent pathways of development and rooted in the notion of intelligent governance which can be expressed in the idea of 'letting go' competences that are better administered elsewhere. It is also

other levels of govern-
some but execrated by
1991 and Jessop, 1993).
its 'national champion'
the French government's
1981, the state's economic
rise of on the one hand,
(World Trade Organiza-
omic institutions. But new
available space and time.
nic 'sovereignty' but maybe
ioethics, and environmental

ere is a strong, leading role
ng the many enterprise sup-
ate, associational interests in
onomic evolution has led to
regional econo͟ ͟ed by a rich institutional and
associational base and capable of compε͟ͳͷ ccessfully on the international
stage, there is less need for a strong, interventionary state in economic terms.
But there may be a case for strong intervention in terms, for example, of environmental policies. It is a question of priorities, capacities, and competence.

In what follows we shall attempt to tie together the master themes of the
book in respect of evolutionary economic theorization, the centrality of innovation and interactive learning to industrial and institutional creativity, the importance in a globalizing economic context of decentralized industrial and other
public policies to regions, and the importance of regions as economic bases for
firms that are increasingly disposed towards agglomeration, externalization, and
specialization. This will be a prelude to our conclusions on the policy implications of this analysis, along the lines adumbrated above.

THE EVOLUTIONARY PERSPECTIVE ON REGIONAL ECONOMIC DEVELOPMENT

Evolutionary economics has four grandparents: Schumpeter, Veblen, Marx, and
Hayek (Witt, 1991). Clearly, we don't have space to elaborate that statement
here but we can supply brief justification for the assertion and draw out the
theoretical implications that have guided our analysis thus far. In doing this we
shall also draw attention to some interesting, but ultimately vitiated insights
coming from so-called 'new growth theory', especially elements of the work
of Krugman (1991; 1995), which add to the confidence we have in the evolutionary perspective for the purposes we set ourselves. These were, it will be
recalled, to attempt to understand the evolutionary origins of diverse regional

economic development pathways, and the role of innovation and learning in industry and institutions as motivators of the evolutionary processes observed.

Each of the grandparents mentioned is associated with a school of intellectual thought and in many ways it is to the contemporary interpreters to whom attention is best diverted. Probably the neo-Schumpeterian school has been the most prolific, closely followed by the neo-institutional heirs to Veblen with respect to their contribution to evolutionary economic theory. While the neo-Marxian school has probably been intellectually most influential, its policy relevance seems to be in deep decline. Conversely, though there has perhaps been least written and least influence intellectually from the Austrian school with whom Hayek is associated, its policy influence has been practically hegemonic for two decades from the mid-1970s. As we are interested here in their contribution to evolutionary economic theory, it is to the neo-Schumpeterians and institutionalists that we shall devote greater attention though certainly not ignoring the others.

Schumpeterian and Neo-Schumpeterian Perspectives

Schumpeter's great insight, which he ascribed to reading Marx (Schumpeter, 1942/1975), was that capitalism is not characterized by a tendency towards equilibrium but rather the opposite. He saw its chief characteristic to be constant movement and change with periods of evolutionary, incremental development punctuated by 'gales of creative destruction' caused by innovations. The latter he saw in his early years as the product of the genius of heroic entrepreneurs who, following a period of struggle to get their innovation to market, would habitually find they had released a burst of growth as imitators and adaptors 'swarmed' to take advantage of the market opportunity that the work of the originator had opened up. Where innovations were radical and clustered in time they were largely responsible for business cycles. Later, Schumpeter came to see the R&D engineers of large corporations as having usurped the entrepreneurial role with the rise of oligopolistic companies.

As well as influencing in a major way the theory of 'growth poles' pioneered by Perroux (1950), which became a mainstay of regional economic development planning in the 1960s, Schumpeter's theoretical work on innovation has been of primary importance to the advances made by neo-Schumpeterians such as Freeman, Nelson, Lundvall, and Rosenberg in innovation theory. Neoclassical economics has neglected technological change of the endogenous variety, claiming that it was to be best understood as an exogenous input acquired as needed from market purchase. It was only with the work of Solow (1957), a key progenitor of new neoclassical growth theory, that technology began to be examined as an important factor in productivity growth in its own right. When Arrow's (1962) theory of 'learning-by-doing' was combined with Lucas's (1988) work concerning the impact of technological 'learning-by-doing' upon the contribution of human capital to productivity growth, neoclassical economists realized

that the so-called 'Solow residual' explained as much as 80–90 per cent of productivity growth in advanced industrial economies as arising from the effects of
innovation. This, of course, was a massive endorsement of Schumpeterian insights
(Freeman, 1994*b*). Latterly, Romer (1990) has completed the theorems that
demonstrate the centrality of technological change to productivity growth based
on *increasing* returns to scale and *imperfect* competition, hitherto somewhat
heretical notions to neoclassicals.

Yet, as Freeman (1994*b*) notes, the neoclassical approach still retains unrealistic assumptions and measurement problems. Instead of innovation they focus
on technology and thus take little account of organizational innovation. Nor can
they explain the interactions between changes in institutional norms, product or
process innovation, and variations in the decision to invest (e.g. European banks'
risk-aversion to innovation as compared to American risk-accommodating
attitudes). Among the major advances made in neo-Schumpeterian innovation
theory and research are:

- discovery of the major contribution to the economic performance of firms
  made by *incremental* innovations not just *radical* ones;
- recognition of the importance to productivity growth of transmission of
  fundamental *scientific* findings into firms by new recruits from universities
  or research institutes;
- understanding of the centrality to successful firm innovation of social interaction through *networks* involving diverse innovation actors;
- realization of the fundamental role played by innovation *users* in the
  development of successful innovation and associated firm performance
  improvements;
- correction of the misperception in government, industry, and academia that
  innovation is a linear process, and successful promotion of the new understanding that it is a process based on systemic *interaction* among diverse
  innovators (Freeman, 1994*a*).

Each of these advances is linked by the leitmotiv of associative, co-operative,
learning-based creativity occurring through exchange amongst social interlocutors
rather than by single, heroic entrepreneurs. To that extent neo-Schumpeterian
work marks a significant advance in interpreting Schumpeter. For, as Freeman
(1994*b*) suggests, what is now clear is that Schumpeter had produced the outline elements of a theory of *entrepreneurship* rather than a theory of innovation. It is the latter to which many neo-Schumpeterians have successfully
contributed from the 1970s onward.

Veblen and the Institutionalists

Thorstein Veblen once famously asked: 'Why is economics not an evolutionary
science?' (Veblen, 1919; Hodgson, 1993). The problem as he and others saw it
was that, following Marshall and the marginalists, economics had been colonized

by the mechanical metaphor of static equilibrium, exogenous impulses for change, and a desiccated notion of humanity as 'rational economic man'. This was in spite of Marshall's own desire that the biological sciences should be the ultimate inspiration for economic imagery, but at the time mathematization in mechanics was superior to that in biology, so the former prevailed. Whether or not any analogy is necessary in a mature science is a moot question, though it is arguable that the concept and word 'evolution' predates that of 'biology' and that the latter has also colonized the former to an unhealthy degree. In any case Veblen rejected the imagery of *homo oeconomicus* and sought to develop an institutional perspective in which inertia and habit punctuated by the creativity of idle curiosity better captured individual and firm action. Veblen adopted the view that history was opaque, even absurd, and that there was no overwhelming trend or tendency towards a higher purpose in events. Alternatively, and extremely importantly for the future of economic development theory, Veblen invented the concept of '*cumulative causation*', later taken up by Young (1928), Myrdal (1957), and Kaldor (1972) with considerable effect. Hodgson (1996) quotes Veblen on this as follows: 'an evolutionary economics must be a theory of a process of cultural growth as determined by the economic interest, a theory of a cumulative sequence of economic institutions stated in terms of the process itself' (Veblen, 1919: 77). Thus Veblen sought a theory of transformation and change, as did Schumpeter and Marx, not a theory of stasis and equilibrium.

After a lengthy period of relative quiescence, except for contributions such as those of Commons (1934), who elaborated further the concept of diverse pathways to economic growth and development being institutionally determined, it is perhaps the work of 1995 Nobel Prize winner Douglass North (1993) that best characterizes the institutional economic position and its appropriateness to some of the key issues we have posed in this book thus far. North emphasizes *trust*, *co-operation*, and *institutions* in his analysis. For him, institutions are equated with rules and behavioural norms, including the manner in which they are enforced, together comprising structured human action. Two kinds of enforcement structure actions: *conventions* which help us manage day-to-day co-ordination, like being a 'trustworthy person'; and *rules of the game* which constrain choice in transactions (e.g. anti-trust legislation). So, institutions shape the economic landscape of incentive and opportunity by defining allowable practice and they create the setting in which *organizations* are embedded. The point of institutions is to minimize *transactions* costs which, North holds, accounted for 45 per cent of US GDP in 1970. High-trust institutional frameworks are thus economically efficient, as is co-operation amongst profit-seeking individuals who North (1993), citing game-theory experiments, says usually prefer co-operation when they engage in repeat plays amongst small numbers of individuals who share a high level of information regarding past performance. This is supported too by the work of Axelrod (1984) and Andersen (1994) who show prisoner's and trader's dilemmas being most simply and regularly resolved by the making of an altruistic first move followed by mimicking the opponent's every subsequent move. The winning game that most simply achieves this was developed by Anatol Rapoport and is known as 'Tit-for-Tat'.

Lastly, there is an interesting school of radical institutionalists who eschew both neoclassical growth theory, and, more tellingly, Williamsonian (1985) neo-institutional transactions costs theory which is dismissed as 'a narrow field of game theory' (Dugger, 1989). This critique is complemented by that of Granovetter (1985) who referred to it as reminiscent of structural-functional sociological theory of the 1940s where 'whatever organization form is most efficient will be the one observed' (Granovetter, 1985: 503). This also, argues Granovetter, under-mines Williamson's use of the concept 'bounded rationality' which conflates satisficing behaviour with optimization (Simon, 1955). Williamson's response is that bounded rationality does not imply satisficing behaviour (which explodes Simon's original formulation) and he accepts that his work is functionalist, a kind of 'explanation' that says 'worms exist so birds can eat them'. Dugger and the Texas school of radical institutionalists will have none of this, which is dismissed as 'ersatz institutionalism'.

Rather, true to the Veblenian origins of the perspective they adopt, their stress is on the study of economic development as a *cumulative process* capable of leading down as well as up the evolutionary curve. Their programme involves seeking to disclose the social *irrationality* in which dominant interests mas-querade as general. Hence they are disposed to illuminate the ways in which economic institutions gain legitimacy via the exercise of social *power* and status, and to influence the 'absurdity' of indeterminate evolutionary economic pro-cesses through egalitarian policy instruments formed in inclusive and democratic ways. Apart from their preference for a strong, 'thick' state, particularly in accomplished economies, to 'replace the market with economic planning', which risks killing the innovatory goose on which even neoclassicals admit so much growth now depends, there is rich stimulus for the institutionalist contribution to evolutionary thinking from radical institutional analysis.

Marx and Hayek

Yoking these two economic thinkers together for their contribution to evolu-tionary theorization may seem perverse but their polarities are linked by an ulti-mately vitiating reductionism. Marx, of course, anticipated Schumpeter in much of his thought about the turbulent, protean nature of capitalist development. But great though many of Marx's insights into the nature of capitalist exploitation were, his scheme had no place for the analysis of individual creativity, entre-preneurial or innovatory. The master category of Marxian analysis is class, and wealth arises from class exploitation. Development and change thus occur when the forces and relations of production in one mode or combination come into contact with those from a less developed mode of production. Interesting and fruitful as that notion of contact between institutionally diverse combina-tions of social and technical forces can be, and Veblen and others hinted at its potential analytical richness, critics such as Hodgson (1996) identify precisely the generality of Marx's perspective as its weak point since it is incapable of differentiating diverse evolutionary developmental pathways, something we have shown to be absolutely necessary to the understanding of regional economic development.

Two other weaknesses exist in the Marxian view from the evolutionary perspective. First, there is the pervasiveness, in Marxian analysis of capitalist society, of capitalist social relations. Everything is steeped in capitalist relations of exploitation and competition, leaving no room for the estimation of co-operation such as that found in families, and between cultural or religious organizations. For Marx, capitalist society is a trust-free zone and we feel that to be, theoretically and empirically, an untenable position. Secondly, the stage-theory of development in Marx's historiography seems to us unduly mechanistic and teleological, a feat that few minds could have brought off, but one, sadly, that obfuscates more than it clarifies.

Hayek and the Austrian School of Economics also have an abstract, universal principle sustaining their economic theory but it is not class exploitation or capital but the market and the free individual. The principal reason why evolutionists do not give short shrift to this reductionist thesis, with its view of human motivation as solely profit-motivated and of markets as the main institutional imperative for spontaneous social order, is its sense of economic development as a creative, undetermined, and unpredictable, cumulative process of the interplay of individual, albeit opportunistic, actions. To the extent that institutions evolve out of this negotiated order they do so as conventions which take on the form of routines, like the emergence of money from the norms of the barter economy. It is more reliable, portable, and convenient and thus it endures as long as it eases the functioning of the market. Such institutions as the state, however, are seen as 'impurities' despite the evidence (e.g. Polanyi, 1944) that without them, markets would be self-devouring.

Thus we come to the point at which the key elements of the evolutionary economic perspective can be summarized. Running through the four schools of thought that comprise it, and emphasizing the specific interest of this book in the regional dimension of economic change, are the following key features (see, for a more generic itemization, Andersen, 1994):

- the objects of interest are *processes* of change that are determinate, cumulative, and pursue diverse economic development pathways;
- such processes are typified by *disequilibrium* situations in the various markets and institutions that comprise economies. Change is cumulative and path-dependent;
- because individuals and organizations have imperfect information, the more radical the change they confront the more they seek solutions in local *agglomerations*;
- processes of *innovation*, radical and incremental, and imitation are of fundamental importance to processes of economic evolution;

- *institutions* in the sense of conventions, norms, rules, and routines include those which embed co-operative, associational practices that enhance efficiency through egalitarian practices;
- economic change is effected in large part by social processes of interactive industrial and institutional *learning*, sometimes involving the organizational form of networks and/or systems;
- the foundations for evolutionary theorising are resolutely *non-mechanical* and, preferably, non-biological in origin, the ultimate aim being the construction of non-analogous theory.

These represent the basic building-blocks for an evolutionary theorization of regional economic development, towards which end this book represents a preliminary step. However, before passing to a reprise of our emphasis upon *innovation*, we wish to pay a brief visit to the opposition camp of the so-called 'new neoclassicals', particularly Krugman whose recent forays bring new growth theory closer to a possible and potentially powerful *rapprochement* with evolutionary economics (Krugman, 1991; 1995; 1996).

Krugman's Theory of Monopolistic Development

The particular interest of Krugman's work for this book is his desire to take the spatial dimension of economic theorization very seriously, unlike his recent neoclassical ancestors. More to the point, he focuses on regional disequilibrium, deploying Marshallian and Veblenian concepts of externalities and cumulative causation to understand industrial location and path dependence *inter alia*. Krugman starts his analysis with international trade, and explains the burgeoning phenomenon of inter-industry trade *specialization* among developed economies in terms of increasing returns to scale and imperfect competition. Once firms find a niche, cumulative causation leads to lock-in and path-dependence because of increasing returns. This is institutionally supported by neo-mercantilist states at all levels, including the regional.

Agglomerations form for similar reasons, imperfect knowledge and increasing returns from specialization making local optimization imperative. Innovative agglomerations gain from cumulative backwash effects and the development of complementary backward and forward linkages. Accordingly, agglomerations, most of which take the form of cities, gain competitive advantage because they are monopolies. This is a consequence of their superiority in intra-industry trade in different, but tradable specializations and divergent development paths. Of course, new innovator regions or agglomerations render such fortunate locations vulnerable. This leads to Krugman's latest position in which such dynamics produce over time a shifting backwards and forwards of advantage for a specific, predictable agglomeration. This occurs up to the point where the centripetal forces which caused it change to centrifugal forces as the agglomeration becomes too competitive or too costly a location. Other regions or other locations in the same region thus become advantaged.

The problems which render Krugman's approach unconvincing are those characteristic of neoclassicism more generally. First, imperfect knowledge and competition are treated *as if* they were perfect to enable the model to function; thus we are almost back to square one. Secondly, he seems to want to have both cumulative causation producing disequilibrium and centrifugal forces relieving the backwash effects of cumulative causation, that is, disequilibrium, as only temporary phenomena while restoration to equilibrium is the norm. But the two concepts of cumulative causation and equilibrium are incompatible. But thirdly, and most importantly, as Freeman (1994*b*) says, such models suffer from familiar problems of an incapacity to deal with institutional factors, organizational innovation, and the nexus between them and investment outcomes. If the world were as Krugman predicts, it would be full of abandoned cities and derelict regions; that it isn't is testimony to the QWERTY-effect of society's institutional attachment to, in neoclassical terms, economically irrational behaviour (David, 1985).

NATIONAL SYSTEMS OF INNOVATION

An important source of inspiration for this exploration of the institutional and organizational bases of 'associational economics' lay in the neo-Schumpeterian community of researchers who, inspired also by Friedrich List's (1859) concept of the national system of political economy, developed the idea of National Innovation Systems (NIS). As Nelson and Rosenberg (1993) have remarked, the growth slowdown of the 1970s and the rise of Japan and other Asian economies, led Western analysts and policy-makers to look at the effectiveness of their mechanisms for managing and promoting technological change in line with: 'A strong belief that the technological capabilities of a nation's firms are a key source of their competitive prowess, with a belief that these capabilities are in a sense national, and can be built by national action' (Nelson and Rosenberg, 1993: 3). To that end, the programme of research reported in Nelson (1993) studied the NISs of fifteen countries, looking for similarities and differences and how they explained national variation in economic performance overall.

A key question in this endeavour was definitional, for example to what extent was it meaningful to explore 'national systems' (meaning *states* that are national in the sense of France, Germany, and Japan) during an era when technology appeared to be becoming increasingly transnational? Innovation, too, was subject to question, at least conceptually, for many of the contributors to the programme, not least Rosenberg and Freeman, had led the challenge to orthodox representation of the innovation process as linear, flowing from (scientific) concept to (technological) consumer. In its place they had argued for an interactive model of the process in which consumers (or users) could be the stimulus for innovation as much as researchers and in which design, production, or marketing managers also played crucial roles, as might public research organizations.

This implied the idea of 'system', what was referred to as the 'set of institutions whose interactions determine the innovative performance, in the sense above, of national firms' (Nelson and Rosenberg, 1993: 4). In the parlance used here, institutions is used loosely and mainly refers to what we would call, after Johnson and Gregersen (1996) 'organizations'. Similarly, Freeman (1987) defines an NIS as 'the network of institutions in the public and private sectors whose activities and interactions initiate, import, modify and diffuse new technologies' (Freeman, 1987: 1). To which most neo-Schumpeterians would certainly add organizational process innovations and, maybe, the opening up of new markets and regions (Andersen, 1994; Edquist, 1997*b*).

While Nelson's (1993) book reported on a vast amount of information concerning the different innovation configurations operating in advanced and developing economies, there are two striking weaknesses, possibly interconnected, in their pioneering study. First, from the outset, the project appears to have lacked a coherent research design in which each study-country's research team is given the task of generating answers to the same basic questions or data relating to the same indicators. Secondly, however, the resulting picture is unclear because explanations of innovation system configuration and economic performance tend to be couched in terms of other, subsidiary variables. These can include correlating strong economic performance with either relatively high defence expenditure in the USA and Sweden (but not Britain) or relatively low defence expenditure, as in Germany and Japan, which does not help understanding very much.

However, if empirical drift is a problem in the Nelson (1993) work, theoretical drift is the equivalent problem in the other main report on NISs edited by Lundvall (1992). This book is very strong on developing the new and extremely useful theory of *interactive learning* as the basis for analysing the NIS phenomenon. Contributions such as those of Johnson on institutional learning, Andersen on evolution and agglomeration, and Lundvall's own introduction and discussion (with Dalum) of public policy for innovation, are exemplary conceptual and analytical treatments of functionally important questions relating to the concept of NIS. But there are no actual national innovation system studies in the book. Were the Lundvall (1992) and Nelson (1993) endeavours to have been combined around a careful research design the result might have been considerably more impressive.

The reality of NISs, though, as we saw in Chapter 1, is that there are major differences in the organization of innovation systems in different countries. Furthermore, these differences can only be explained in terms of complex interactions of social, economic, and technical changes over geographical space. The problem as we see it is that NIS research may have focused on the wrong spatial level. It is a common misconception among evolutionary (and non-evolutionary) economists in general and those interested in innovation systems in particular, that only the state-national level is of importance analytically. Yet the results of the NIS programme at least leave open the possibility that this is insufficient or even inadequate. One common conclusion, namely that firms are the most important innovation organizations, should give caution to those who nevertheless wish mainly to focus on the national level. Firms are increasingly forced towards sub-national interactions amongst suppliers and innovation support organizations, especially where *tacit* knowledge is being exchanged, and pulled towards global, or at least transnational, interactions for learning of a more *codified* nature, acquisition of more standardized inputs, and, of course, for sales. To his credit, Freeman (1995) is one of the few to recognize the importance of the *regional* scale of interaction for innovation in his approval for work demonstrating the importance of 'local infrastructure, externalities, especially in skills and local labour markets, specialised services and not least, mutual trust and personal relationships' (Freeman, 1995: 21) in underpinning 'national systems' from the beginning. We consider this to be a timely corrective to the hype surrounding 'techno-globalization' as the most salient trajectory for innovation systems integration of the future. The point is that all three levels—global, national, and regional—have their relative importance and the research challenge is to tease out how and in what ways.

Innovation and Smaller Firm Support

We argued these points in our first chapter and return to them here, but in the process we wish also to raise questions concerning state intervention, which in most countries remains strongest for *innovation policy* at the state-national level as it has traditionally for *industrial policy*. The latter seems everywhere to be moribund, or where, as in France, still based on the promotion of 'national champions', ineffective. For the present and foreseeable future, the exigencies of a global monetarist ideology built on the imperatives of fiscal, monetary, and budgetary rectitude, have made public expenditure towards supporting or picking winners profoundly unfashionable. 'Natural selection' is seen as a cheaper and politically less risky option, more suited to the neo-liberal turn that has gone furthest in the UK and USA but inevitably exerted influence even in countries still characterized by the ethics of 'social partnership'. There is something of a dilemma here, as we note from the outset. If there is no overt industry policy but an overt innovation support policy remains in place, who is the beneficiary? As Edquist (1994) points out for the case of Sweden, it tends to go in support of firms that have already demonstrated their capacity to conform to the 'survival of the fittest'. Much the same can be said for European Union framework support for the corporate sector with disproportionate amounts being spent on Siemens, Olivetti, and Bull, largely due to their lobbying powers. Yet, in one case—Siemens—such assistance can scarcely be said to be capable of making a significant difference, due to its massive coffers and R&D budget, whereas for the other two, it is usually a case of good money being thrown after bad.

Our strong belief, and one for which there is growing support in terms of academic analysis and emergent policy, is that the vast majority of innovation support expenditure should be directed at and through the regional state level. There are three convincing reasons for this. First, as already implied, there is little justification for giving large sums to large firms whose internal R&D budgets tend to dwarf public innovation subventions to them. Moreover, as Edquist (1994) argues, it is not infrequently the case that such recipients are themselves innovative not in tomorrow's but rather in yesterday's industries. Secondly, it is far better to support firms that find it hard to access venture capital because of risk-aversion by banks. Such businesses increasingly play a crucial role as suppliers of specialist know-how, products, and even organizational processes to large firms. They are largely small and medium-sized enterprises. And thirdly, why not support the only sector of the advanced economies identified by OECD (1994a) as having job-growth potential for the foreseeable future: not the large private sector, not the public sector, but, once more, the small and medium-sized enterprise sector and, particularly, the innovative start-ups or surviving new technology business firms?

Such firms warrant the kind of 'infant industry' support that Nelson (1993) says characterized much innovation expenditure by public authorities throughout the fifteen NIS countries surveyed. But this is overwhelmingly directed towards larger rather than smaller enterprises. What we have in mind here, and will say more about later, is the need for creating policy which recognizes the rather 'upside-down' (Handy, 1989) nature of economic relationships in the post-Fordist age, but also the insecurities associated with it. Instead of a *dirigiste* 'picking-winners' policy on the one hand, or a neo-liberal, arm's length, 'survival of the fittest' policy on the other, we see reason in regional innovation interventionism. Thus, assistance would be given over a time-limited start-up period to, for example, 'academic entrepreneurs' (i.e. graduates or academics starting up new business) retaining close association with their parent faculty, but also partly or wholly in receipt of orders for business, sub-contracted from a single or a number of larger associated firms, who thus provide security and access to valued know-how during the difficult start-up period for new, knowledge- or technology-intensive business.

This kind of systemic innovation support is clearly much better handled by competent bodies operating at the sub-central rather than the country level of governance and administration. We have argued that this is the lowest strategic level at which key resources of tacit knowledge exchange, trust, and credibility among firms and agencies operate, not least because of the relative proximity of actors. It must be equally evident that a specific, exemplary policy initiative such as the one outlined requires a number of policy-specific institutions and organizations to be present 'in the system' for it to function and that such a base is not equally distributed. This is especially apposite in a country like Britain with its highly concentrated knowledge and innovation infrastructure centred on London, though it is rather less relevant in more decentralized systems such as Germany and moderately decentralized Italy and Spain. We wish to be clear on this specific point that an innovation-support policy remains an innovation policy not an employment policy, and *a fortiori* not a regional equalization policy. The last two are policy problems in need of their own associational policy formulation by policy networks of actors of consequence to those spheres who may, in part, include those of consequence to regionalized innovation support. This is a point we develop later in terms of the 'Third Sector'.

As we said at the outset, these are issues involving tacit knowledge exchange between actors from different constituencies (large business, small business, academia, associations, regional government, expert agencies, outside experts, and so on). They may have to engage not only in what we called, after Argyris and Schon (1978), first and second-order feedback loops involving goal achievement and goal adjustment, but also first, second, or even third-order rule deliberation as follows:

If realized results lie below the aspiration level . . . Search is triggered. Search . . . is assumed to be governed by second-order 'meta rules': search or learning rules. Triggering the second-order rules may lead to a replacement of the 'old' first-order rules by new ones. There may also be third-order rules that instruct . . . How 'to learn'. (Vromen, 1995: 79)

Such interchanges, which are fundamentally learning processes, demand high-trust exchange relationships among members of diverse constituencies who, over time, have developed a networking propensity, a common language, shared institutional norms, and the capability to invoke legitimate authority and resources to implement evolutionary policy pathway adjustments. This is not a garden that can be designed from the window of a jumbo jet at 30,000 feet (or its equivalent in Whitehall or Washington, DC) as Robin Murray once memorably put it (Murray, 1991).

As we showed in Chapter 2, this kind of focused, trust-building, and longer-term associational practice in localized settings, has become a characteristic of many leading-edge larger firms, following the selective learning they have embarked upon to adjust to new rules of engagement with Japanese and other Asian competitors. The rethinking of principal-agent relationships in respect of corporate governance, bringing the 'stakeholder' idea into a picture hitherto shareholder-dominated, signifies a shift in at least recognition of a problem regarding the degree of exclusivity often practised in Anglo-Saxon business regimes. Similarly, Hedlund's (1993) ideas on the superiority of heterarchic over hierarchical organizational systems in contexts where change, instability, and uncertainty are high and rapid knowledge-transfer and learning are imperative, are complementary to our perspective. So too are ideas affirming the decentralization of competence and capability in the corporation of the future.

Moreover, with even such a hitherto centralized core competence as R&D being reconfigured along more integrated, communication-enhancing, and transfer-minded lines in leading corporations, involving differentiated structures of localization for tacit-knowledge exchange and virtual networking for more codified interaction, the innovatory organizational trend becomes very clear. Beyond the factory-laboratory too, and into the supply chain, high-trust, partnership relationships, often associated with real or virtual proximity, dependent upon task-specificity, are commonly associated with high-performance companies in dynamic industries. The challenge, for governance systems outside the corporate sphere, to learn and apply appropriate good practice from exemplar administrations is a daunting one, but one, we have argued, that can be met. An important way in which it can be met is through a thorough revaluation of the role of the *regional* dimension, on the one hand, and the *associational* dimension, on the other, in advancing the innovative capacity of the public sphere. A key effect of this should be to help break down historic and systemic barriers between public and private spheres. This will encourage functional transfer of key responsibilities from the private to the public and vice versa, as deemed appropriate in terms of agreed priorities and resource capabilities.

THE REGIONAL NEXUS

We have made a strong case for the importance of 'the regional' in terms of the delivery of innovatory services and ideas primarily, in our analysis, for purposes of enterprise support. Given our analysis of decentralizing tendencies in much of the corporate sector's 'leading edge' and signs of attenuation in budgets for certain public functions—most notably industry policy—that had hitherto been the province of national governments, we wish at this point to explore in further detail the fundamentally *regional* phenomenon of *agglomeration*. Our argument, it will be recalled, is that regions are strengthening their *offensive* development capacity. This is an uneven process and the trajectories regions are following in this respect are diverse. Indeed our selection of regions for in-depth study was governed by precisely this interest in divergent pathways. Thus Baden-Württemberg is an 'artificial' region of Germany that has nevertheless developed a strong identity from its economic development as a leading mechanical engineering and automotive agglomeration and a constitutionally secure and established governance structure which often acts in association with industry. Emilia-Romagna is also 'artificial' but operates in a comparable way, with a relatively weak, though democratic governance structure, making the most of its limited powers to provide enterprise support and promotion for its micro-agglomerations in diverse industrial districts. In both cases strong elements of socio-political cohesiveness and identity derive from economic politics.

The Basque Country and Wales are different. They are historic nations with strong cultural distinctiveness, institutional norms, and organizational forms that lend identity to them within their particular 'national' states. From this base each has evolved a regional state apparatus, that of the Basque Country with a parliament since 1981, recovering the organic parliamentary tradition destroyed by the totalitarian Francoist state and the Nazi bombing of Gernika. These regional state apparatuses grew in strength in response to pressure from below, caused largely by deindustrialization of the old, resource-based sectors on which their cultural and economic development paths were dependent. But the trajectory of escape from regional 'lock-in' has differed. This is because in the case of the Basque Country, political violence gives Madrid the excuse to discourage potential inward investors, so the Basques must pursue a difficult policy of endogenous growth based on small and medium enterprises. The much milder threat of nationalism persuaded London to allow Wales the governance capacity to shift its path-dependence from coal and steel to high-performance engineering precisely by pursuing a strategy of attracting foreign investment, then laying the foundations for cluster-building through the elaboration of localized smaller enterprise supply-chain linkages.

These developmental processes are the product of complex interactions between cultural and economic forces, expressed both politically and apolitically through associational organization and interaction. But they cannot easily be seen, as some strains of evolutionary economics would, as a 'natural selection' process producing 'the survival of the fittest'. That tautology, which defines fitness in terms of evidence of survival and vice versa is simply meaningless in the context of regional development. And this has obvious repercussions for the use of that analogy with respect to firms. Of far more relevance here is a notion of evolution which is culturally and politically rooted in a concept of 'selective learning' as elaborated by Vromen (1995). In Chapter 3 we showed how this happens, referring to and developing the ideas of Schon (1973) and Argyris and Schon (1978) on feedback loops, whereby advanced regional organizations monitor, engage in reflexive behaviour, learn, and, operating through associational policy networks, implement actions appropriate to the task in hand. In Vromen's (1995) analysis *learning* is the selection mechanism by means of which *innovation* brings forth the mutation of one path-dependence for another. In Schumpeterian terms such innovations are *transmitted* or transferred by imitation.

Thus, the nexus of processes we discussed in Chapters 1 and 2, occasioned by the rise of new competition from Japan, produced conditions in which economic performance came to depend more and more on a capacity to support and maintain *externalized* relationships among economic actors of different sizes and types. More than that, we have argued, following Malmberg and Maskell (1997) and Krugman (1995), that such externalization is also accompanied by increasing *specialization*. This is because of the growth of intra-industry trade or the locational attractions of specific geographic spaces, where a high level of *tacit-knowledge* interchange is necessary. To which can be added the Veblen–Myrdal cumulative causation cycle that ensures where and when agglomeration of consequence exists, and regional governance organizations that help promote the specialities of the region. As de Vet (1993) notes, empirically this tends to attract further investment from foreign capital thus globalizing but also enhancing the *specialization* and *externalization* assets of that economy.

Agglomeration facilitates inter-firm learning, especially in respect of tacit but also newly codified knowledge and information. To the extent that such inter-actions build on a basis of *trust* between, at the least, 'families' of firms, *trans-action costs* à la North (1993) or Williamson (1985) will be reduced owing to a lessening of the requirement for transaction search, selection, and legal con-tract expenditures. In propitious circumstances such trust-building will come to take the form at one level of Northian 'conventions', such that actors come to recognize other actors as reliable, trustworthy, 'as good as their word', and so on. At a higher level, a *microconstitution* of acceptable, desirable, and outlawed practices, norms, and routines becomes institutionalized. To the extent that this acts as a form of *microregulation*, conventions can be said to have evolved into 'rules of the game' whereby considerable reliance is placed on the practices of members of the network which would, if breached, be psychologically, socially, and economically costly. To the extent, further, that such conventional or regulatory microconstitutional norms and understandings evolve, we can talk meaningfully about the existence of a *collective social order* having become institutionalized.

This is a preferable way of explaining the kind of collective social orders of rules and conventions that underpin both the Emilian industrial districts and the Baden-Württemberg industrial system, than the Hayekian notion of a sponta-neous social order emerging from the atomistic, yet creative, interactions of individuals in contested market situations. It is equally preferable to the Marxian idea of a particular social order being the product of a combination of dom-ination by a given mode of production and its associated institutional capacity for inducing false consciousness. And evolutionary process-thinking, in which selective learning from experimentation with a range of responses to the 'shock therapy' of rapid deindustrialization in the Basque Country and Wales, is help-ful in suggesting how, within severe constraints, specific adjustment trajector-ies of consequence to regional economic regeneration actually emerged.

In all cases the sustaining or rebuilding of *agglomerations* has been the para-mount economic policy concern. Even before the idea of business clusters became popular with policy-makers, following Porter (1990) who showed agglom-eration to be the source of competitive advantage, these regions had long experience of their economic virtues and vices. The mighty engineering cluster of the Neckar valley and Stuttgart, the remarkable mini-clusters of Emilia, the declining steel, metallic, and shipbuilding cluster of the Bilbao region and the large south and smaller north Wales clusters of coal, steel, and metals pro-cessing, have been the hearts of these regional economies, in some cases for a century or more. In our two 'cultural regions' of the Basque Country and Wales they energized a process of cultural if not political institution-building in the period around the turn of the nineteenth century. In our 'artificial regions', that process has occurred during the last half of the twentieth century.

But, of course, as traditional regional development analysis and policy said, agglomerations can be vulnerable if they are too narrowly focused. If based on small firms they may be prey to acquisition, concentration, and external control, classically as was the fate of the South Wales tin-plate industry. If they evolve as relatively self-sufficient islands their risk is that of introversion, deafness to dissent, path-dependence, and lock-in associated with a failure to innovate that may be fatal. The formerly predominating industry of textiles and clothing in Baden-Württemberg is a textbook example of this, Basque shipbuilding is another.

Finally, agglomerations can be vulnerable to new competition which may simply take markets and wipe competitors out. Straw hats went out of fashion in Carpi but the community managed to apply selective learning and shift the local trajectory to knitwear, an industry which has survived the onslaught of Asian competition by innovation in fashion design and production technology. The Baden-Württemberg machine-tool industry is currently assailed by Asian competition which is stripping away the lower-cost end of the market and causing such celebrated firms as Traub (Germany's fourth largest) to seek a suitor for acquisition and to shift manufacturing to Chemnitz in former East Germany (Marsh, 1996a). The recent work of Krugman (1995) invites us to contemplate a major increase in the speed with which specialized industrial locales experience 'creative destruction'. Those that are massively engaged in intra-industry trade of the kind precisely captured in the Baden-Württemberg case (export of expensive cars and machinery, import of cheaper variants) will, he argues, enter cycles of decline and be replaced elsewhere by the slightly more innovative competitor locale.

What is clear is that co-location is not enough to give agglomerations sustained capacity to survive and prosper. So in what ways does *proximity* matter and what are the limitations of its influence? In Malmberg and Maskell's (1997) careful assessment of the advantages of proximity to industrial systems there are three key features, each with its evolutionary roots in the insights of Marshall (1916), and each associated with a distinctive school of thought. The first emphasizes path-dependence and cumulative causation though, interestingly, the initial locational rationale for an agglomeration can be superseded in the cumulative causation process, as externally or internally generated innovations or contextual changes occur over time. Here, following Arthur (1994), are found the strong *horizontal* linkages which, through emulation by 'spin-off', add to the diversity of available inputs.

Secondly, the externality effect from economies based on proximity through agglomeration confers advantage in respect of transaction costs (Scott, 1996). In the negative these are reduced where customer–supplier trust is high and the latter reliably expects that the order from the former will not change six times before it is finally placed to a near-impossible delivery schedule. In the positive dimension there is less need for normal overhead costs such as those related to legalization of contracts, contract enforcement, contract compliance, and so on. Equally, exchange and co-operation will reduce the costs of intangible (e.g. tacit knowledge) and tangible (e.g. codified knowledge) transactions. Primarily, these advantages of agglomeration externalities operate in the *vertical* plane. The possibilities for proximate, regular, project-based simultaneous engineering of product or process design, where teams composed of distinctively skilled professionals combine to innovate, enhance advantage. Similarly, 'simultaneous scheduling' where customer and supplier know intimately each other's demand and supply requirements lowers the cost of logistics, including transportation.

Thirdly, the milieu (Maillat, 1995) or institutional infrastructure of norms, rules, and routine practices amongst the production community, adds to the socio-cultural and political assets available to help sustain and move forward the activities of the agglomeration. This is the environment from which advantage is supported by unlocking the learning and innovation capacity contained in 'social capital' (Putnam, 1993). The investment of social capital is not confined primarily to either the *lateral* or *horizontal* dimensions of inter-linkage but is capable of being deployed in support of either or both. One of the more celebrated cases of the latter was the way the Jura watch-making community pushed at the relatively open door of the Swiss government who were inclined in favour of promoting a generic microelectronics industry support-programme, which was then mainly accessed by former watchmakers to escape their 'lock-in' problem and shift path-dependence into microelectronics manufacture and supply (Crevoisier, 1993).

Offsetting the destructive forces that may assail the too 'monocultural' industrial agglomeration and posing difficulties for Krugman's (1995) hypermobility thesis, are three distinctive processes, two active and one passive. The first active one, the most important, is the selective learning and innovation capacity of firms, especially smaller and medium-sized ones that, as we have seen, may increasingly be conceived as the backbone of the contemporary externalized, specialized agglomeration. Thus, instead of the Traub strategy of selling assets and exporting manufacturing, we may consider another Baden-Württemberg machine-tool firm's response to the struggle for survival. Index, a specialist machining-centre producer, has moved towards 'simultaneous scheduling' by opening its new Esslingen warehouse on Saturdays, unheard of in weekend-working-free German engineering. Learning from Robert Bosch, his previous employer, the chief executive has presided over a growth to 65 per cent of revenue from machine designs of less than five years old. To do this, teams combining production, design, and marketing professionals have been formed to improve in-house communication on innovation. The firm has resolutely refused to cut prices or go downmarket but it has reduced production costs by designing standardized modules and purchasing rather than making electronic control systems. As outsourcing increased by 33 per cent from 1990 to 1995 so production costs were reduced by up to 20 per cent. The main area of job loss has been in the new, automated warehouse which now employs sixteen compared to the previous forty (Marsh, 1996*b*).

The second active process capable of offsetting systemic degradation of agglomerations, is the activation of social and political capital through associational activities. In Chapter 3, we noted that regions with appropriate governance mechanisms had moved from a defensive to a more offensive posture in regard to their economic constituencies. The regional state agencies are the legitimate facilitators of this process but not the sole actors in the policy-appreciation, monitoring, and implementation spheres, that give expression to *regional reflexivity* functions. We outlined the ways these processes were activated in the four case regions, usually involving President's commissions, sometimes on a periodic basis. But such commissions of inquiry, where they are inclusive of other interests of consequence to the problems being faced, are metaphorical islands that are really the peaks of a submerged mountain range of cumulative and sedimented social action.

The third, passive defence that agglomerations possess is that to which Malmberg and Maskell (1997) refer as 'asset stock accumulation'. In other words, the neo-Schumpeterian assumption that information diffuses rather like a free good, enabling imitators rapidly to swarm into the market opened up by the radical innovator, may need some attention. The argument against rapid imitation is that know-how embodied in the tacit knowledge of the innovator is difficult to tap without an asset of equivalent value to exchange. But more importantly, although it may leak out, as codified knowledge did amongst our Emilia-Romagna clothing industry case studies, a successful innovator will have moved on to the next application, and thus will have 'kept ahead of the game'. Specific channels of communication through which innovators are likely to operate in relation to customers and suppliers will add to these 'time-compression diseconomies' faced by would-be imitators. The advantage to outside users (as distinct from potential imitators) of privileged access to, for example, process technology innovations from Japan, is testified to in the case of Benetton, as described by Belussi (1996).

One final point remains to be reiterated with respect to the learning and innovatory capacities of agglomerations. Localized learning is not enough. There is, first, a distinction to be made between strategic and routine learning by firms (Glasmeier and Fuellhart, 1996). While there is not the simple equation these authors imply between strategic and distant, routine and local, nevertheless some strategic learning is bound almost by definition to be non-proximate where the source is elsewhere and unique (e.g. Silicon Valley for IT and peripherals). By contrast, in the case of routine learning, as with the transfer of knowledge for using new models of machine studied by Gertler (1995), the absence of acculturation by the distant user to the nuances prevalent in the producer community is a barrier to successful take-up. This is mirrored in the introverted customer–supplier relations we identified in the Baden-Württemberg engineering product markets in Chapter 4. Interestingly, as this unravels somewhat with Asian market penetration (Mueller and Loveridge, 1995, Herrigel, 1996), little is heard of communication, cultural, or nuancing barriers, suggesting that machine-tool communities understand machine tools while those that lack them but nevertheless need to use them, as Gertler (1995) describes in the Canadian situation, have problems of 'absorptive capacity' (Cohen and Levinthal, 1990). As we noted in Chapter 3, capacity to learn is contingent on the level of previous learning, and distance can mean 'out of sight, out of mind'.

So, there is no one best way. Agglomeration is not a panacea, though its present advantages, appropriately secured, seem to outweigh its disadvantages in an era of externalization and specialization. Even so, hitherto secure Baden-Württemberg sees its innovative capacity challenged by Asian producers as, to some extent, does Emilia-Romagna. Contrariwise, the Basque Country's enforced endogenous development raises its engineering product innovation capability, while for Wales small firm process innovation is enhanced by close contact with foreign multinationals seeking localized agglomeration externalities.

WHAT POLICY LESSONS ARE TO BE LEARNED?

It is clear that the evolutionary perspective informing our analysis allows for diverse developmental pathways. Accordingly, there may be many more-or-less appropriate policy instruments that can be implemented to suit the economic circumstances specific regions confront. Consequently, there will be no universalistic measures such as 'growth poles', 'infant industry protection', or 'mobilization of indigenous potential' recommended in what follows. This would go completely against the grain of our argument. This is that our objects of interest are diverse evolutionary processes of change typified by disequilibrium conditions, from which industrial agglomeration can be an important resultant and stimulant of firm and institutional learning and innovation, at and beyond the regional level. Explicit in this analysis is the viability of a view of human nature that despite 'selfish genes' is capable of co-operative, even altruistic practices. There are many circumstances in which such practices are both more equitable and efficient than those associated with 'arm's length' competitive exchange as conceived to be the norm in neoclassical orthodoxy.

However, there are some policy-relevant, general deductions we are prepared to reiterate from our preceding argument. We are convinced that, for the foreseeable future, product, process, and institutional innovation will continue to make the major contribution to productivity growth in all economies. However, the Piagetian point that learning capability increases exponentially must always be borne in mind. Hence, we think innovation-poor regions and countries will continue to slip behind the innovation-rich ones unless preferentially assisted. But we have also argued, as the national systems of innovation research found, that there is no correlation between innovativeness and the size of, for example, a country or region's R&D budget. Denmark, a country of an arguably regional scale and position, geographically and economically, demonstrates that a relatively low R&D input can be compensated for through practising the principles of a 'learning economy' (Lundvall and Johnson, 1994). These involve the promotion of firms that enhance learning capabilities by networking, lateral information exchange, inter-firm staff mobility, and the reflexivity of learning organizations; also, governance systems that promote the means, incentives, capability, access, and intelligence to learn. From this perspective: 'Firms start to learn how to learn' (Lundvall and Johnson, 1994: 26) and 'the role of government in the learning economy becomes one of supporting learning processes' (ibid. 38).

Nevertheless, we part company from Lundvall and Johnson (1994) to some degree in dissenting from their view that this is most suitably organized by states rather than at regional level. We recognize the possible counter-argument to our own position for small countries such as Denmark, but in general we think policy interventions of the kind we have been discussing are most appropriately co-ordinated regionally. In this we are by no means alone, as recent contributions on learning regions (Florida, 1995*b*), the wealth of regions (Storper and Scott, 1995), and regional motors of the global economy (Scott, 1996) testify. We not only advocate but see, nowhere more than in our regional case analyses, a shift towards *decentralized industrial policy*, a trend also recommended by the World Bank, OECD, and European Union. This is perhaps not so surprising since decentralized industrial policy is relatively inexpensive and has shown good signs in many instances of bearing fruit, though it is also a well-tried way for states to offload responsibilities in circumstances they find difficult to manage.

We also think, as argued earlier in this chapter, that the 'national economy' will become controlled less by sovereign states and more by global corporations (which, nevertheless, will be more and more dependent on regional agglomerations). This will be augmented by supranational 'state' organizations like the European Union (which will become more dependent on regionalized policy delivery mechanisms). We strongly add to this the view that large firms should receive minimal industrial or innovation support subsidy since, by and large, they either waste it by being non-innovative (Edquist, 1994) or, being innovative, do not experience significant benefits from it in their overall research and innovation budgets. The one exception to this rule we would make is that a share in such support may be warranted where the large firm, including inward investors, can demonstrate a significant role in a network of SMEs so that state aid is not 'captured' by a single firm.

INNOVATION AND REGIONAL DEVELOPMENT: THE EU REPERTOIRE

Nowhere has the regional role in innovation been more forcefully championed than in the European Union (EU). After a series of internal battles between rival directorates over the past decade, the European Commission has finally accepted that its policies for innovation (in the form of the Framework Programme for research and technological development, RTD) cannot be entirely divorced from its policies for regional development (the Structural Funds). Perhaps the clearest statement of this position is the *Green Paper on Innovation*, which provoked a widespread debate about the problems and prospects for innovation in the EU (European Commission, 1995*a*). We shall focus on this debate to highlight the scope and limits of the region as an arena for promoting innovation and development.

The Green Paper identifies a series of factors—cultural, financial, regulatory, and technical—which act as barriers to innovation in the EU. The net effect, according to the Commission, is that the EU is today afflicted by three key weaknesses: (1) it invests proportionately less than the USA and Japan in RTD; (2) there is too little co-ordination between the various stages of the RTD process; and (3) it has a limited capacity to convert scientific and technological knowledge into commercially successful products and services. The latter two weaknesses can be thought of as a 'knowledge transfer' problem which in turn signals a weak networking capacity, that is, an inability to collaborate for mutually beneficial ends. To overcome these problems the Commission argues that the EU needs to enhance 'the capacity of institutions and firms to invest in R&D, in education and training, in information, in cooperation, and more generally in the intangible' (European Commission, 1995*a*).

To redress the 'innovation deficit' the Commission launched an Action Plan for Innovation, involving EU, national, and regional initiatives aimed at three areas: to foster a more robust innovation culture; to establish a better regulatory framework for innovation; and to forge a stronger interface between research and innovation (European Commission, 1996*a*). Regional action is accorded an important role in this multi-level strategy, and some of the key regional tasks are summarized in Table 8.1. In the Commission's view the rationale for regional action is that:

The local or regional level is in fact the best level for contacting enterprises and providing them with the necessary support for the external skills they need (resources in terms of manpower, technology, management and finance). It is also the basic level at which there is a natural solidarity and where relations are easily forged. It is therefore the level at which small enterprises can be encouraged and helped to pool their strengths in partnerships in order to compete with bigger enterprises with greater resources or to make the most of the opportunities which these enterprises can offer. (European Commission, 1995*a*)

While we broadly concur with this rationale, we take issue with the Commission's view that there is a 'natural solidarity' at the regional level which renders collaboration easy. Far from being easily forged, collaboration is the result not of mere physical proximity but of conscious decisions on the part of regional actors to pursue the route of associational action. Indeed, the lesson of all the efforts to promote innovation in the less favoured regions (LFRs) of the EU is that these efforts deliver little or nothing unless there is adequate investment in social capital. Hence in the evolution of regional innovation policy, from the

TABLE 8.1. Strengthening the regional dimension of innovation

---

- To foster co-operation among enterprises (large and small) and strengthen groupings based on technology or sector in order to realize the potential of local know-how (in traditional activities as well as for top-of-the-range products);
- to encourage an internationally minded approach among enterprises (in liaison with research centres and support services), facilitating acceptance of foreign investment with high value-added and introducing procedures to absorb technology from other countries;
- to improve or add to business support structures by introducing:
  - tools for analysing the stated or unstated needs of enterprises;
  - one-stop shops for access to information and services;
  - mechanisms to facilitate dialogue between the various local partners involved in innovation and the follow-up and monitoring of aid measures;
  - networks to link and rationalize support services (like the Nearnet and Supernet networks in the United Kingdom or the technology dissemination networks in France);
- to reinforce university-industry co-operation in order to facilitate transfers of technology, knowledge and skills.

Source: European Commission (1995*a*).

STRIDE programme in 1990 to the Regional Innovation Strategies of 1997, we see an important shift from supply-side initiatives to a more interactive process in which consensus-building and collective learning are deemed to be the key elements (Morgan, 1997; Landabaso, 1997). With the coming reform of the Structural Funds in 1999, innovation-based measures are set to become more important and, since these involve knowledge-related skills rather than road-building skills, these measures will make more exacting demands on regional institutional capacity.

Through the operation of the Structural Funds, the main instrument for promoting spatial cohesion in the EU, the European Commission has played an important role in fostering regional consciousness, not least by raising the status of the regions as an institutional partner in the design and delivery of the Structural Funds, working alongside member states and the Commission itself in a tripartite partnership. While LFRs could do much more for themselves as regards institutional capacity-building, which includes the tasks identified in Table 8.1, these regions cannot regenerate themselves solely through their own efforts because the scale of the problems far outweighs their internal capacities and because the current policy repertoire, at both EU and national levels, inadvertently works against them.

At the EU level, the Structural Funds cannot hope to compensate for the internal deficiencies of the LFRs or bridge the gap between poor and prosperous regions. Large as they seem, with 170 billion ECU for the period 1994–9, these Funds actually account for just 0.45 per cent of GDP in the EU. What compounds the plight of the LFRs is that the Framework Programme, the main instrument for promoting research and technological development (RTD) in the

EU, is a *de facto* regional policy for the prosperous regions, where the key centres of excellence are located. Indeed, almost 50 per cent of all RTD activity in the EU is concentrated in just twelve 'islands of innovation', the so-called 'Archipelago Europe', running from London to Milan and embracing Amsterdam/ Rotterdam, Ile de France, the Ruhr, Frankfurt, Stuttgart, Munich, Lyon/Grenoble, and Turin (European Commission, 1996*b*). This spatial allocation attests to the significance not of cohesion criteria but of the imperatives of competitiveness, which is the dominant priority in the EU policy repertoire for the Single European Market. However, if the LFRs are to be better equipped to meet the challenge of innovation, then the Fifth Framework Programme, which begins in 1999, will have to ensure that these RTD resources are not so spatially skewed to the core regions of 'Archipelago Europe'.

The European Commission frankly concedes that 'solidarity in the Union begins at home', a reference to the continuing significance of national action in achieving spatial cohesion. It also admits that national action is the single most important mechanism for fostering innovation, not least because the Framework Programme accounts for just 4 per cent of publicly funded RTD in the European Union (European Commission, 1996*b*). The spread of neo-liberal policies at the national level, however, further compounds the problems of the LFRs because member states have progressively reduced their own commitments to social and economic cohesion in the name of deregulation. This underlines the significance of the nation state as an actor in social and economic renewal, a point which is neglected by both 'regionalists' and 'supra-nationalists' (Amin and Tomaney, 1995).

In designing new strategies for innovation and cohesion—two of the key challenges facing Europe today—we need to recognize the limits of unilateral action on any one spatial scale, be it regional, national, or supranational. Each has its merits for certain activities, but successful strategies will often depend on an interpolation of all three, as proposed by recent theories of multi-level governance systems (Jeffery, 1996).

The EU is clearly the most appropriate level at which to design and police pan-European regulatory standards for social, economic, and environmental welfare. No national state, for example, let alone a region, has the power to prevent footloose multinationals from exploiting locational tournaments for mobile investment, fuelling an ever-rising spiral of subsidy offers from jobs-starved localities. A more robust regulatory system to contain these tournaments is now emerging at the EU level, triggered by the case of Renault, which closed a profitable plant in Belgium in 1997 and sought state aid to modernize its Spanish plant. This is also the level at which to promote cross-border RTD collaboration, to design pan-European infrastructures, and to disseminate new developmental practices through inter-regional exchanges.

The national level will remain an important arena for promoting innovation and securing social and spatial cohesion, though the central state, to be effective, will have to work in and through a multi-level governance system, with EU institutions above and regional authorities below. This means that the central state can no longer expect to operate in the old hierarchical ways, since it has neither the legitimacy nor the competence to do so. The traditional hierarchy, with the central state at the apex, is being modified because 'change at the bottom is no longer expected to come about through change at the top', although 'change at the top is called for to consolidate and develop the achievements of initiatives at the bottom' (Lipietz, 1992). If developmental strategies are to be rendered more effective, the central state should treat regional authorities not as a threat to its sovereignty, which is often more apparent than real, but as partners in a common endeavour that neither side can accomplish on its own. For example, if the unique assets of the central state reside in its capacity to fund developmental initiatives and to empower others, regional authorities can lay claim to equally valuable assets, like their unrivalled knowledge of their regions and their ability to forge durable, high-trust relations with other regional actors.

Where the parties are able and willing to recognize their interdependence the central state's role will tend to be 'less hierarchical, less centralized and less dirigiste in character' (Jessop, 1997). To repeat a point we made in Chapter 1, in the discussion of associational strategies, the central state is not necessarily rendered less powerful if it engages in less *direct* intervention. By doing less and enabling more it can actually help to build new capacities for action amongst its partners, especially amongst its regional partners, and this is nowhere more important than in the LFRs, where the barriers to innovation are as much to do with institutional capacity as with technological competence. This strategy, of doing less and enabling more, may even be forced on central states by tight public budgets and the growth of the 'new governance', which refers to the proliferation of self-organizing inter-organizational networks (Rhodes, 1994). The great danger, of course, is that central states will simply pursue the first part of this strategy (i.e. doing less), which is precisely what has happened under neo-liberal strategies of deregulation, and this poses severe problems for both innovation and cohesion strategies in the LFRs.

While the new regional innovation strategies in the LFRs are moving in the right direction, these bottom-up initiatives need to be complemented and nurtured by stronger top-down support from national and supranational initiatives with respect to investment, training, technology-transfer, and institutional capacity-building. As important as they are, these new innovation strategies cannot hope to address all the problems of the LFRs, particularly mass unemployment and social exclusion. To address these problems we need to recognize that conventional economic growth no longer offers a credible solution for the long-term unemployed in our societies. Among other things this problem requires more innovative *labour market* concepts, like the 'socially useful third sector' (Lipietz, 1992), the 'sheltered economy' (Freeman and Soete, 1994) and the 'intermediate labour market' (Wise Group, 1994). The common thread running through these concepts is the idea of marrying idle hands with unmet social needs, an idea which is being explored by the European Commission as part of its new approach to cohesion (European Commission, 1995*b*). If it is to operate on an EU-wide basis, however, this third sector strategy will need to combine local knowledge of supply and demand with national and supranational political support, because it presupposes radical reform of current welfare regulations. Rather than dismissing regional innovation policy for not addressing the problems of social exclusion, which it is not designed to do, it is far better to think of a repertoire of policies for the LFRs which afford parity of esteem to economic renewal and social justice (Morgan, 1997*a*).

This twin-track approach is essential to the future integrity of the European Union. The spectre facing the EU as it wrestles with economic and monetary union is that, to gain entry, member states have to meet stringent convergence criteria with respect to debt and deficits, a stance which could lock the entire Union into a deflationary regime with sombre consequences for the LFRs. In the worst scenario this could induce a race to the bottom, in which regions seek to outdo each other by offering the lowest social costs and the highest public subsidies to attract mobile capital in an ever more desperate and debilitating scramble for jobs at any price. The key challenge for regions, member states, and the EU will be to contain this spectre by offering an alternative scenario based upon a twin-track strategy for economic renewal through innovation and social justice through job creation.

CONCLUSIONS AND IMPLICATIONS

We would argue strongly for a mode of policy appreciation and delivery that is far more inclusive, indeed the term we advocate is *associational*, than it was under the hegemony of more *dirigiste* state postures in the 1960s and 1970s or the more *neo-liberal* mode of the 1980s and early 1990s. In Chapter 3 we praised the *associational*, 'negotiated economy' approach practised in Denmark, as described by Amin and Thomas (1996). This was because, unlike the QUANGO model of arm's-length state intervention practised in Britain in general and Wales in particular, associational interactivity is accountable if there are democratic institutions and organizations to clarify rules and police indiscretions in a transparent manner and on a regular basis. The devolution of parliamentary power to distinctive polities with legitimate demands is a sign of intelligence of the multidimensional kind we discussed in Chapter 3, in particular, the intelligence to know when to 'let go' of functions that are better performed at subsidiary levels.

This can only happen in a satisfactory manner when the recipient region has been endowed, or has acquired, the capacity for significant supralocal policy deliberation and delivery. Such organizations in our regional case analyses as SPRI in the Basque Country, the Steinbeis Foundation in Baden-Württemberg, ERVET and CITER in Emilia-Romagna, and the WDA in Wales have developed, occasional setbacks notwithstanding, the substantive credibility that they are bodies competent to enhance their regional economies through the pursuit of decentralized industry policies. In more established regional parliamentary settings, they show the capability to meet policy commitments, pursue democratically determined policy themes, and, to varying degrees, function on the basis of inclusive policy networks. These latter bring in representatives *of consequence* to the policy theme in question, as sources for learning and policy evolution whether indirectly through commissions of inquiry or directly in respect of urgent policy questions. The case of the regional automotive industry business association in the development of small-firm innovation support through 'model-projects' in Baden-Württemberg, the Emilian associationalism in tackling the need to develop an innovative CAD-CAM system for the clothing industry, and the mediating role of the Mondragon system in Basque industry and innovation policy, are testimony to the power and advantage of incorporating and empowering 'local knowledge'.

We conclude by highlighting the policy themes and action lines which our research has strongly suggested to us to be appropriate spheres for decentralized industry policy of the kind to which we have alluded in the book thus far. Regional governance systems will, it will be recalled, prioritize these and other themes differentially. First, we find the regional level to be highly suitable for organizing *vocational training* at all levels. Because of the increasingly distinctive skills needs of regionally specialized economies, probably only the regional level now has the appropriate purview of labour market demand and supply relationships in the current period. Wales, for example, is genuinely hampered in its pursuit of a manufacturing growth strategy based on inward investment by a central government education and training policy governed by the more academic requirements of a post-industrial, metropolitan society in London and south-east England. Baden-Württemberg, by contrast, can tailor its needs for industrially experienced graduates by establishing distinctive vocational universities with an industrial, not, as yet, a financial services, bias.

Secondly, *innovation*—not to be confused with R&D—we also believe has to be supported by policies formed at regional level. This is given added weight by our stress on the need for innovation support to be given overwhelmingly to smaller firms, start-ups, and the like. This is to be shared with those organizations such as research laboratories, universities, or even large firms that can show themselves to be essential to the security and durability of networks of small firms confronting the challenges of innovation and selective learning. Regional administrations may find it essential to include, associationally, expert representation in decision processes that may stimulate the need for mild competitive bidding of the kind familiar to virtually all actors in the innovation-financing field.

Thirdly, *business intelligence*, enterprise support and general funding assistance, advice and signposting comprise a sphere in which our case analyses convince us that the regional level is the appropriate one for co-ordination, in association with local public and private representative and associational bodies. The role of the EITE centres, covering technology-related services in the Basque Country, offer numerous lessons for those seeking solutions to the problem of implanting an innovation stimulus in a less-favoured region with a tradition of scholarly teaching rather than leading-edge, industrially relevant research in the university sector. The Steinbeis Foundation, too, is an innovative technology service specializing in brokering technological problem-solving through a dense network of higher education institutes. Steinbeis could not have worked in the Basque Country, or Emilia, or Wales because it was tailored to a rich variety of higher education institutes rather than, as in Spanish and Italian cases, having to substitute for them. We are clearly in the world of divergent pathways of evolutionary development in respect of business services.

Finally, our own not-so-radical innovation is to add to our three pillars of decentralized industry policy a fourth, *environmental sustainability*. This is already a pressing issue ripe with problems, rich in learning possibilities, and potentially fruitful in respect of innovatory products, processes, new markets, and new regional opportunities. We would argue that environmental recovery has been the jewel in the crown of the Welsh Development Agency despite the hype surrounding inward investment. A generation of expertise in restoring nineteenth-century industrial dereliction to pristine greenness is hard to criticize. Our criticism would be that insufficient business benefits have arisen from this experience, unlike the case of the Ruhr (Cooke, 1995). Our other case regions too have problems and opportunities ranging from poisoned industrial land in the Spanish and German cases to massive effluent problems in the Emilian dairy industry. Firms increasingly need to learn how to learn in this new field in which both global and local co-operation are evolutionary imperatives.

REFERENCES

Adler, P. (1993), ' "The Learning Bureaucracy": New United Motor Manufacturing, Inc', *Research in Organizational Behavior*, 15: 111–94.
—— (1997), 'Beyond Autonomy: The Socialization of Production', in J. Durand (ed.), *Teamwork in the Automotive Industry*, Oxford: Oxford University Press.
Alaez, R., Bilbao, J., Camino, V., and Longas, J. (1996), *El Sector De Automocion: Nuevas Tendencias en la Organizacion Productiva*, Madrid: Editorial Civitas.
Albert, M. (1993), *Capitalism Against Capitalism*, London: Whurr Publishers.
Aichholzer, G., and Schienstock, G. (eds.) (1994), *Technology Policy: Towards an Integration of Social and Ecological Concerns*, Berlin: de Gruyter.
Alchian, A. (1950), 'Uncertainty, Evolution and Economic Theory', *Journal of Political Economy*, 58: 201–21.
Allen, T., and George, V. (1989), 'Changes in the Field of R&D Management over the Past 20 Years', *R&D Management*, 19/2: 103–13.
Amin, A. (1994), 'Santa Croce in Context or How Industrial Districts Respond to the Restructuring of World Markets', in R. Leonardi and R. Nanetti (eds.), *Regional Development in a Modern European Economy: The Case of Tuscany*, London: Pinter, 170–86.
—— (1996), 'Beyond Associative Democracy', *New Political Economy*, 13: 259–79.
—— Bradley, D., Gentle, C., Howells, J., and Tomaney, J. (1994), *Regional Incentives and the Quality of Mobile Investment in the Less Favoured Regions of the EC*, Progress in Planning, 41/1: 1–112.
—— and Thomas, D. (1996), 'The Negotiated Economy: State and Civic Institutions in Denmark', *Economy and Society*, 25: 255–81.
—— and Thrift, N. (1995), 'Institutional Issues for the European Regions: From Markets and Plans to Socioeconomics and Powers of Association', *Economy and Society*, 24/1: 41–66.
—— and Tomaney, J. (1995), 'The Regional Dilemma in a Neo-liberal Europe', *European Urban and Regional Studies*, 2: 171–88.
Amsden, A. (1989), *Asia's Next Giant: South Korea and Late Industrialization*, New York: Oxford University Press.
Andersen, E. (1994), *Evolutionary Economics: Post-Schumpeterian Contributions*, London: Pinter.
Aoki, M., and Rosenberg, N. (1987), 'The Japanese Firm as an Innovating Institution', Dept of Economics, Stanford University, California.
Archibugi, D., and Pianta, M. (1992), *The Technological Specialization of Advanced Countries*, London: Kluwer.
—— —— (1996), 'Innovation Surveys and Patents as Indicators', in OECD (ed.), *Innovation, Patents and Technological Strategies*, Paris: OECD.
Argyris, C., and Schon, D. (1978), *Organisational Learning: A Theory of Action Perspective*, Reading, Mass.: Addison-Wesley.
Aronsson, P. (1995), 'The Desire for Regions: The Production of Space in Sweden's History and Historigraphy', *Interregiones*, 4: 49–90.
Arribas, J. (1994), Communication Manager, Labein, Bilbao, interview, 26 Apr.
Arrow, K. (1962), 'The Economic Implications of Learning by Doing', *Review of Economic Studies*, 29: 155–73.
—— (1974), *The Limits of Organization*, New York: Norton.
Arthur, B. (1994), *Increasing Returns and Path Dependence in the Economy*, Ann Arbor: Michigan University Press.

Ashton, D. (1996), 'Education, Skill Formation and Economic Development: The Singaporean Approach', Centre for Labour Market Studies, University of Leicester (mimeo).

Auer, P., and Riegler, C. (1990), *Post-Taylorism: The Enterprise as a Place of Learning Organisational Change*, Stockholm: The Swedish Work Environment Fund.

Axelrod, R. (1984), *The Evolution of Cooperation*, London: Penguin.

Bartlett, C., and Ghoshal, S. (1986), 'Tap Your Subsidiaries for Global Reach', *Harvard Business Review*, 64/6: 87–94.

—— —— (1989), *Managing Across Borders: The Transnational Solution*, Boston: Harvard Business School Press.

—— —— (1990), 'Managing Innovation in the Transnational Corporation', in C. Bartlett, Y. Doz, and G. Hedlund (eds.), *Managing the Global Firm*, London: Routledge, 215–55.

Bartlett, C., and Ghoshal, S. (1994), 'Beyond Strategy, Structure, Systems to Purpose, Process, People', in P. B. Duffy (ed.), *The Relevance of a Decade*, Boston: Harvard Business School Press.

Becker, C., and Pfirrmann, O. (1993), *Cooperative R&D Strategies in Microsystems Technology* (in German), Berlin: GIB.

Bellandi, M. (1992), 'The Incentives to Decentralised Industrial Creativity in Local Systems of Small Firms, *Revue d'Economie Industrielle*, 59: 99–110.

—— (1996), 'Innovation and Change in the Marshallian Industrial District', *European Planning Studies*, 4: 353–64.

Bellini, N. (1993), 'The Management of the Economy in Emilia-Romagna: The PCI and the Regional Experience', in R. Leonardi and R. Nanetti (eds.), *The Regions and European Integration: The Case of Emilia-Romagna*, London: Pinter, 109–23.

Belussi, F. (1996), 'Local Systems, Industrial Districts and Institutional Networks: Towards a New Evolutionary Paradigm of Industrial Economics', *European Planning Studies*, 4: 1–15.

Bennett, R. (1995), *Engaging the Business Community*, London: Association of British Chambers of Commerce.

—— Wicks, P., and McCoshan, A. (1994), *Local Empowerment and Business Services*, London: University College London Press.

Benton, L. (1990), *Invisible Factories: The Informal Sector and Industrial Development in Spain*, Albany, NY: SUNY Press.

Benz, A. (1989), 'Intergovernmental Relations in the 1980s', *Publius: The Journal of Federalism*, 19: 203–20.

Berger, S., and Dore, R. (eds.) (1996), *National Diversity and Global Capitalism*, Ithaca, NY: Cornell University Press.

Berggren, C. (1995), 'Japan as Number Two: Competitive Problems and the Future of Alliance Capitalism After the Burst of the Bubble Boom', *Work, Employment and Society*, 9/1: 53–95.

Berle, A. A., and Means, G. C. (1933), *The Modern Corporation and Private Property*, London: Harcourt Brace.

Best, M. (1990), *The New Competition*, Cambridge: Polity.

Bianchi, P., and Giordani, M. (1993), 'Innovation Policy at the Local and National Levels: The Case of Emilia-Romagna', *European Planning Studies*, 1: 25–42.

—— and Gualtieri, G. (1993), 'Emilia-Romagna and its Industrial Districts: The Evolution of a Model', in R. Leonardi and R. Nanetti (eds.), *The Regions and European Integration: The Case of Emilia-Romagna*, London: Pinter, 83–108.

Bilbao, C. (1995), 'Competitiveness through Clusters in the Basque Country', Paper to the Regional Technology Plan Workshop on Industrial Clusters, 3 March, Leipzig.

Blair, M. (1995), *Ownership and Control: Rethinking Corporate Governance for the Twenty-First Century*, Washington, DC: The Brookings Institution.

Boddy, M., and Fudge, C. (1984), *Local Socialism*, London: Macmillan.

Boekholt, P. (1994), 'Methodology to Identify Regional Clusters of Firms and their Needs', TNO, Apeldoorn, The Netherlands (mimeo).

Boyer, R. (1996), 'The Convergence Hypothesis Revisited: Globalization but Still the Century of Nations?' in Berger and Dore (1996), 29–59.

Braczyk, H., Schienstock, G., and Steffensen, B. (1995), 'The region of Baden-Württemberg: A Post-Fordist Success Story?' in E. Dittrich, G. Schmidt, and R. Whitley (eds.), *Industrial Transformation in Europe: Process and Contexts*, London: Sage, 203–33.

Braverman, H. (1974), *Labor and Monopoly Capital*, New York: Monthly Review Press.

Brown, J. S. (1991), 'Research that Reinvents the Corporation', *Harvard Business Review*, Jan.–Feb.

Bruce, P. (1991), 'State Still Accounts for Half of GDP', *Financial Times*, 15 Mar.

Brusco, S. (1982), 'The Emilian Model: Productive Decentralisation and Social Integration', *Cambridge Journal of Economics*, 6: 167–84.

—— and Pezzini, M. (1990), 'Small-Scale Enterprise in the Ideology of the Italian Left', in F. Pyke, G. Becattini, and W. Sengenberger (eds.), *Industrial Districts and Inter-firm Cooperation in Italy*, Geneva: International Institute for Labour Studies, 142–59.

—— (1990), 'The Idea of the Industrial District: Its Genesis', in F. Pyke, G. Becattini, and W. Sengenberger (eds.), *Industrial Districts and Inter-firm Cooperation in Italy*, Geneva: International Institute for Labour Studies.

Burawoy, M. (1979), *Manufacturing Consent*, Chicago: University of Chicago Press.

Burns, T. (1989), 'The Deusto Springboard', *Financial Times*, 30 Nov.

—— and Stalker, G. M. (1961), *The Management of Innovation*, London: Tavistock Publications.

Cadbury, A. (1992), *Report of the Cadbury Committee on the Financial Aspect of Corporate Governance*, London: Gee.

Campbell, M. (ed.) (1990), *Local Economic Policy*, London: Cassell.

Cantwell, J. (1995), 'The Globalization of Technology: What Remains of the Product Cycle Model?' *Cambridge Journal of Economics*, 19/1: 155–74.

Cassell, M. (1994), 'Lament of the Big Spenders', *Financial Times*, 10 Jan.

Cawson, A., Morgan, K., Webber, D., Holmes, P., and Stephenson, A. (1990), *Hostile Brothers: Competition and Closure in the European Electronics Industry*, Oxford: Clarendon Press.

Chandler, A. (1962), *Strategy and Structure*, Cambridge, Mass.: MIT Press.

Charkham, J. (1995), *Keeping Good Company: A Study of Corporate Governance in Five Countries*, Oxford: Oxford University Press.

Chislett, W. (1994), *Spain: At a Turning Point*, Madrid: Banco Central Hispano.

Clark, G., and Dear, M. (1984), *State Apparatus*, London: Allen & Unwin.

Clark, K., and Fujimoto, T. (1991), *Product Development Performance: Strategy, Organisation and Management in the World Auto Industry*, Boston: HBS Press.

Coase, R. (1937), 'The Nature of the Firm', *Economica*, 4: 386–405.

Cohen, E., and Bauer, M. (1985), *Les Grandes Manœuvres Industrielles*, Paris: Belfond.

Cohen, W., and Levinthal, D. (1990), 'Absorptive Capacity: A New Perspective on Learning and Innovation', *Administrative Sciences Quarterly*, 35: 128–52.

Cole, R. (1979), *Work, Mobility and Participation: A Comparative Study of American and Japanese Industry*, Berkeley: University of California Press.

—— (1994), 'Different Quality Paradigms and their Implications for Organizational Learning', in M. Aoki and R. Dore (eds.), *The Japanese Firm*, Oxford: Clarendon Press, 66–83.

Commons, J. (1934), *Institutional Economics—Its Place in Political Economy*, New York: Macmillan.

Cooke, P. (1984), 'Region, Class and Gender: A European Comparison', *Progress in Planning*, 22: 86–146.

Cooke, P. (ed.) (1995), *The Rise of the Rustbelt*, London: University College London Press.

—— (1996*a*), 'Reinventing the Region: Firms, Clusters and Networks in Economic Development', in P. Daniels and W. Lever (eds.), *The Global Economy in Transition*, London: Longman, 310–27.

—— (1996*b*), 'Building a Twenty-First Century Regional Economy in Emilia-Romagna', *European Planning Studies*, 4: 53–61.

—— (1997), 'Regions in a Global Market', *Review of International Political Economy*, 4: 348–79.

—— Alaes Aller, R., and Etxebarria, G. (1991), *Regional Technological Centres in the Basque Country*, Centre for Advanced Studies in the Social Sciences, Cardiff: University of Wales.

—— and da Rosa Pires, A. (1985), 'Productive Decentralisation in Three European Regions', *Environment and Planning A*, 17: 527–54.

—— Etxebarria, G., Morris, J., and Rodrigues, A. (1989), 'Flexibility in the Periphery: Regional Restructuring in Wales and the Basque Country', *Regional Industrial Research Report No. 3*, Cardiff: University of Wales.

—— and Morgan, K. (1990), 'Learning Through Networking: Regional Innovation and the Lessons of Baden-Württemberg', *Regional Industrial Research Report No. 5*, Cardiff: University of Wales.

—— —— (1991*a*), 'Industry, Training and Technology Transfer: The Baden-Württemberg System in Perspective', *Regional Industrial Research Report No. 6*, Cardiff: University of Wales.

—— —— (1991*b*), 'The Intelligent Region: Industrial and Institutional Innovation in Emilia-Romagna', *Regional Industrial Research Report No. 7*, Cardiff: University of Wales.

—— —— (1991*c*), 'Technology Transfer and Regional Policy', in Cheese, J. (ed.), *Attitudes to Innovation in Germany and Britain: A Comparison*, London: Centre for the Exploitation of Science and Technology, 48–58.

—— —— (1992), *Regional Innovation Centres in Europe*, Report to the Department of Trade and Industry, Cardiff: University of Wales.

—— —— (1993), 'The Network Paradigm: New Departures in Corporate and Regional Development', *Environment and Planning D: Society and Space*, 11: 543–64.

—— —— (1994*a*), 'Growth Regions Under Duress: Renewal Strategies in Baden-Württemberg and Emilia-Romagna', in A. Amin and N. Thrift (eds.), *Globalization, Institutions and Regional Development in Europe*, Oxford: Oxford University Press, 91–117.

—— —— (1994*b*), 'The Regional Innovation System in Baden-Württemberg', *International Journal of Technology Management*, 9: 394–429.

—— —— (1994*c*), 'The Creative Milieu: A Regional Perspective on Innovation', in M. Dodgson and R. Rothwell (eds.), *The Handbook of Industrial Innovation*, Aldershot: Edward Elgar, 25–32.

—— —— and Price, A. (1993), 'The Future of the *Mittelstand*: Collaboration versus Competition', *Regional Industrial Research Report No. 13*, Cardiff: University of Wales.

Cossentino, F., Pyke, F., and Sengenberger, W. (eds.) (1996), *Local and Regional Response to Global Pressure: The Case of Italy and its Industrial Districts*, Geneva: International Institute for Labour Studies.

Cram, L. (1994), 'The European Commission as a Multiorganization', *Journal of European Public Policy*, 1: 195–217.

Crevoisier, O. (1993), 'Spatial Shifts and the Emergence of Innovative Milieux: The Case of the Jura Region between 1960 and 1990', *Environment and Planning C: Government and Policy*, 11: 419–30.

Dalum, B. (1992), 'Export Specialisation, Structural Competitiveness and National Systems of Innovation', in Lundvall (1992), 191–225.

—— (1995), 'Local and Global Linkages: The Radiocommunications Cluster in Northern Denmark', Department of Business Studies, University of Aalborg (mimeo).

David, P. (1985), 'Clio and the Economics of QWERTY', *American Economic Review*, 75: 332–7.

Dehnbostel, P. (1996), 'Germany: Innovative Approaches to Vocational Education and Training', paper to ESRC Symposium on Comparative Skill Formation Processes, University of Bristol, May.

Dei Ottati, G. (1994), 'Cooperation and Competition in the Industrial District as an Organizational Model', *European Planning Studies*, 2: 371–92.

—— (1996), 'Economic Changes in the District of Prato in the 1980s: Towards a more Conscious and Organized Industrial District', *European Planning Studies*, 4: 35–52.

Delbridge, R., Oliver, N., Turnbull, P., and Wilkinson, B. (1990), 'Supplier Relations in the UK Automotive Components Industry', Cardiff Business School.

del Castillo, J. (1989), 'Social Rigidities as a Factor of Decline in Old Industrial Regions', in del Castillo *et al.* (1989), 135–54.

—— (1994), Departamento de Economia Aplicado, Universidad del Pais Vasco, Bilbao, interview, 27 Apr.

—— Crespo, M. and Musto, S. (eds.) (1989), *Spatial Aspects of Technological Change*, Bilbao: Universidad del Pais Vasco, 37–58.

Deming, W. E. (1986), *Out of Crisis*, Cambridge, Mass.: MIT Centre for Advanced Engineering Study.

Department of Trade and Industry (1992), *A Prospectus for One Stop Shops for Business*, London: DTI.

—— (1994), *Competitiveness: Helping Business To Win*, London: DTI.

Dertouzos, M., Lester, R., and Solow, R. (1989), *Made in America*, Cambridge, Mass.: MIT Press.

de Vet, J. (1993), 'Globalisation and Local and Regional Competitiveness', *STI Review*, 13: 89–121.

Devlin (1972), *Report of the Commission of Inquiry into Industrial and Commercial Representation*, London: HMSO.

Dickson, M. (1992), 'All For One and One For All', *Financial Times*, 3 Sept.

Doeringer, P., and Terkla, D. (1990), 'How Intangible Factors Contribute to Economic Development', *World Development*, 18/9: 1295–1308.

Dore, R. (1986), *Flexible Rigidities*, London: The Athlone Press.

Dosi, G. (1988a), 'The Nature of the Innovation Process', in Dosi *et al.*, *Technical Change and Economic Theory*, London: Pinter.

—— (1988b), 'Sources, Procedures and Microeconomic Effects of Innovation', *Journal of Economic Literature*, 36: 1126–71.

—— and Coriat, B. (1994), 'Learning How to Govern and Learning How to Solve Problems: On the Co-Evolution of Competences, Conflicts and Organizational Routines', paper to the Prince Bertil Symposium, Stockholm, June.

—— Freeman, C., and Fabiani, S. (1994), 'The Process of Economic Development: Introducing Some Stylised Facts and Theories on Technologies, Firms and Institutions', *Industrial and Corporate Change*, 3/1: 1–45.

—— Nelson, R., Silverberg, G., and Soete, L. (eds.) (1988), *Technical Change and Economic Theory*, London: Pinter.

Dugger, W. (ed.) (1989), *Radical Institutionalism: Contemporary Voices*, London: Greenwood Press.

Dunning, J. (1993), *Multinational Enterprise and the Global Economy*, Wokingham: Addison-Wesley.

Dyer, J. (1996), 'How Chrysler Created an American Keiretsu', *Harvard Business Review*, July–Aug., 42–56.

Edquist, C. (1994), 'Technology Policy: The Interactions between Governments and Markets', in Aichholzer and Schienstock (1994), 67–94.

—— (1997a), 'Introduction: Systems of Innovation Approaches—Their Emergence and Characteristics', in Edquist (1997b), 1–35.

—— (ed.) (1997b), *Systems of Innovation: Technologies, Institutions and Organizations*, London: Pinter.

—— Hommen, L., and McKelvey, M. (1996), *Product versus Process Innovation, Productivity Growth and Employment*, paper to EAEPE Conference, Antwerp, 7–9 Nov.

EITE (1994), *Annual Report*, EITE, Parque Tecnologico, Zamudio.

Eltis, W. (1995), *How Much of the UK Competitiveness Gap Has Been Closed?* London: Foundation for Manufacturing and Industry.

Eraut, M. (1996), 'Skills, Competence and Transfer: Towards Clarifying Meanings and Inferences, and a New Conceptual Framework', University of Sussex (mimeo).

Esser, J. (1989), 'Does Industrial Policy Matter? *Land* Governments in Research and Technology Policy in Federal Germany', in C. Crouch and D. Marquand (eds.), *The New Centralism: Britain Out of Step in Europe?* London: Macmillan, 94–108.

European Commission (1991), *The Regions in the 1990s*, Brussels: Commission of the European Communities.

—— (1994a), *Competition and Cohesion: Trends in the Regions*, Brussels: Commission of the European Communities.

—— (1994b), *The Regional Technology Plan: Guidebook*, Brussels: Commission of the European Communities.

—— (1995a), *Green Paper on Innovation*, Brussels: Commission of the European Communities.

—— (1995b), *Local Development and Employment Initiative*, Brussels: Commission of the European Communities.

—— (1996a), *First Action Plan for Innovation in Europe*, Brussels: Commission of the European Communities.

—— (1996b), *First Cohesion Report*, Brussels: Commission of the European Communities.

Evans, P. (1992), 'The State as Problem and Solution: Predation, Embedded Autonomy and Structural Change', in S. Haggard and R. Kaufman (eds.), *The Politics of Economic Adjustment*, Princeton: Princeton University Press, 139–81.

Evans, R., and Harding, A. (1997), 'Regionalisation, Regional Institutions and Economic Development', *Policy and Politics*, 25/1: 19–30.

Fagerberg, J. (1995), 'User-Producer Interaction, Learning and Comparative Advantage', *Cambridge Journal of Economics*, 19/1: 243–56.

Ferlie, E., and Pettigrew, A. (1996), 'The Nature and Transformation of Corporate Headquarters', *Journal of Management Studies*, 33/4: 495–523.

Ferreiro, J., Serrano, F., and Bilbao, J. (1995), *Japanese Direct Investment in the Basque Country*, Bilbao: Departamento de Economia Aplicada, Universidad del Pais Vasco.

Firn, J. (1975), 'External Control and Regional Development: The Case of Scotland', *Environment and Planning A*, 3/4: 393–414.

Florida, R. (1995a), 'The Industrial Transformation of the Great Lakes Region', in Cooke (1995), 162–76.

—— (1995b), 'Towards the Learning Rregion', *Futures*, 27: 527–36.

Foss, N. (1993), 'Theories of the Firm: Contractual and Competence Perspectives', *Journal of Evolutionary Economics*, 3/2: 127–44.

Fox, A. (1974), *Beyond Contract: Work, Power and Trust Relations*, London: Faber and Faber.

Franchi, M. (1994), 'Developments in the Districts of Emilia-Romagna', paper to Conference on 'Industrial Districts and Local Economic Development in Italy: Challenges and Policy Perspectives', Bologna, May.

Freeman, C. (1982), *The Economics of Industrial Innovation*, London: Pinter.

—— (1987), *Technology Policy and Economic Performance—Lessons from Japan*, London: Pinter.

—— (1994a), 'Critical Survey: The Economics of Technical Change', *Cambridge Journal of Economics*, 18: 463–514.

—— (1994b), 'Innovation and Growth', in M. Dodgson and R. Rothwell (eds.), *The Handbook of Industrial Innovation*, Cheltenham: Edward Elgar, 78–93.

—— (1995), 'The "National System of Innovation" in Historical Perspective', *Cambridge Journal of Economics*, 19: 5–24.

—— and Soete, L. (1994), *Work for All or Mass Unemployment*, Pinter: London.

Fürst, D., and Kilper, H. (1995), 'The Innovative Power of Regional Policy Networks: A Comparison of Two Approaches to Political Modernization in North Rhine-Westphalia', *European Planning Studies*, 3: 287–304.

Future Commission (1993), *Economy 2000* (in German), Stuttgart: Future Commission.

Garmise, S. (1997), 'Making a Difference? Regional Government, Economic Development and European Regional Policy', *International Planning Studies*, 2/1: 63–81.

Garrahan, P., and Stewart, P. (1992), *The Nissan Enigma*, London: Mansell Publishing.

Geddes, M., and Benington, J. (eds.) (1992), *Restructuring the Local Economy*, London: Longman.

Gertler, M. (1995), 'Being There: Proximity, Organization and Culture in the Development and Adoption of Advanced Manufacturing Technologies', *Economic Geography*, 71: 1–26.

Giddens, A. (1984), *The Constitution of Society*, Cambridge: Polity.

Glasmeier, A., and Fuellhart, K. (1996), 'What do we Know about How Firms Learn?' Department of Geography, Penn State University, PA16802 (mimeo).

Gobierno Vasco (1994a), *Cluster de Componentes de Automocion: Una Vision Para El Futuro*, Vitoria: Basque Government.

—— (1994b), *Cluster De Maquina Herramienta: Una Vision Para El Futuro*, Vitoria: Basque Government.

Goitia, J. A. (1995), Centro de Formacion, Otalora, Mondragon Cooperative Corporation, Mondragon, interview, 28 Apr.

Götz, K. (1993), *Intergovernmental Relations and State Government Discretion*, Baden-Baden: Nomos.

Grabher, G. (1993a), 'The Weakness of Strong Ties: The Lock-in of Regional Development in the Ruhr Area', in Grabher (1993b), 255–77.

—— (ed.) (1993b), *The Embedded Firm: On the Socio-Economics of Industrial Networks*, London: Routledge.

Gramsci, A. (1971), *Selections From Prison Notebooks*, London: Lawrence & Wishart.

Granovetter, M. (1973), 'The Strength of Weak Ties', *American Journal of Sociology*, 78/6: 1360–80.

—— (1985), 'Economic Action and Social Structure: The Problem of Embeddedness', *American Journal of Sociology*, 91: 481–510.

Granstrand, O., Hakanson, L., and Sjolander, S. (1993), 'Internationalisation of R&D: A Survey of Some Recent Research', *Research Policy*, 22/5: 413–30.

Greenwood, D., and Gonzales Santos, J. (1991), *Industrial Democracy as Process: Participatory Action Research in the Fagor Cooperative Group of Mondragon*, Van Gorcum, Assen.

Griffiths, J. (1990), 'Fizz on the Shopfloor', *Financial Times*, 22 May.

—— (1995), 'Nissan in Project to Help Suppliers Raise Standards', *Financial Times*, 13 Dec.

Hadjimichalis, C. (1986), *Uneven Development and Regionalism*, London: Croom Helm.

Handy, C. (1989), *The Age of Unreason*, London: Arrow.

—— (1994), *The Empty Raincoat: Making Sense of the Future*, London: Hutchinson.

Hanratty, N. (1995), 'Innovation Policy in the Basque Autonomous Region', unpublished manuscript, Department of City and Regional Planning, University of Wales, Cardiff.

Harrison, B. (1994), 'The Italian Industrial Districts and the Crisis of the Cooperative Form: Part I', *European Planning Studies*, 2: 3–22.

Harvie, C. (1994), *The Rise of Regional Europe*, London: Routledge.

Häusler, J., Hohn, H., and Lütz, S. (1993), 'The Architecture of an R&D Collaboration', in Scharpf, F. (ed.), *Games in Hierarchies and Networks: Analytical and Empirical Approaches to the Study of Governance Institutions*, Frankfurt: Campus; Boulder, Colo.: Westview Press, 211–50.

Hausner, J. (1994), 'Imperative vs. Interactive Strategy of Systematic Change in Central and Eastern Europe', *Review of International Political Economy*, 2.

Hayek, F. (1945), 'The Use of Knowledge in Society', *American Economic Review*, 35/4: 519–30.

—— (1988), *The Fatal Conceit: The Errors of Socialism*, Chicago: University of Chicago Press.

Hedlund, G. (1986), 'The Hypermodern MNC: A Heterarchy?' *Human Resource Management*, 25: 9–25.

—— (1993), 'Assumptions of Hierarchy and Heterarchy: An Application to the Multinational Corporation', in S. Ghoshal and E. Westney (eds.), *Organization Theory and the Multinational Corporation*, London: Macmillan.

—— (1994), 'A Model of Knowledge Management and the N-Form Corporation', *Strategic Management Journal*, 15: 73–90.

Heidenreich, M. (1996), 'Beyond Flexible Specialization: The Rearrangement of Regional Production Orders in Emilia-Romagna and Baden-Württemberg', *European Planning Studies*, 4: 401–20.

—— and Krauss, G. (1997), 'The Production and Innovation Regime of Baden-Württemberg: Between Past Successes and New Challenges', in P. Cooke, H. Braczyk, and M. Heidenreich (eds.), *Regional Innovation Systems*, London: University College London Press.

Heinze, R., and Schmid, J. (1996), 'Industrial Change and Meso-corporatism—A Comparative View on Three German States', *Discussion Paper 96–2*, Bochum: Ruhr University.

Held, D. (1991), 'Democracy, the Nation State and the Global System', *Economy and Society*, 20: 138–72.

Henderson, D. (1995), *Innovation and Technology Support Infrastructure in Wales*, Centre for Advanced Studies in the Social Sciences, Cardiff: University of Wales.

Herrigel, G. (1989), 'Industrial Order and the Politics of Industrial Change: Mechanical Engineering', in P. Katzenstein (ed.), *Industry and Politics in West Germany*, Ithaca, NY: Cornell University Press, 185–220.

—— (1996), 'Crisis in German Decentralized Production', *European Urban and Regional Studies*, 3: 33–52.

Heseltine, M. (1993), Speech on Trade Associations, Confederation of British Industry, 17 June.

Hesse, J. (1990), *Meso-level Government Within a Federal System: The Case of the West German Länder*, Speyer, MS.

Hill, S., and Munday, M. (1994), *The Regional Distribution of Foreign Manufacturing Investment in the UK*, London: Macmillan.

Hines, P. (1992), 'The Role of Intermediaries in the Supply Network', *Logistics Today*, May.

—— (1994), *Creating World Class Suppliers*, London: Pitman.
Hing, A. (1997), 'Industrial Restructuring and Regional Networking in Singapore', in H. Braczyk, P. Cooke, and M. Heidenreich (eds.), *Regional Innovation Systems*, London: University College London Press.
Hirschman, A. (1958), *The Strategy of Economic Development*, New Haven: Yale Univerity Press.
—— (1970), *Exit, Voice and Loyalty: Responses to Decline in Firms, Organizations and States*, Cambridge, Mass.: Harvard University Press.
—— (1986), *Rival Views of Market Society and Other Recent Essays*, New York: Viking.
Hirst, P. (1994), *Associative Democracy*, Amherst, Mass.: University of Massachusetts Press.
Hobday, M. (1995), *Innovation in East Asia: The Challenge to Japan*, Aldershot: Edward Elgar.
Hodgson, G. (1988), *Economics and Institutions*, Cambridge: Polity.
—— (1993), *Economics and Evolution: Bringing Life Back into Economics*, Polity: Cambridge.
—— (1995), 'Evolutionary and Competence-Based Theories of the Firm', The Judge Institute of Management Studies, University of Cambridge.
—— (1996), 'Varieties of Capitalism and Varieties of Economic Theory', *Review of International Political Economy*, 3: 381–434.
Hormaeche, J. (1995), Deputy Manager, Technology Transfer Centre, Robotiker, Zamudio, interview, 29 Nov.
Houlder, V. (1995), 'Revolution in Outsourcing', *Financial Times*, 6 Jan.
—— (1996), 'Intangible Asset', *Financial Times*, 21 May.
House of Commons (1992), *The Trade Gap in Food and Drink*, Agriculture Committee, London: HMSO.
—— (1994), *Competitiveness of UK Manufacturing Industry*, Trade and Industry Committee, London: HMSO.
—— (1995), *Regional Policy*, Trade and Industry Committee, London: HMSO.
House of Lords (1985), *Overseas Trade*, Select Committee on Overseas Trade, London: HMSO.
Humphrey, J., and Schmitz, H. (1996), 'Trust and Economic Development', Institute of Development Studies Discussion Paper 355, Brighton.
Hutton, W. (1995), *The State We're In*, London: Jonathan Cape.
—— (1996), *The State We're In*, London: Vintage.
IFS (1995), *Industrial Tourism in the UK: The Ten Most Visited Plants*, Bedford: IFS.
Ikei (1995), *SME Policy in the Basque Country*, San Sebastian: Ikei.
Inagami, T. (1988), *Japanese Workplace Industrial Relations*, Tokyo: Japan Institute of Labour.
Innovation Advisory Board (1990), *Promoting Innovation and Long Termism*, London: IAB.
Instituto de Maquina-Herramienta (1992), Memoria del IMH, Elgoibar.
Invest in Britain Bureau (1995), *Annual Review*, London: DTI.
Isaksen, A. (1996), 'Towards Increased Regional Specialisation? The Quantitative Importance of New Industrial Spaces in Norway, 1970–1990', *Norsk Geografisk Tidsskrift*, 1.
ISTAT (1988), *Innovation Statistics for Italian Industry* (in Italian), Dec., Rome: ISTAT.
Isusi, I. (1991), 'The Role of Regional Governments in Technology Transfer to SMEs: Case Studies of the Basque Country, Catalonia and Limburg', Unpublished M.Sc. thesis, Department of City and Regional Planning, University of Wales, Cardiff.
JAW (1992), 'Japanese Automobile Industry in the Future', Tokyo.
Jeffery, C. (ed.) (1996a), 'Farewell the Third Level? The German *Länder* and the European Policy Process', *Regional and Federal Studies*, 6/2: 56–75.
—— (1996b), The territorial dimension, in G. Smith, W. Patterson, and S. Padgett (eds.), *Developments in German Politics 2*, Manchester: Manchester University Press, 85–98.

Jessop, B. (1993), 'Towards a Schumpeterian Workfare State? Preliminary Remarks on Post-Fordist Political Economy', *Studies in Political Economy*, 40: 7–39.
—— (1994), 'Post-Fordism and the State', in A. Amin (ed.), *Post-Fordism: A Reader*, Oxford: Blackwell, 251–79.
—— (1997), 'The Future of the National State: Erosion or Reorganisation', Department of Sociology, University of Lancaster.
Johnson, B. (1992), 'Institutional Learning', in Lundvall (1992), 23–44.
—— and Gregersen, B. (1996), 'The Institutional Set-up of National Systems of Innovation and Economic Integration', *Journal of Industry Studies*, 3.
—— Kristensen, A., and Christensen, J. (1991), *Modes of Usage and Diffusion of New Technologies and New Knowledge*, FAST Paper 220, Brussels: European Commission.
Johnson, C. (1982), *MITI and the Japanese Miracle*, Stanford, Calif.: Stanford University Press.
Jurgens, U. (1995), 'Group Work and the Reception of Uddevalla in the German Car Industry', in Sandberg (1995).
—— Malsch, T., and Dohse, K. (1993), *Breaking From Taylorism*, Cambridge: Cambridge University Press.
Kaldor, N. (1972), 'The Irrelevance of Equilibrium Economics', *Economic Journal*, 82: 1237–55.
Karacs, I. (1996), 'German Unions Confront Meltdown', *Independent on Sunday*, 28 Apr.
Katzenstein, P. (ed.) (1978), *Between Power and Plenty: Foreign Economic Policies of Advanced Industrial States*, Cambridge, Mass.: Harvard University Press.
Kay, J. (1994), 'Is There a Competitive Advantage of Nations?' ESRC Lecture, London.
—— and Silberston, A. (1995), 'Corporate Governance', *National Institute Economic Review*, Aug., 84–97.
Kearney, A. T. (1994), *Partnership or Power Play?* Manchester: A. T. Kearney.
Keating, M., and Loughlin, J. (eds.) (1997), *The Political Economy of Regionalism*, London: Frank Cass.
Keep, E., and Mayhew, C. (1994), 'UK Training Policy: Assumptions and Reality', paper to TUC Conference on Looking Forward to Full Employment, Congress House, 5 July.
Keman, H. (ed.) (1993), *Comparative Politics: New Directions in Theory and Method*, Amsterdam: Vrije University Press.
Kitson, M., and Michie, J. (1996), 'Britain's Industrial Performance Since 1960: Underinvestment and Relative Decline', *Economic Journal*, 106: 196–212.
Kline, S., and Rosenberg, N. (1986), 'An Overview of Innovation', in R. Landau and N. Rosenberg (eds.), *The Positive Sum Strategy*, Washington: National Academy Press, 275–305.
Körfer, H., and Latniak, E. (1994), 'Approaches to Technology Policy and Regional Milieux—North Rhine Westphalia', *European Planning Studies*, 2: 303–20.
Krugman, P. (1991), *Geography and Trade*, Cambridge, Mass. and London: MIT Press.
—— (1995), *Development, Geography and Economic Theory*, Cambridge, Mass. and London: MIT Press.
—— (1996), 'What Evolutionists can Teach Economists and Vice Versa', paper to European Association for Evolutionary Political Economy (EAEPE) conference on 'Work, Unemployment and Need: Theory, Evidence, Policies', Antwerp, 7–9 Nov.
Lamming, R. (1993), *Beyond Partnership: Strategies for Innovation and Lean Supply*, Hemel Hemstead: Prentice Hall.
—— (1994), *A Review of the Relationship between Vehicle Manufacturers and Suppliers*, London: Department of Trade and Industry.
Landabaso, M. (1997), 'The Promotion of Innovation in Regional Policy', *Entrepreneurship and Regional Development*, 9: 1–24.

Lane, C., and Bachmann, R. (1996), 'The Social Constitution of Trust: Supplier Relations in Britain and Germany', *Organization Studies*, 17/3: 365–95.

Langlois, R. (1991), 'Schumpeter and the Obsolescence of the Entrepreneur', Department of Economics, University of Connecticut.

Lascelles, D., and Dale, B. (1989), 'Examining the Barriers to Supplier Development', *International Journal of Quality and Reliability Management*, 7/2: 46–56.

Lash, S., and Urry, J. (1994), *Economies of Signs & Space*, London: Sage.

Latniak, E., and Simonis, G. (1994), 'Socially Oriented Technology Policy in Germany: Experiences of a North Rhine-Westphalian Programme', in Aichholzer and Schienstock (1994), 223–48.

Lavia, C., Olazaran, M., and Urrutia, V. (1995), *Los Sistemas De Ciencia Y Tecnologia De La Comunidad Autonoma Vasca Y Navarra*, Donostia: Eusko Ikaskuntza.

Lawson, G., and Morgan, K. (1991), *Employment Trends in the British Engineering Industry*, Watford: Engineering Industry Training Board.

Leonardi, R. (1993), 'The Regional Reform in Italy: From Centralized to Regionalized State', in R. Leonardi (ed.), *The Regions and the European Community*, London: Frank Cass, 217–46.

Lipietz, A. (1977), *Le Capital et son Espace*, Paris: Maspero.

—— (1987), *Mirages and Miracles*, London: Verso.

—— (1992), *Towards a New Economic Order*, Cambridge: Polity.

List, F. (1859), *The National System of Political Economy* (trans. 1904), London: Longman.

Locke, R. (1995), *Remaking the Italian Economy*, Ithaca, NY and London: Cornell University Press.

Lopez Egana, J. A. (1995), 'R&D in the Research Centres', paper to the Eusko Ikaskuntza Conference on Science, Technology and Social Change in the Basque Country, Zamudio, 29 Nov.–1 Dec.

Lorenz, C. (1995), 'In Two Minds', *Financial Times*, 10 Nov.

Lucas, G. (1988), 'On the Mechanics of Economic Development', *Journal of Monetary Economics*, 22: 3–42.

Luhmann, N. (1979), *Trust and Power*, Chichester: Wiley.

Lundvall, B. A. (1988), 'Innovation as an Interactive Process: From User-Producer Interaction to the National System of Innovation', in Dosi *et al.*, 349–69.

—— (ed.) (1992), *National Systems of Innovation: Towards a theory of innovation and interactive learning*, London: Pinter.

—— (1994), *The Learning Economy: Challenges to Economic Theory and Policy*, paper to the EAEPE Conference, Copenhagen, 27–9 Oct.

—— and Johnson, B. (1994), 'The Learning Economy', *Journal of Industry Studies*, 1: 23–41.

Macbeth, D., and Ferguson, N. (1994), *Partnership Sourcing*, London: Pitman.

Maillat, D. (1995), 'Territorial Dynamic, Innovative Milieus and Regional Policy', *Entrepreneurship and Regional Development*, 7: 157–65.

Malerba, F. (1993), 'The National System of Innovation: Italy', in Nelson (1993), 230–60.

Malmberg, A., and Maskell, P. (1997), 'Towards an Explanation of Regional Specialization and Industry Agglomeration', *European Planning Studies*, 5: 25–42.

Marin, B., and Mayntz, E. (eds.) (1991), *Policy Networks: Empirical Evidence and Theoretical Considerations*, Frankfurt: Campus; Boulder, Colo.: Westview Press.

Marquand, H. (1936), *South Wales Needs a Plan*, London: Allen and Unwin.

Marsh, P. (1996a), 'Troubled Traub Searches for Suitor', *Financial Times*, 1 Oct., 23.

—— (1996b), 'Sharp Look at the Tools of the Trade', *Financial Times*, 16 Oct., 23.

Marshall, A. (1916), *Principles of Economics*, London: Macmillan.

—— (1919), *Industry and Trade*, London: Macmillan.

Marx, K. (1970), *Capital*, i, London: Lawrence & Wishart.

—— and Engels, F. (1970), *The German Ideology*, London: Lawrence and Wishart.

Massey, D. (1984), *Spatial Divisions of Labour*, London: Macmillan.

Mayes, D. (1995), 'Conflict and Cohesion in the Single European Market—A Reflection', in A. Amin and J. Tomaney (eds.), *Behind the Myth of European Union*, London: Routledge, 1–9.

Mead, G. (1993), 'High-Tech Glimpse of the Future', *Financial Times*, 24 Nov.

Miller, P., and O'Leary, T. (1994), 'The Factory as Laboratory', *Science in Context*, 7/3: 469–96.

Mintzberg, H. (1994), *The Rise and Fall of Strategic Planning*, New York: Prentice Hall.

Mondragon Co-operative Corporation (1992), *Annual Report*, Mondragon: Guipuzcoa.

Morgan, K. O. (1983), *Rebirth of a Nation: Wales 1880–1980*, Oxford: Oxford University Press.

Morgan, K. (1983), 'Restructuring Steel: The Crises of Labour and Locality in Britain', *International Journal of Urban and Regional Research*, 7: 175–201.

—— (1989), 'Telecom Strategies in Britain and France: The Scope and Limits of Neo-liberalism and Dirigisme', in M. Sharp and P. Holmes (eds.), *Strategies for New Technology*, Hemel Hempstead: Philip Allan, 19–55.

—— (1994), 'Reversing Attrition? The Auto Cluster in Baden-Württemberg', 'Working Paper No. 37', Stuttgart: Center for Technology Assessment.

—— (1996), 'Learning By Interacting: Inter-Firm Networks and Enterprise Support', OECD (ed.), *Networks of Enterprises and Local Development*, Paris: OECD, 53–66.

—— (1997a), 'The Learning Region: Institutions, Innovation and Regional Renewal', *Regional Studies*, 31: 491–503.

—— (1997b), 'The Regional Animateur: Taking Stock of the Welsh Development Agency', *Regional and Federal Studies*, 7/2.

—— Cooke, P., and Price, A. (1992), 'The Challenge of Lean Production in German Industry', *Regional Industrial Research Report No. 12*, Cardiff: University of Wales.

—— and Rees, G. (1994), 'Vocational Skills and Economic Development', Occasional Paper No. 3, Department of City and Regional Planning, University of Wales, Cardiff.

—— and Roberts, E. (1993), 'The Democratic Deficit: A Guide to Quangoland', *Papers in Planning Research No. 151*, Department of City and Regional Planning, University of Wales, Cardiff.

—— and Sayer, A. (1988), *Microcircuits of Capital: Sunrise Industry and Uneven Development*, Cambridge: Polity.

Mueller, F., and Loveridge, R. (1995), 'The "Second Industrial Divide"? The Role of the Large Firm in the Baden-Württemberg Model', *Industrial and Corporate Change*, 4: 555–82.

Münchau, W. (1996), 'German Work Consensus turns to Conflict', *Financial Times*, 25 Apr.

Munday, M. (1991), 'Integrated Materials Management: Beyond Component Quality', *Logistics Today*, July/Aug.

Murray, F. (1983), 'The Decentralisation of Production—The Decline of the Mass Collective Worker?' *Capital and Class*, 19: 74–99.

Murray, R. (1991), *Local Space*, Manchester: Centre for Local Economic Strategies.

Muzyka, D., Breuninger, H., and Rossell, G. (1997), 'The Secret of New Growth in Old German *Mittelstand* Companies', *European Journal of Management*, 31: 125–38.

Myrdal, G. (1957), *Economic Theory and Underdeveloped Regions*, London: Duckworth.

Nakamoto, M. (1995), 'Knocked off the Road Again', *Financial Times*, 20 Apr.

Nakamoto, M. (1996), 'Carmaker To End Some Outsourcing', *Financial Times*, 28 May.

National Economic Development Office (1991), *The Experience of Nissan Suppliers: Lessons for the UK Engineering Industry*, London: NEDO.

National Science Foundation (1994), *Science Indicators 1993*, Washington, DC: NSF.

Nelson, R. (1990), 'Capitalism as an Engine of Progress', *Research Policy*, 19: 193–214.

—— (1991), 'Why Do Firms Differ and How Does It Matter?' *Strategic Management Journal*, 12: 61–74.

—— (ed.) (1993), *National Innovation Systems*, Oxford: Oxford University Press.

—— (1995), 'Recent Evolutionary Theorising about Economic Change', *Journal of Economic Literature*, 33: 48–90.

—— (1996), 'Evolutionary Theorizing About Economic Change', in N. Smelser and R. Swedberg (eds.), *The Handbook of Economic Sociology*, New York: Sage, 108–36.

—— and Rosenberg, N. (1993), 'Technical Innovation and National Systems', in Nelson (1993), 3–22.

—— and Winter, S. (1982), *An Evolutionary Theory of Economic Change*, Cambridge, Mass.: Harvard University Press.

Nieto, A. (1984), *La Organizacion del Desgobierno*, Barcelona: Editorial Ariel.

Nishiguchi, T. (1994), *Strategic Industrial Sourcing: The Japanese Advantage*, Oxford: Oxford University Press.

Noble, D. (1977), *America By Design: Science, Technology and the Rise of Corporate Capitalism*, Oxford: Oxford University Press.

Nomura, M. (1993), 'Farewell to "Toyotism"? Recent Trends of a Japanese Automobile Company', *Actes du Gerpisa*, 6: 37–76.

Nooteboom, B. (1996), 'Towards a Cognitive Theory of the Firm', School of Management and Organization, Groningen University.

Nonaka, I., and Takeuchi, H. (1995), *The Knowledge-Creating Company*, Oxford: Oxford University Press.

Norman, P., and Münchau, W. (1996), 'Daimler Ends its 45-year Run of Payouts', *Financial Times*, 4 Apr.

North, D. (1993), 'Institutions and Economic Performance', in U. Mäki, B. Gustafsson, and C. Knudsen (eds.), *Rationality, Institutions and Economic Methodology*, London: Routledge, 242–64.

OECD (1986), *Review of Innovation Policies*, Paris: OECD.

—— (1989), *OECD Science and Technology Indicators Report*, Paris: OECD.

—— (1991), *OECD Economic Surveys: Spain*, Paris: OECD.

—— (1992), *Technology and the Economy: The Key Relationships*, Paris: OECD.

—— (1994*a*), *The OECD Jobs Survey*, Paris: OECD.

—— (1994*b*), *OECD Economic Surveys: Spain*, Paris: OECD.

Office of National Statistics (1996), *New Earnings Survey*, London: ONS.

Office of Science and Technology (1995), *Technology Foresight: Progress Through Partnership*, London: OST.

Ohmae, K. (1990), *The Borderless World*, New York: Harper.

—— (1993), 'The Rise of the Region State', *Foreign Affairs*, 72: 78–87.

—— (1996), *The End of the Nation State*, New York: Free Press.

Oliver, N., Jones, D., Delbridge, R., and Lowe, J. (1994), *Worldwide Manufacturing Competitiveness Study: The Second Lean Enterprise Report*, Anderson Consulting.

Ormaechea, J. M. (1991), *The Mondragon Cooperative Experience*, Mondragon: MCC.

Osmond, J. (1978), *Creative Conflict: The Politics of Welsh Devolution*, Llandysul: Gomer Press.

—— (1994) (ed.), *A Parliament for Wales*, Llandysul: Gomer Press.

Ostrom, E. (1992), 'Community and the Endogenous Solution of Commons Problems', *Journal of Theoretical Politics*, 4: 343–51.

Paasi, A. (1986), 'The Institutionalisation of Regions: A Theoretical Framework for Understanding of the Emergence of Regions and the Constitution of Regional Identity', *Fennia*, 164: 1–28.

Parliamentary and Scientific Committee (1992), *The Implications and Consequences of Japan's Emerging Lead in Technology*, London: The Royal Society.

Patel, P., and Pavitt, K. (1994), 'National Innovation Systems: Why They Are Important and How They Might Be Measured and Compared', *Economics of Innovation and New Technology*, 3: 77–95.

Pavitt, K., and Patel, P. (1991), 'Large Firms in the Production of the World's Technology: An Important Case of Non-Globalisation', *Journal of International Business Studies*, 22: 1–21.

Pelikan, P. (1988), 'Can the Imperfect Innovation Systems of Capitalism Be Outperformed?', in Dosi *et al.* (1988), 370–98.

Perroux, F. (1950), 'Economic Spaces', reprinted in F. Perroux (1969), *The Twentieth Century Economy* (in French), Paris: Presses Universitaires, 25–39.

Piaget, J. (1971), *Structuralism*, London: Routledge.

Piore, M., Lester, R., Kofman, F., and Malek, K. (1994), 'The Organization of Product Development', *Industrial and Corporate Change*, 3/2: 405–34.

Polanyi, K. (1944), *The Great Transformation*, Boston: Beacon Press.

Polanyi, M. (1958), *Personal Knowledge*, Chicago: Chicago University Press.

—— (1966), *The Tacit Dimension*, London: Routledge and Kegan Paul.

Porter, M. (1990), *The Competitive Advantage of Nations*, New York: The Free Press.

Powell, W. (1990), 'Neither Market Nor Hierarchy: Network Forms of Organization', *Research in Organizational Behavior*, 12: 74–96.

—— (1996), 'Trust-Based Forms of Governance', in R. Kramer and T. Tyler (eds.), *Trust in Organizations*, London: Sage, 51–67.

Prais, S. (1993), *Economic Performance and Education: The Nature of Britain's Deficiencies*, Discussion Paper No. 52, London: National Institute of Economic and Social Research.

Prodi, R. (1993), 'The Single European Market: Institutions and Economic Policies', *European Planning Studies*, 1: 13–24.

Prospektiker (1994), *Evaluacion de los Planes Tecnologicas de la Comunidad Autonoma del Pais Vasco*, Zarautz: Prospektiker.

Putnam, R. (1992), *Making Democracy Work: Civic Traditions in Modern Italy*, Princeton: Princeton University Press.

Pyke, F. (1994), *Small Firms, Technical Services and Inter-firm Cooperation*, Geneva: International Institute for Labour Studies.

Rehfeld, D. (1995), 'Disintegration and Reintegration of Production Clusters in the Ruhr Area', in Cooke (1995), 85–102.

Reichheld, F. (1996), *The Loyalty Effect*, Boston: Harvard Business School Press.

Rhodes, R. (1988), *Beyond Westminster and Whitehall: The Sub-Central Governments of Britain*, London: Unwin Hyman.

—— (1994), 'The New Governance: Governing Without Government', *Political Studies*, 44/4: 652–67.

Riester, W. (1994), *Minority Report on the Future Commission 'Economy 2000' Study*, Stuttgart: Future Commission.

Robertson, P., and Langlois, R. (1995), 'Innovation, Networks and Vertical Integration', *Research Policy*, 24: 543–62.

Romer, P. (1990), 'Endogenous Technological Change', *Journal of Political Economy*, 98: S70–S102.

Rosenberg, N. (1976), *Perspectives on Technology*, Cambridge: Cambridge University Press.

—— (1991), 'Critical Issues in Science Policy Research', *Science and Public Policy*, 18/6: 335–46.

—— and Nelson, R. (1994), 'American Universities and Technical Advance in Industry', *Research Policy*, 23: 323–48.

Rosenfeld, S. (1995), *Industrial-Strength Strategies*, Washington, DC: The Aspen Institute.

Roth, S. (1992), *Japanization or Going Our Own Way: New 'Lean Production' Concepts in the German Automobile Industry*, Frankfurt: IG Metall.

Rothwell, R., and Zegveld, W. (1985), *Reindustrialization and Technology*, Harlow: Longman.

Royal Society for the Encouragement of Arts, Manufactures and Commerce (1995), *Tomorrow's Company: The Role of Business in a Changing World*, London: RSA.

Rubbini, I. (1986), Address to Conference on Italy's industrial renaissance, New York, 21–22 October (mimeo).

Ruigrok, W., and Van Tulder, R. (1995), *The Logic of International Restructuring*, London: Routledge.

Sabel, C. (1982), *Work and Politics: The Division of Labour in Industry*, Cambridge: Cambridge University Press.

—— (1989), 'Flexible Specialization and the Re-emergence of Regional Economies', in P. Hirst and J. Zeitlin (eds.), *Reversing Industrial Decline? Industrial Structure and Policy in Britain and her Competitors*, Oxford: Berg, 17–70.

—— (1992), 'Studied Trust: Building New Forms of Co-operation in a Volatile Economy', in F. Pyke and W. Sengenberger (eds.), *Industrial Districts and Local Economic Regeneration*, Geneva: International Institute for Labour Studies, 215–50.

—— (1993), 'Constitutional Ordering in Historical Context', in F. Scharpf (ed.), *Games in Hierarchies and Networks*, Frankfurt: Campus; Boulder, Colo.: Westview.

—— (1994), 'Learning By Monitoring: The Institutions of Economic Development', in N. Smelser and R. Swedberg (eds.), *Handbook of Economic Sociology*, Princeton: Princeton University Press, 137–65.

—— (1995), 'Experimental Regionalism and the Dilemmas of Regional Economic Policy in Europe', paper to international seminar on 'Local Systems of Small Firms and Job Creation', OECD, Paris, June.

—— Herrigel, G., Deeg, R., and Kazis, R. (1989a), 'Regional Prosperities Compared: Massachusetts and Baden-Württemberg in the 1980s', *Economy and Society*, 18: 374–403.

—— Kern, H., and Herrigel, G. (1989b), *Collaborative Manufacturing: New Supplier Relations in the Automobile Industry and the Redefinition of the Industrial Corporation*, Cambridge, Mass: Sloan School of Management, MIT.

Sadler, D. (1996), 'Europeanisation of Production Systems in the Automotive Industry: The Role of Supply Chain Management Strategies', presented to the EMOT Workshop on Learning and Embeddedness: Evolving Transnational Firm Strategies in Europe, University of Durham, 27–29 June.

Saez, J. I. (1994), Director, Unidad De Estrategia Tecnologica, SPRI, Bilbao, Interview, 29 Apr.

Sako, M. (1992), *Prices, Quality and Trust*, Cambridge: Cambridge University Press.

—— and Helper, S. (1996), *Does Trust Improve Business Performance?* Paper to the Society for the Advancement of Socio-Economics, University of Geneva, 12–14 June.

—— Lamming, R., and Helper, S. (1995), 'Supplier Relations in the UK Car Industry: Good News-Bad News', *European Journal of Purchasing and Supply Management*, 1/4: 237–48.

Salmon, K. (1991), *The Modern Spanish Economy*, London: Pinter.

Sandberg, A. (ed.) (1995), *Enriching Production: Perspectives on Volvo's Uddevalla Plant as an Alternative to Lean Production*, Aldershot: Avebury.

Saxenian, A. (1994), *Regional Advantage: Culture and Competition in Silicon Valley and Route 128*, Cambridge, Mass.: Harvard University Press.

Sayer, A., and Walker, R. (1992), *The New Social Economy*, Oxford: Blackwell.

Scharpf, F. (1976), 'Theory of *Politikverflechtung*', in F. Scharpf, B. Reissert, and F. Schnabel (eds.), *Politikverflechtung: Theory and Empirics of Cooperative Federalism in Germany* (in German), Kronberg: Scriptor, 3–30.

—— (1988), 'The Joint Decision Trap: Lessons from German Federalism and European Integration', *Public Administration*, 66: 239–78.

Schmidt, W. (1991), 'The State Constitution—Its Development since 1953', in H. Wehling (ed.), *The German Southwest: Baden-Württemberg; History, Politics, Economy and Culture*, Stuttgart: Köhlhammer, 58–78.

Schoenberger, E. (1996), 'The Firm in the Region and the Region in the Firm', in T. Barnes and M. Gertler (eds.), *Regions, Institutions and Technology*, London: Routledge.

Schon, D. (1973), *Beyond the Stable State: Public and Private Learning in a Changing Society*, Harmondsworth: Penguin.

Schumpeter, J. (1934), *The Theory of Economic Development*, Cambridge, Mass.: Harvard University Press.

Schumpeter, J. (1942/1975), *Capitalism, Socialism and Democracy*, New York: Harper Torchbooks.

—— (1943), *Capitalism, Socialism and Democracy*, London: George Allen and Unwin.

Scott, A. (1988), *New Industrial Spaces*, London: Pion.

—— (1996), 'Regional Motors of the Global Economy', *Futures*, 28: 391–411.

—— (1997), 'From Silicon Valley to Hollywood: The Multimedia Industry in California', in H. Braczyk, P. Cooke, and M. Heidenreich (eds.), *Regional Innovation Systems*, London: UCL Press.

Scott, P., and Cockrill, A. (1997), 'Training for Multiskilling in Small and Medium Sized Engineering Companies: A Welsh-German Comparison', *Regional Industrial Research Report No. 21*, Cardiff: University of Wales.

Segal Quince Wicksteed Ltd. (1996), 'Evaluation of Source Wales: Report to the WDA', Cardiff.

Semlinger, K. (1993), 'Economic Development and Industrial Policy in Baden-Württemberg: Small Firms in a Benevolent Environment', *European Planning Studies*, 1: 435–64.

Senge, P. (1990), *The Fifth Discipline: The Age and Practice of the Learning Organization*, London: Century Business.

Serrano, F., Ferreiro, J., and Bilbao, J. (1993), *El Sector Publico Vasco: Costes Y Duplicaciones*, Bilbao: Circulo De Empresarios Vascos.

Sharpe, L. (1993), *The Rise of Meso Government in Europe*, London: Sage.

Shimizu, K. (1995), 'Humanization of the Production System and Work at Toyota Motor Co and Toyota Motor Kyushu', in Sandberg (1995).

Shotton, R., and Miege, R. (1994), *The Regional Technology Plan: Why and How?* RTP Newsletter No. 1, Brussels.

Simon, H. J. (1955), 'A Behavioural Model of Rational Choice', *Quarterly Journal of Economics*, 69: 99–118.

—— (1962), 'The Architecture of Complexity', *Proceedings of the American Philosophical Society*, 106: 467–82.

Simon, H. (1992), 'Lessons from Germany's Mid-sized Giants', *Harvard Business Review*, Mar.–Apr.

Simonian, H. (1996), 'Relentless Driver of Change', *Financial Times*, 29 Aug.

Solow, R. (1957), 'Technical Change and the Aggregate Production Function', *Review of Economics and Statistics*, 39: 312–20.

SPRI (1993), *Competitividad de la Comunidad Autonoma del Pais Vasco Para la Implantacion Industrial*, Bilbao: SPRI.

—— (1994*a*), *La Industrial Vasca en 1993*, Bilbao: SPRI.

—— (1994*b*), *Basic Industrial Sectors in the Basque Country: Car Component Sector*, Bilbao: SPRI.

—— (1994*c*), *Basic Industrial Sectors in the Basque Country: Machine Tools Industry*, Bilbao: SPRI.

—— (1995), *Reorientacion Estrategica Y Tecnicas Operativas (RETO)*, Bilbao: SPRI.

Stigler, G. (1951), 'The Division of Labour is Limited by the Extent of the Market', *Journal of Political Economy*, 69: 213–25.

Stöhr, W. (1989), 'Territorial Innovation Complexes', in del Castillo *et al.* (1989), 37–58.

Storper, M. (1995), 'The Resurgence of Regional Economies, Ten Years After: The Region as a Nexus of Untraded Interdependencies', *European Urban and Regional Studies*, 2: 191–221.

—— and Scott, A. (1995), 'The Wealth of Regions: Market Forces and Policy Imperatives in Local and Global Context', *Futures*, 27: 505–26.

Streeck, W. (1989), 'Successful Adjustment to Turbulent Markets: The Automobile Industry', in P. Katzenstein (ed.), *Industry and Politics in West Germany*, Ithaca, NY: Cornell University Press, 113–56.

—— (1995), *German Capitalism: Does It Exist? Can It Survive?* Köln: Max-Planck Institut Für Gesellschaftsforschung.

—— (1996), 'Lean Production in the German Automobile Industry: A Test Case for Convergence Theory', in Berger and Dore (1996).

—— and Schmitter, P. (1985), *Private Interest Government: Beyond Market and State*, London: Sage.

Sturm, R. (1994), *Economic Regionalism in a Federal State: Germany and the Challenge of the Single Market*, Occasional Paper No. 1, Tübingen: European Centre for Federalism Research.

Sydow, J. (1996), 'Flexible Specialisation in Regional Networks', in U. Staber, N. Schaefer, and B. Sharma (eds.), *Business Networks: Prospects for Regional Development*, Berlin: de Gruyter, 24–40.

Tabb, W., and Sawers, L. (eds.) (1984), *Sunbelt/Snowbelt*, Oxford: Oxford University Press.

Takeuchi, H., and Nonaka, I. (1986), 'The New New Product Development Game', *Harvard Business Review*, Jan.–Feb., 137–46.

Taylor, F. W. (1967), *The Principles of Scientific Management*, New York: W. W. Norton.

Terazono, E. (1993), 'Feeling the Pinch', *Financial Times*, 23 Nov.

Thrift, N. (1987), 'The Fixers: The Urban Geography of International Commercial Capital', in J. Henderson and M. Castells (eds.), *Global Restructuring and Territorial Development*, London: Sage, 203–33.

Times Higher Education Supplement (1996), 'Ideas of Marches', 26 Apr.

Trades Union Congress (1996), *Draft Report to Congress 1996 on Stakeholding*, London: TUC.

Turner, L., and Auer, P. (1994), 'A Diversity of New Work Organization: Human-Centred, Lean and In-Between', *Industrielle Beziehungen* 1/1: 39–61.

UNCTAD (1994), *World Investment Report*, New York: UN.

Varaldo, R., and Ferrucci, L. (1996), 'The Evolutionary Nature of the Firm within Industrial Districts', *European Planning Studies*, 4: 27–34.

Veblen, T. (1919), 'Why is Economics Not an Evolutionary Science?' *Quarterly Journal of Economics*, 12: 373–97 and in *The Place of Science in Modern Civilization and Other Essays* (reprinted 1990), New Brunswick: Transactions.

Velasco, R. (1989), 'Reindustrialisation and Regional Policy in the Basque Country', in del Castillo *et al.* (1989), 191–212.

—— (1994*a*), Departamento de Economia Aplicada, Universidad del Pais Vasco, Bilbao, interview, 26 Apr.

238   *References*

Velasco, R. (1994*b*), 'El Ajuste Incesante De La Economia Vasca', *Papeles De Economia Espanola*, 59.
von Hippel, E. (1988), *The Sources of Innovation*, Cambridge, Mass.: MIT Press.
Vromen, J. (1995), *Economic Evolution*, London: Routledge.
Wade, R. (1990), *Governing The Market: Economic Theory and the Role of Government in East Asian Industrialization*, Princeton: Princeton University Press.
—— (1996), 'Globalization and Its Limits: Reports of the Death of the National Economy Are Greatly Exaggerated', in Berger and Dore (1996), 60–88.
Waller, D. (1993), 'A Shine on its Financial Face', *Financial Times*, 14 July.
Walton, R. (1985), 'From Control to Commitment in the Workplace', *Harvard Business Review*, Mar.–Apr., 77–84.
Welsh Local Government Association (1996), *Evidence to House of Lords Select Committee on Relations Between Central and Local Government*, London: HMSO.
Wheelwright, S., and Clark, K. (1992), *Revolutionizing Product Development*, New York: Free Press.
White, D. (1995), 'A Change of Culture for the Basque Cooperatives', *Financial Times*, 7 June.
White, G. (ed.) (1988), *Developmental States in East Asia*, London: Macmillan.
Whyte, W., and Whyte, K. (1988), *Making Mondragon: The Growth and Dynamics of the Mondragon Cooperative Complex*, Ithaca, NY: Cornell University Press.
Wickens, P. (1987), *The Road to Nissan*, London: Macmillan.
Wilkes, S., and Wright, M. (eds.) (1987), *Comparative Government-Industry Relations*, Oxford: Clarendon Press.
Williams, J. (1980), 'The Coalowners', in D. Smith (ed.), *A People and a Proletariat*, London: Pluto Press.
Williams, K., Haslam, C., Williams, J., Adcroft, A., and Sukhder, J. (1992), *Factories or Warehouses? Japanese Manufacturing FDI in Britain and the US*, Occasional Papers on Business, Economy and Society No. 6, Polytechnic of East London.
Williamson, O. (1975), *Markets and Hierarchies: Analysis and Antitrust Implications*, New York: The Free Press.
—— (1985), *The Economic Institutions of Capitalism*, New York: The Free Press.
Windhoff-Héritier, A. (1993), 'Policy Network Analysis: A Tool for Comparative Political Research', in H. Keman (ed.), *Comparative Politics: New Directions in Theory and Method*, Amsterdam: Vrije University Press, 143–60.
Winter, S. (1988), 'On Coase, Competence and the Corporation', *Journal of Law, Economics and Organization*, 4/1: 163–80.
Wise Group (1994), *Annual Review*, Glasgow.
Witt, U. (1991), 'Reflections on the Present State of Evolutionary Economic Theory', in G. Hodgson and E. Screpanti (eds.), *Rethinking Economics: Markets, Technology and Economic Evolution*, Cheltenham: Edward Elgar, 83–102.
Wolf, M. (1996), 'No Answer in Germany', *Financial Times*, 16 Apr.
Womack, J., and Jones, D. (1996), *Lean Thinking*, New York: Simon and Schuster.
—— Jones, D., and Roos, J. (1990), *The Machine That Changed the World*, London: Macmillan.
Young, A. (1928), 'Increasing Returns and Economic Progress', *Economic Journal*, 38: 527–42.
Zanfei, A. (1996), 'Technology and the Changing Organization of Transnational Firms', presented to the EMOT Workshop on Learning and Embeddedness: Evolving Transnational Firm Strategies in Europe, University of Durham, 27–9 June.
Zumarraga, L. (1994), Sub-Director General De Promocion Tecnologica, SPRI, Bilbao, interview, 29 Apr.

INDEX